ROMMEL AND CAPORETTO

ROMMEL AND CAPORETTO

by

John and Eileen Wilks

LEO COOPER

First published in Great Britain in 2001 by
LEO COOPER
an imprint of
Pen & Sword Books Ltd
47 Church Street
Barnsley
South Yorkshire
S70 2AS

© Wilks & Wilks, 2001

ISBN 0 85052 772 4

A catalogue record for this book is
available from the British Library

Typeset in 10/11 Amasis by Phoenix Typesetting, Ilkley, West Yorkshire

Printed in England by CPI UK

Contents

Maps

Acknowledgements

We gratefully acknowledge the assistance of the Ufficio Storico of the Stato Maggiore dell' Escercito which much facilitated our studies. We are also most grateful for the assistance we received during visits to the Biblioteca Centrale Militare in Rome, and especially for the expert help and advice of Ajutante Luigi Diana.

We also received invaluable assistance from Herr Wolf-Albrecht Kainz, a student of German military uniforms and of the part played by the military forces of the Kingdom of Wurttemberg in the First World War. We thank him for discussions during two visits to Ludwigsberg, for access to his archives, for permission to reproduce photographs from his collection, and for his kind hospitality.

We are indebted for discussions with Dr Marco Rech of Seren del Grappa who has made a study of the German archives concerning Rommel and Caporetto, as set out in his book *Da Caporetto al Grappa*. We are also grateful for his kindness in taking us to Val Stizzon to photograph Monte Fontasecca.

We acknowledge the facilities provided by the British Library, and the Library of the Imperial War Museum, and in Oxford the Bodleian Library and the Libraries of Magdalen College, Oriel College and Pembroke College. We also have much appreciated discussions with Professor Mack Smith concerning the political climate in Italy at that time.

We thank the Ufficio Storico for permission to reproduce the photographs in Plates 7, 8, 14, 22; and Herr Kainz for permission to reproduce those in Plates 1, 2, 12, 16, 17, 18, 20, 21, 25, 27, 31. The sketch on page 174 is reproduced by permission of the Hauptstaatarchiv Stuttgart.

Introduction

Erwin Rommel remains the best remembered enemy general from the Second World War. Yet few are aware that Rommel had fought in Italy in 1917 at the Battle of Caporetto, and by his exploits at that time established himself as one of the most notable young officers in the German Army. Indeed his performance then has been described 'as extraordinary an example of skill and daring as can be found in the annals of modern warfare'.[1]

Throughout the spring and summer of 1917 the armies of Italy, then an ally of France and Britain, had launched a series of offensives against the Austro-Hungarian forces. The Italians had made only modest advances, but by September the Austrian High Command concluded that it could not withstand a further offensive, and appealed to Germany for assistance. Seven German divisions were sent as the spearhead of an Austro-German Army to strike against the Italians on the upper Isonzo river in the Julian Alps, and on 24 October this army launched the offensive known as the Battle of Caporetto.

For the Italians, Caporetto was an unexpected and unparalleled reverse, and they were forced to withdraw from the Isonzo to the River Piave, 50 or 70 miles further back, and only 20 miles from Venice. Rommel was then a young lieutenant in a battle which in three days broke through the main Italian defences in the mountains, and then developed into a war of movement across the Venetian plain and through the mountains beyond. During the first three days, in command of only two or three infantry companies and the associated machine-gun companies, he captured some 9,000 Italian troops. Then, two weeks later, he achieved the surrender of a further 10,000.

Such successes would hardly have been possible on the Western Front, but the Battle of Caporetto arose from a combination of somewhat unusual circumstances, including inter alia the very mountainous nature of the ground, and the failure of the Italians to recognize the weaknesses of their front in the mountains until too late. This book describes how the German offensive made the most of various Italian weaknesses, and presented Rommel with opportunities, which he seized with a skill, determination and courage that few could match.

1

There are two official accounts of the larger aspects of the Battle of Caporetto, one from either side, which give excellent factual and critical accounts of the whole campaign, although neither is available in English. The first, published during 1926 and 1927, is the book by General Konrad Krafft von Dellmensingen, *Der Durchbruch am Isonzo*. General Krafft was the Chief of Staff of the Austro-German Army, and had access to the official German archives, and his book forms part of the Official German History. Shortly after its publication, General Cadorna, the former Chief of Staff of the Italian Army and virtually the Commander-in-Chief at the time of Caporetto, described it as an 'account told with clarity and precision',[2] and it is now available in an excellent translation into Italian by Pieropan.

On the Italian side, generals and others, soon after the war produced various accounts, often self-justifying, but the official Italian account of the battle was not forthcoming until the publication of the relevant volume of *L'Esercito Italiano nelle Grande Guerra*, the Official Italian History (IOH) published only in 1967. This impressive work, prepared under the direction of Lieutenant General Ferdinand di Lauro, provides a comprehensive and critical account of events with some 730 pages of text, 500 pages of documents, a series of excellent maps and photographs. Since its publication various studies have been made incorporating information from the IOH, particularly the books by Silvestri, Melograni and Pieropan, but the IOH remains the one essential Italian account of the Battle of Caporetto.

The above histories describe the whole battle on a very large canvas, on which Rommel's achievements receive no more than a passing remark or footnote. However, we have first-hand and first-rate accounts of Rommel's actions, because he eventually turned out to be 'a born writer as well as a born fighter'.[3] After the war Rommel spent four years (1929–33) as an instructor at the Infantry School at Dresden. A typical lecture on battlefield tactics would start with a first-hand account of one of his actions during the war, and be followed by an analysis of what assessments and decisions he had made during the action, and what lessons could be learnt. In 1931 the Commandant of the School wrote that his lectures were always a 'delight to hear' and also included 'a lot of ideological food for thought'. A year later the senior instructor commented that he was 'respected by his colleagues, worshipped by his cadets'.[4]

Like many other lecturers, Rommel worked his lecture notes into a book, *Infanterie greift an*, which was published in 1937. Military textbooks on battlefield tactics for junior officers seldom excite much public interest, but *Infanterie greift an* became an immediate best-seller, providing an extremely good read for the general public, an inspiration for young men thinking of a military career, and in addition 'probably one of the best infantry manuals ever written'.[5] A copy of the twelfth (1942) edition, in the present authors' possession is inscribed 'found in German defences Calais summer 1945'. This was an impressive book which still presents one not only with some appreciation of Rommel's extraordinary stamina, moral and physical courage, and determination, but with respect for his ability to size up and analyse a situation, and to respond immediately with an imaginative solution.

In addition, there are two other first-hand accounts from the German side. The until recently unpublished diary of the German commander, General Otto von Below, is now available (in Italian) in Fadini's book *Caporetto dalla parte del vincetore*. Also, Major Sproesser, the Commanding Officer of the Wurttemberg Mountain Battalion in which Rommel served, has edited and partly written a history of the battalion, *Die Geschichte der Württembergischen Gebirgsschützen* (The History of the Wurttemberg Mountain Troops) published in 1933, in which he deals at length with the campaign in Italy.

Finally, we note that Rommel's descriptions of his actions in *Infanterie greift an* besides being a very good account, are in the nature of things almost the only account. Hence for our account of Rommel on the Kolovrat, on Matajur and at Longarone, we rely primarily, but not entirely, on Rommel's own account. Two English translations are available. The first, made by the United States Army during the Second World War, was published, somewhat abridged, in 1944 in the American *Infantry Journal*, and this account was reprinted in 1990 under the title *Infantry attacks*. Meanwhile an unabridged edition, retranslated by J.R. Driscoll, appeared in 1979 under the title *Attacks*, and our references usually refer to this work. However, all direct quotations have been translated from the German edition of 1942. (As Rommel's book is laid out clearly and chronologically with many section headings, we have not thought it necessary to give such detailed page references here as elsewhere.)

3

Austria seeks German help

1.1   The War to October 1917

Italy declared the war on the Austro-Hungarian Empire, or Austria for short, in May 1915, and then for two and a half years tried to make significant inroads into Austrian territory but this turned out to be very difficult. The frontier with Austria was about 400 miles long, and except for about 20 miles lay either in mountainous or very mountainous country. It had been drawn many years previously, much to the military advantage of the Austrians, so that a short advance would take them into the Italian plain. On the other hand, if the Italians were to advance, they would find themselves going deeper and deeper into increasingly difficult mountain country. In fact the only part of the frontier not mountainous was the last twenty miles between Gorizia and the sea (Map 1). Hence the Italian plan in 1915 was to attack across the lower reaches of the River Isonzo with the aim of capturing Trieste, and then perhaps Ljubljana and Vienna.

The pre-war frontier below Gorizia, where the Isonzo emerges from the mountains, ran along the watershed five to eight miles to the west of the river, and gave only a poor line of defence to the Austrians. Therefore the Austrian command had arranged to defend this sector by withdrawing to previously prepared positions mainly, though not entirely, on the east bank of the Isonzo. The town of Gorizia which commanded the entry to the upper Isonzo valley and the road to the east leading to Ljubljana, was on the east bank, but strongly protected by positions on the surrounding hills.

Below Gorizia, the ground on the east side of the river rises to the Carso, a green but infertile limestone plateau which extends down to the coast. Although of no great altitude, the Carso formed the type of defensive barrier so eagerly sought by the warring armies on the plains of France. Moreover, the Austrians had already constructed bunkers and gun positions in the hard limestone rock (only inches below a thin layer of soil) to obtain gave good protection against attack.

Italy declared war on 24 May, at a time of her own choosing, when the Austrians were heavily engaged with the Russians, and their Italian

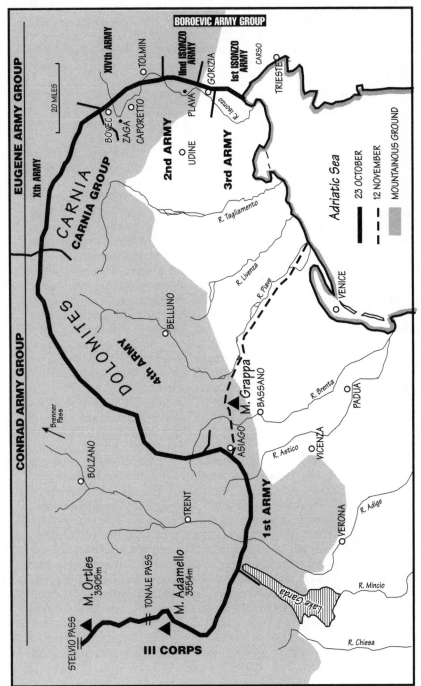

1. The Italian front before and after Caporetto.

frontier was only weakly defended. However, the Italian Armies were not yet ready for a major action, and the first stage of the war was not an Italian onslaught on the Austrians but the so-called *primo balzo*, essentially a readjustment of positions on both sides,[1] as the Austrians moved back to positions on their main defence line.

The first Italian offensive opened on 23 June against the Austrian positions between Gorizia and the sea, and continued intermittently as the first four Battles of the Isonzo until 2 December. According to Cyril Falls, the Italian infantry 'showed splendid courage in hopeless tasks'.[2] By the end of the year the Italians had suffered losses and casualties amounting to about 180,000, but had made virtually no progress. However, two significant gains were made higher up the Isonzo.

Two miles above Gorizia, the Isonzo is narrowly confined in a narrow valley between steep-sided hills, rising up to 600m or so, which continue for the next fifteen miles. Hard fighting had obtained a small bridgehead across the river opposite the village of Plava, at the foot of a rough road leading up to the Bainsizza, an upland plateau on the east of the river between Tolmin and Gorizia, varying in altitude between about 500 and 800 metres. The bridgehead was, however, very limited in size, and dominated by Austrian positions higher up.

The most spectacular advance was further north, between Tolmin and Bovec (formerly Flitsch or Plezzo). Italian mountain troops, the alpini, had crossed the river and occupied the high ridge on the east bank, including the highest point Monte Nero (now Krn, 2224m). This advance gave a substantial bridgehead on the far bank, but one of limited value as the mountains beyond formed a formidable obstacle to further progress to the east. Moreover, this new Italian line was not entirely satisfactory, particularly north of Tolmin where it ran across a high and steep mountain slope with the Austrian positions above the Italians.

During the winter the Italians decided to concentrate their principal effort in 1916 against Gorizia and the Carso, but this programme was soon interrupted by a full-scale Austrian offensive in the mountains between the Rivers Adige and Brenta (Map 1), which aimed to break through to the plain, and arrive behind the Italian armies on the Isonzo. On 15 May, fourteen divisions, supported by a strong force of artillery, launched the so-called Strafexpedition. Despite strong resistance the Italians were forced to give ground, and by the end of the month had been pushed to the very edge of the mountain plateau overlooking the plain of Italy. Then epic Italian resistance at many points along the line prevented any breakthrough into the plain. On 16 June the Austrians decided to break off the attack, and by 26 June had drawn back some distance to a new prepared defence line.

To meet the threat posed by the Strafexpedition, the Italian

Comando Supremo, General Cadorna, had assembled a reserve 5th Army on the plain to face any Austrian forces breaking out from the mountains, and he now ordered a series of counter-attacks. But in spite of many attempts from 27 June to 24 July, and heavy losses, no great progress was made in driving the Austrians further back. The battle had worn itself out. The Italians had lost 35,000 dead, 75,000 wounded and 45,000 missing, 155,000 in all, while the Austrian losses were estimated at more than 80,000.

By the end of July Cadorna was able to return troops to the Isonzo in order to take part in the 6th Battle of the Isonzo which opened on 4 August. The main success was the capture of Gorizia. South of Gorizia the line was pushed somewhat further into the Carso, but three subsequent battles in September, October and November made little further progress, except for advances of up to three miles on the northern half of the Carso.

(The year 1916 also saw some spectacular actions on the peaks and snowfields of the Adamello group and amid the rock walls and pinnacles of the Dolomites, as each side struggled to maintain control of the high ground on either side of important road passes. The Italian mountain troops, the alpini, succeeded in pushing back their Austrian counterparts for some distance both across the glaciers and in the Dolomites, but the ground was too severe to permit anything approaching a breakthrough. Yet each side needed to be present in the mountains to prevent serious incursions by the other.)

After a pause during the winter, the war of attrition resumed again in 1917. During the 10th Battle of the Isonzo (12 May to 8 June) the Italians attacked across the river between Plava and Gorizia, and on the southern edge of the Carso against Monte Hermada (324m). The losses were very heavy and the gains very moderate, the most important being a significant enlargement of the bridgehead across the Isonzo opposite Plava, and an advance of two to three miles on the southen edge of the Bainsizza.

Cadorna now turned to the Asiago front on the Asiago plateau (Map 1), and on 10 June launched an offensive against the Austrian line running north from Asiago for about eight miles up to Monte Ortigara (2105m). Two corps were engaged, deploying 59 battalions, but made very little progress. The large stony summit area of Ortigara was occupied on 25 June but the Italians were forced back to their start line by 29 June. The Italian losses against well-constructed and ably defended Austrian positions amounted to over 23,000 in dead, wounded and missing. The specially enlarged 52nd Division suffered particularly with over 13,000 casualties out of an initial strength of about 35,000.

Finally, on 18 August the Italian 2nd and 3rd Armies launched the

11th Battle of the Isonzo involving 52 divisions, attacking both on the Carso and across the river between Plava and Gorizia. This, the last, largest and most successful of all the offensives, made some progress on the Carso, and between Plava and Gorizia advanced distances of up to five miles into the Bainsizza.

At first sight the results of two and a half years fighting on the Isonzo were very modest. The great hopes of sweeping on to Trieste and even to Ljubljana and Vienna had not been fulfilled. The Italian army had lost about 200,000 men dead, and very many more wounded, but was virtually no nearer to Trieste. Even so, the results of the 11th Battle with its casualties totalling about 26,000 dead and 96,000 wounded, compared not unfavourably with those obtained by the British Army struggling in the mud of Passchendaele at about the same time. The Italians had found themselves caught in the same tactical morass which had forced the armies of Germany, France and Britain into immobile trench warfare on the Western Front. Wars of movement had become wars of attrition in which battles with enormous casualties produced only miniscule changes of position.

Nevertheless, Italy had played a considerable role in this war of attrition, and by September 1917 the Austrian High Command feared that they might be overwhelmed by another Italian attack on the scale of the 11th Battle. In particular, they were concerned that any extension of the latest Italian gains on the Bainsizza could threaten the flank of their positions on the Carso, and they therefore appealed to Germany for help.

1.2 The Austrian Appeal and the Upper Isonzo

The request for German assistance in the autumn of 1917 was not the first time that Austria had sought to attract German forces to Italy. In December 1916, the then Chief of the General Staff of the Austrian Armies, General Franz Conrad von Hötzendorff, had suggested that the best strategy for the Central Powers in 1917 would be a joint Austro-German attack on Italy. The proposal found some support at the German GHQ, and at conference on 23 January General Conrad proposed a double offensive, with the main assault from the Trentino, preceded by an attack across the Isonzo in the region of Caporetto. However, the Germans said they were unable to spare troops from their other fronts, and would not agree to any such operation.[3]

A further factor was the death of the old Emperor Franz Joseph on 21 November 1916, and the succession of his young nephew Karl, whose main preoccupation was to end the war before the ruin of the Austrian Empire. Hence Conrad, who had always been an ardent advocate of war with Italy, was promoted Field Marshal, invested with the high honour of The Grand Cross of the Military Order of Maria Theresa, and dismissed from his post as Chief of the General Staff. General Arz, Conrad's Chief of Staff, then took over as Chief of the General Staff, and Conrad at Karl's insistence assumed command of the Army Group of the Tyrol in the Trentino.

The next step towards the Battle of Caporetto came during the 11th Battle of the Isonzo (18 August – 12 September) when the Austrians were hard pressed and losing ground on the Bainsizza. They then believed that a counter-offensive was necessary to regain their previous positions, otherwise they would be forced to draw back a considerable way to obtain a new defence line, and would lose their bridgehead opposite Tolmin, where their line ran on the west bank for about five miles. Therefore on 29 August General Arz's aide, General Waldstätten, visited the German High Command with a proposal for a joint counter-offensive against Italy.[4]

Both sides had already found that it was very difficult to make any significant advances on either the Carso or the Bainsizza. Hence the Austrians had returned to Conrad's earlier suggestion of an attack across the upper Isonzo, and they now proposed a joint offensive between Tolmin and Bovec. The planning and execution of the initial stages of the offensive depended very much on the topography of the thirty miles or so of the Isonzo valley from below Tolmin to above Bovec, all now in Slovenia. Map 2 shows that on both sides of the river the topography is determined by a series of mountain ridges, which are indicated schematically.

From about two miles above Gorizia to near Tolmin the Isonzo is closely confined in a narrow valley, then just short of Tolmin, the valley broadens out to give a relatively flat floor about a mile wide. Plate 3, taken from near Tolmin, shows the heavily wooded slopes on the west side of the valley, rising to the summits of Ocna and Na Gradu. Beyond Na Gradu the southern side of the valley is bounded by the long and quite broad ridge known as the Kolovrat, running from Na Gradu (1114m) to Monte Kuk (1243m). Beyond Kuk the ground falls to the village of Livek (690m), and then rises again over successive peaks to the highest point Monte Matajur (1642m) overlooking Caporetto (now known as Kobarid).

Just past Tolmin the sides of the valley close in, leaving a relatively flat floor perhaps half a mile wide. Plate 4 taken about a mile beyond Tolmin, shows the view up the valley with the lower slopes of Mrzli on the right. The north side of the valley, opposite the Kolovrat rises from Tolmin to form a long ridge (Plate 5), drawing back from the river, and rising up to the highest point, Monte Nero (Krn, 2244m) opposite Caporetto.

The village of Caporetto is situated in a wide part of the valley, and

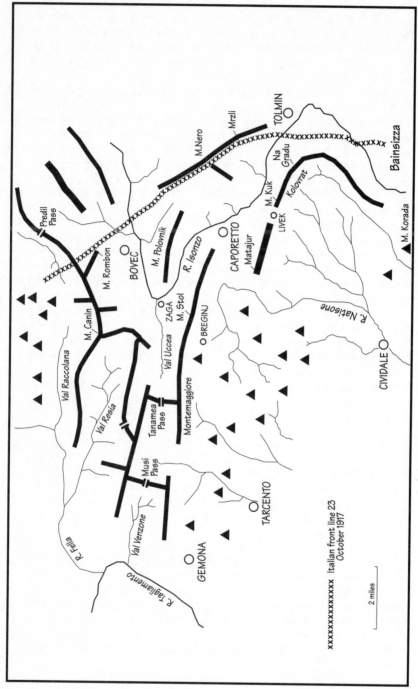

2. Schematic view of the mountain ridges around Caporetto.

Map labels:
R. Tagliamento, R. Fella, Val Venzone, Val Resia, Val Raccolana, M. Canin, Predil Pass, M. Rombon, BOVEC, M. Polovnik, M. Nero, Mrzli, TOLMIN, Bainsizza, Na Gradu, M. Kuk, Kolovrat, M. Korada, LIVEK, Matajur, CAPORETTO, R. Isonzo, M. Stol, ZAGA, Val Uccea, BREGINJ, R. Natisone, CIVIDALE, Montemaggiore, Tanamea Pass, Musi Pass, GEMONA, TARCENTO

xxxxxxxxxxxx Italian front line 23
October 1917

2 miles

is overlooked by an Italian military cemetery, which stands in a prominent position at the foot of a high continuous ridge leading to Monte Stol (1673m) and Montemaggiore (1613m). For the first six miles or so above Caporetto the valley is narrow and vee-shaped, with the slopes of Monte Polovnik to the north falling steeply to the river (Plate 6). The valley then becomes somewhat wider, past Zaga to the village of Bovec, overlooked by Monte Canin (2587m) and Monte Rombon (2208m). For about two miles below and around Bovec the valley floor is about a mile wide until the mountains finally close in again (Plate 9).

Before the war the principal line of communication in this outlying region of the Austrian Empire was the main road which ran from Trieste to Gorizia, and then along the valley of the Isonzo to Bovec, where it left the river to cross the Predil Pass to arrive at Tarvisio, on one of the main road and rail arteries between Austria and north-east Italy. Between Tolmin and Bovec there were only three side roads of any significance. From Tolmin a road, following a side valley to the east, ran to Kranj and Ljubljana in the Sava valley, about thirty miles away. From Caporetto, a road followed the narrow Natisone valley to Cividale, and from Zaga a lesser road passing through Val Uccea eventually arrived at Tarcento.

Finally we note that the topography of the south side of the Kolovrat and Matajur is very different from the forms described above. On this side the mountains descend in a series of long subsidiary ridges running down from the main ridge, like those shown in Plates 10 and 13, dotted with small hamlets and cultivated fields up to a height of seven to eight hundred metres.

The ground around Tolmin and Bovec is obviously not the ideal choice for an offensive, but the Austrians thought that the Italian defence was vulnerable because it had insufficient depth. They argued that the operation would require 13 divisions, 8 to 10 at Tolmin and about 3 at Bovec, and that 8 of the 13 divisions should come from Germany, and should include mountain troops and heavy artillery. It was also suggested that two other German divisions should be deployed very visibly in the Trentino as a decoy.

General Ludendorff, the First Quartermaster-General of the German Army, was not enthusiastic. German troops were not used to the mountains. The aim of the offensive was too limited, no more than to better the tactical positions held by the Austrians. Hence, he would have preferred to continue the offensive in Galicia on the Eastern Front, in order to occupy Moldavia which had a much greater strategic significance. However, General Waldstätten insisted that the Austrian High Command deemed it absolutely essential for the security of their armies that some improvement be made on their positions on the Isonzo. Therefore the German Commander-in-Chief, Field Marshal von Hindenberg, sent a senior German officer, Lieutenant General Konrad Krafft von Dellmingsen, to view the ground and report on the situation.[5]

1.3 General Krafft's Reconnaissance

At the time of Caporetto General Krafft, a Bavarian artillery officer, was fifty-four years of age with a distinguished war record. For the first nine months of the war he had served as the Chief of Staff to Prince Ruprecht of Bavaria, commanding the 6th German Army in Lorraine. Then in early May 1915, when it appeared that Italy might enter the war, Austria became very concerned because most of her troops were on the Eastern Front, and her Italian frontier was only weakly held. Austria sought help from Germany. But almost all the border between Italy and Austria was very mountainous, and Germany had no mountain troops comparable to the Italian alpini and their Austrian counterparts. Hence after Italy's declaration of war on 24 May Krafft (a keen mountaineer who had climbed extensively in the Dolomites) was promoted Lieutenant General, and appointed to the command of a new German division, the Alpine Corps.[6]

The Alpine Corps was constituted of elite troops, partly of Bavarians accustomed to the mountains, but also including formations of south and north German origin, for whom the mountains were a new experience. On the one hand the Corps had a full knowledge of the conduct of war on the Western Front, but on the other hand it had yet to acquire mountain equipment, and experience of the mountains. The Corps arrived in Italy at the beginning of June, and was sent to help defend the frontier in the region of the Dolomites (even though Italy had not yet declared war on Germany!). In the event the Corps saw very little action in Italy, for its orders were to act only defensively, and the Italians launched no large attack against them.[7]

In October 1915 the Alpine Corps left the Dolomites for Serbia to serve as part of an Austrian force under Austrian direction until February 1916 when it moved to France, and was subsequently engaged in the heavy fighting around Verdun. For six weeks in July and August Krafft acted as commander of the Ist Bavarian Corps, and on 1 September received the high military decoration, the Pour le Mérite. Then in the autumn of 1916 the Alpine Corps left France for duty in Romania where it fought successfully in the mountains of Transylvania, often in hard winter conditions. Finally in February 1917 Krafft was posted away from the Alpine Corps to become the Chief of Staff to Duke Albrecht of Wurttemberg, commanding the Army Group in Lorraine between Metz and the Swiss frontier.[8]

After the Austro-German conference on 29 August, Krafft visited

12

the Isonzo from 2 to 6 September, and reported on 8 September that General Waldstätten had quite correctly drawn attention to the state of the Austrian Army. Krafft had by now considerable experience of mountain warfare and judged the proposed offensive to be no easy undertaking. Although the terrain was not truly alpine it would need mountain equipment and pack animals. Also, the substantial height differences that would be involved would demand considerable physical strength on the part of the infantry, and very thorough training.[9]

Even given the necessary forces the task still appeared formidable. The Italians were holding apparently well-prepared positions, with strong points and gun positions. The few good sites for German guns were already dotted by numerous craters produced by Italian shells. The areas available at Tolmin and Bovec for the final concentration of troops prior to the attack were very limited, and vulnerable to enemy artillery fire. The two mediocre roads and the single-track railway through the mountain valleys leading to Tolmin were hardly adequate for bringing up the heavy artillery and vast quantities of men, equipment and ammunition that would be required.

It appeared to Krafft that the Italian positions had too little depth. Moreover, the Austrian army had considerable experience in the mountains. But would such a plan succeed? Krafft now had the responsibility of advising the German GHQ whether or not to adopt a plan which he later described as verging on 'the limits of the possible'. In fact, he believed it could be done, basing his opinion on three considerations: the offensive capacity of the German infantry, the experience and training of the officers in charge, and his opinion that the Italian defence would not be as stout and well organized as that of the French or British. Moreover, the situation of the Austrian Army demanded that some such effort be made.[10]

Ludendorff still had doubts about the project, and was in favour of helping Austria by some action on the Eastern Front. However, the final decision was taken by Field Marshal von Hindenberg, who decided to create a new XIVth Army to make an attack across the Isonzo. The main force would consist of 7 German divisions 'all without exception very experienced units formed from excellent troops',[11] plus 3 Austrian divisions already holding positions on the front line, and a further 2 Austrian divisions. In addition, there would be an Army reserve of another 5 Austrian divisions. The Army would be commanded by the German General Otto von Below, a successful and experienced officer on the Eastern Front and currently an Army Commander on the Western Front, with Lieutenant General Krafft as his Chief of Staff.

1.4 Austro-German Preparations

The XIVth Army was to form part of the Austrian Army Group of the South-West, with the Austrian IInd and Ist Isonzo Armies on its left. The Commander of the Group, Field Marshal the Archduke Eugene, met von Below and Krafft on 15 September, when his Chief of Staff described the Austrian plans for the offensive. According to Krafft, the basic concept of the plan was an 'improvement' of the Austrian positions. To this end, the XIVth Army would advance from Tolmin, its right wing making towards Cividale, and its left wing down the Isonzo towards Monte Korada (Map 2). To the right of the XIVth Army, an autonomous Austrian Corps under General Krauss would advance to Monte Stol and Breginj. At the same time, to the left of the XIVth Army, the two Austrian Armies of the Isonzo would attack frontally but only after the XIVth Army had broken through the Italian line.[12]

To Krafft and von Below, the Austrian objectives were too modest to provide any substantial relief to Austria, and no doubt too modest to justify the presence of such a considerable German army. They also noted that if, as proposed, the Austrian Armies of the Isonzo waited to begin their attack until the XIVth Army had broken through the Italian line, the Italians would be able to deploy all their reserves against the XIVth. In fact Krafft and von Below believed that the minimum objective for all the Armies should be the River Tagliamento.

The Archduke Eugene visited XIV Army HQ on 20 September; good relations were established and it was agreed that all the Armies would aim for the Tagliamento. It was also agreed that the Ist Austrian Corps under General Krauss would form part of the XIVth Army to ensure better coordination of the drive to the Tagliamento. The IInd Austrian Army of the Isonzo to the south of the XIVth would have the initial aim of reaching a line from Monte Korada to Salcano, three miles above Gorizia; the Ist Austrian Army of the Isonzo to the south of the IInd would be ready to take part but in ways not greatly specified.[13] In his diary for 27 September, General von Below noted a conversation with General Boroevic, commanding the Army Group of the IInd and Ist Isonzo Armies, during which Boroevic exclaimed 'We'll never reach the Tagliamento. Never. Never.'[14]

Krafft and von Below recognized the difficulties to be overcome, but unlike Boroevic, believed that German troops and German methods and organization could achieve success. Their optimism was no doubt at least partially due to their knowledge of the new tactics being developed on other fronts. The failure of all the combatants on the Western Front to make significant advances in 1915, and particularly on the Somme and at Verdun in 1916 despite enormous casualties, had forced all the armies to reconsider their methods. By September 1917,

Germany appeared to have taken the lead in developing new tactics for both artillery and infantry techniques.

The French and British armies had usually opened their major offensives with bombardments lasting days or even weeks. Although the effect of these bombardments was not often as great as had been hoped, they certainly gave sufficient notice of the coming attack for the enemy to move up his reserves. On the other hand the Germans had always preferred shorter bombardments for a period of only a few hours, thus gaining the benefits of surprise.

During the years 1916 and 1917 a few artillery officers, particularly Colonel Bruchmüller, experimented to make the German bombardments more effective in various ways: by paying particular attention to bringing up the artillery unseen by the enemy; by developing methods to reduce the primary registration of the guns to a minimum so as to maximize security; by a central control of all the guns for the initial stage of an offensive; by the use of gas as well as high explosive, sometimes up 25 per cent or more of the total fired.[15]

Quite apart from these artillery tactics, the concept of the linear infantry attack was becoming open to question. The first part of 1917 had seen the experimental development of infiltration tactics, in which trained troops probed for weak spots in a line, and then pushed through, leaving any enemy strong points aside, to be dealt with by other troops following up. These various new tactics were most noticeably brought together by General Hutier and his Chief of Artillery, Bruchmüller, at the Battle of Riga on 1 September 1917. Their sudden violent hammer blow against the Russians, followed by a determined and rapid infiltration, achieved a rapid and conspicuous success.[16]

(After Caporetto similar methods were used in the first half of 1918 on the Western Front when the Germans made their final effort to win the war before the Americans arrived in force. Their Michael offensive on 21 March between Arras and Rheims completely disorganized the British Fifth Army, and captured 90,000 prisoners and 1,200 guns. Their offensive on 9 April against the British in Flanders led to the extremely serious situation marked by Haig's famous 'Backs to the Wall' appeal on 12 April. On 27 May similar tactics against the French on the Chemin des Dames resulted in an advance of thirteen miles on the first day of the offensive, the longest advance in a single day since the trenches were dug. By July the front had been pushed back up to forty miles, to within forty miles of Paris. All these German attacks followed the same pattern of a sudden violent hammer blow to break the front followed by determined and rapid infiltration.)

Basic to the XIVth Army's plan of attack was the intention to secure surprise by much careful planning. Hence, the divisions for the initial assault, and their equipment, stores, guns and ammunition would have to be brought up without giving warning to the enemy. The divisions could be concentrated initially in areas around Villach, Ljubljana, and the Sava valley, without much difficulty, but the next thirty or more miles to the front lay through mountainous ground, threaded only by a few roads in steep and narrow valleys where any troop movements could all too easily be observed.

To maintain secrecy, convoys lay concealed during the day, and moved only during the hours of darkness. But the roads to Tolmin were poor, and the only railway was a single track from Bled to Tolmin. Although the roads were grossly overloaded, an efficient system of traffic control maintained the flow, some of the road being divided into blocks, as on a railway, with telephone communication between blocks. There was also a road to Bovec over the Predil Pass (1156m), but the summit was open to Italian fire. Therefore, some 3,000 men were employed in transporting supplies on the electric trains working the underground quarry which lay below the pass, with entrance shafts on either side of the pass. Hence, some 300 tonnes of supplies were transported each day to near Bovec.[17] Further details of the move to the Isonzo are given by Krafft and von Below.

Units of the German Air Force played a vital part in maintaining security during the days of preparation. Hitherto, the Italian Air Force had been able to fly almost unhindered over both sides of the front, and to observe the Austrian positions and movements (provided there was no cloud cover, not infrequent in that part of the world). However, fighter pilots of the German Air Force, working from bases forty miles or so behind the Isonzo, soon established complete air superiority, and there were no more Italian reconnaissance flights. In addition, the Germans were able to make a complete aerial photographic survey of all the Italian front and rear areas. Hence, the cartographic section was able to prepare and distribute accurate maps showing the Italian defences, gun positions, dumps, and lines of communication.[18]

Also at the forefront of the preparations was the deployment of the artillery. Krafft's plan of attack was to begin with an all out onslaught on the Italian defence system, leading to an uninterrupted advance, by night and day, to obtain the high ground all along the line of summits of Monte Canin – Montemaggiore – Mia – Matajur – Jeza – Kum (Maps 2 and 3). The artillery was to provide the key to this break-through. Over a thousand guns would be assembled in the Tolmin sector, with enough ammunition to provide each battery of small calibre with a thousand rounds a day for four days, and a somewhat lesser amount for the medium and large calibres.

To maintain secrecy the guns were brought into position at night, and registration was spread out over a period of six days, followed by two completely quiet days immediately before the assault. At the same time strong artillery action by the Xth, IInd and Ist Armies on either side of the XIVth Army (Map 1), would help limit Italian counter-battery action against the XIVth Army. To obtain the maximum effect from the initial bombardment, all the thousand or so guns of the XIVth Army would be under the sole control of the Artillery Commander, Major General von Berendt, a leading artillery expert. (Control would then revert to the divisions, except for the heavy long-range guns.) Gas was to be used from 02.00 to 04.30 to help paralyse the enemy, and the end of the bombardment was to be marked by heavy mortar fire against the enemy on the valley floor.[19]

As the above preparations went ahead, an elaborate decoy scheme was set up to mislead the Italians. On 13 September the Alpine Corps was posted to the Trentino, where it engaged in patrol activity and sporadic actions employing whole battalions with mountain artillery. Other small parties of Germans appeared elsewhere in the Trentino and on the Carso, while General von Below made a very visible journey through the Trentino. Then, when the Alpine Corps finally moved to the Isonzo front, they were replaced by three German assault battalions from the Western Front who took part in local actions on various fronts in the mountains. To complete the deception radio stations between Lake Garda and Val Sugana broadcast messages suggesting the presence there of a whole new army.[20]

The troops moved up to their final assembly points during the night of 22/23 October for the assault on the 24th. The XIVth Army had encountered surprisingly little Italian interference,[21] but the offensive was now at a most critical phase with the troops massed near the Isonzo in range of the Italian guns.

1.5   Lieutenant Rommel

Among the Germans who came to the assistance of Austria was the young Lieutenant Rommel. Erwin Rommel was born on 15 November 1891, the son of a schoolmaster in Heidenheim in the kingdom of Wurttemberg, a constituent part of Imperial Germany. He joined the 124th Wurttemberg Infantry Regiment as an officer cadet in July 1910, and entered the Imperial War School in Danzig in March 1911. His passing out report in November described him as 'a useful soldier', 'quite good in rifle and drill work', 'adequate in gymnastics, fencing and riding', and 'with immense will-power and enthusiasm . . . con-scientious and comradely. Mentally well endowed'.[22] In January 1912 Rommel was commissioned as a 2nd Lieutenant and for the next two and a half years lived the normal life of a junior officer.

When the war broke out in 1914 the 124th Regiment crossed the German frontier on 18 August, and during the next month advanced

17

against French opposition from the neighbourhood of Longwy to the Argonne district north of Verdun, where it was to remain for some time. Rommel now had the opportunity to put his years of training into effect, and very soon established himself as an expert platoon commander, eager to advance and attack, and sufficiently skilful to obtain success by daring rather than by heavy losses. Hence, he was soon employed for a variety of tasks, and Fraser in his book on Rommel comments that, 'There is no swagger or bravado in Rommel's own account of the earlier soldiering adventure, but the reader has the impression of an officer who was used and over-used whenever a doubt or problem arose.'[23] On 24 September he received a nasty wound in the left thigh from a ricochet bullet while facing three French soldiers with only an empty rifle. He was taken to hospital, and a few days later decorated with the Iron Cross (2nd Class).[24]

Rommel returned to his regiment in January 1915 with his leg still not fully healed. He was given the command of a company, and wrote subsequently: 'There was for me a twenty three year old officer no finer job than that of a company commander. Through direction, clear commands, through constant concern for the men entrusted to you, through self-discipline, and through living together under the same rough conditions a leader can win the confidence of his subordinates in a short time', and when once this is done 'the troops will go with him through fire and water'.[25]

On 29 January he led his company on a raid deep into the French line and captured four bunkers protected by very deep wire defences, and held three of them against a French counter-attack. However, his company had outrun the other companies of the battalion, and he was ordered to withdraw. He was then in a difficult situation for his only line of retreat would come under heavy flanking fire from either side. Therefore, rather than suffer heavy losses, he immediately launched a further attack on the French position, which put the French infantry to flight and disorganized their artillery, and he was able to extricate his whole company except for five men left behind wounded. A few days later 2nd Lieutenant Rommel was awarded the Iron Cross (1st Class), the first lieutenant in the Regiment to gain this coveted award.

Rommel remained with his Regiment in the Argonne sector until September and describes two further attacks by his company on 20 June and 8 September. These do not concern us here, but two other incidents throw some further light on Rommel's character. During May, a more senior lieutenant joined the Regiment, and his seniority automatically entitled him to the command of Rommel's company. The Regimental Commander therefore suggested that Rommel apply for a transfer to another regiment, but Rommel insisted that he wished to stay with his own company, and for the next three months this now

18

well-known and highly decorated officer served as a platoon commander, until he was given command of the 4th Company in July.

Rommel was always eager to attack, but he was always equally mindful of the cost in life of the successes obtained. Referring to some casualties caused by enemy shelling during May, he wrote:

> It is always very painful to take leave of comrades. The dead or severely wounded would be brought back – I will never forget that rifleman whose leg was hit by a fragment of a French mortar. At sunset he was carried past me along a narrow trench in a bloody groundsheet. Grief at the loss of these young men, such splendid trustworthy soldiers, overwhelmed me. I pressed his hand to encourage him. But he said 'Herr Lieutenant it is nothing serious. I will soon be back in the Company, even if I have to walk with a wooden foot.' The gallant rifleman was not again to see the rising of the sun. He died on the way to the hospital. His conception of duty was typical of the spirit of the Company.[26]

The end of September marked the end of Rommel's service with the 124th Regiment for he was promoted Lieutenant and posted as a Company Commander and a founder member of a new specialist unit, the Wurttemberg Mountain Battalion (WMB). The formation of the WMB may well have had its origin in a certain rivalry between the neighbouring states of Bavaria and Wurttemberg. The formation of a ski battalion of ski enthusiasts in Bavaria in October 1914 had been followed by the creation of the Wurttemberg Ski Company No.1 in December. Similarly after the formation of the Bavarian-based Alpine Corps in May 1915, the Wurttemberg Ministry of War established a new specialized unit, the Wurttemberg Mountain Battalion, in October 1915.[27] Although nominally a battalion, the new unit had an establishment of six rifle companies, each of 200 rifles commanded by a lieutenant assisted by four 2nd lieutenants, together with three machine-gun companies, and was thus considerably larger than a normal battalion, approaching the size of a regiment. The command of this specialist unit was entrusted to Major Theodore Sproesser, a career officer previously commanding a battalion of the 125th (Wurttemberg) Infantry Regiment, then forty-five years of age, assisted by a staff which included a captain and a lieutenant.

The basic idea behind the WMB was to create a unit capable of working in the mountains autonomously, providing all its own essential services. Each of the six rifle companies would be trained to carry out operations independently, with its own fire support provided by one or more of the three machine-gun (MG) companies each with six heavy machine guns. Then for a given operation, there could be ad hoc combinations of two or more rifle companies plus one or more MG companies, which would be directed by one of the commanders of the rifle companies involved. Hence a company commander, normally a lieutenant, could find himself with two rifle companies and one MG company, or more, a command approaching that of a normal battalion.

The chain of command in the WMB was unusually direct. Each of the nine company commanders reported directly to Major Sproesser who maintained a close watch on the objectives and progress of the companies. Sproesser's own philosophy is reflected in his orders of 5 November 1917, insisting that all detachments and companies give maximum attention to the following points:

(a)   Maintain pressure at the head of the attack.

(b)   Install and maintain communications day and night (telephone, cyclists, runners).

(c)   Send written messages with simple sketches or prompt messages carried by reliable runners.

(d)   The staff (adjutant or night duty officer, telephonist) to be vigilant at night.

(e)   Mark the route for the next detachments.

(f)   No unnecessary captured material to be carried.

(g)   All must be inspired by the need to press on. Pursuit without rest saves bloody losses.[28]

Major Sproesser's first task on assuming his new command was to establish the structure, efficiency and morale of the Battalion. In May 1915 the Wurttemberg Ski Company had been renamed the Wurttemberg Mountain Company, and the members of this company were transferred to the new battalion. However, most of Sproesser's troops had come following an invitation from the Wurttemberg War Ministry, to all officers and men with expertise in moving on snow, to request a transfer to the new battalion. Hence when the WMB first mustered, at Munsingen in Wurttemberg at the beginning of October, it included officers and men from fifteen or more different units, and from different parts of the service, in a variety of uniforms.[29]

During October and November company commanders, including Rommel, set about training their companies of already experienced soldiers to work together in their new teams. Meanwhile Sproesser and his staff were setting up the administrative and support structure which would enable the Battalion to move and fight in the mountains as an autonomous body using only its own resources. Foremost among these was the transport section to bring up supplies and equipment either by horse-drawn wagons or by pack animals on mountain tracks, including veterinary officers and the supply of fodder for the animals. Also horses for the company commanders. The signal section was responsible for maintaining communications and was trained to lay telephone lines during an attack to maintain contact between the Battalion Commander and his companies. There was also a medical section which included a doctor with each company.

Sproesser was evidently a strict commander who set high standards, and by 24 November the whole WMB was able to parade, with 1500 rifles and 8 machine guns, before King William of Wurttemberg, so that he could 'see for himself what excellently equipped and efficient troops had been formed in a few weeks'.[30] The Battalion then left for the neighbourhood of the Arlberg Pass, and during December spent all the hours of daylight skiing on steep slopes, with and without heavy packs.

In the evening the company sat together in the large bar. The company band under Father Hugel played the latest hits, and mountain songs were sung. All this was very different from my time in the Argonne. I soon learnt that in this informal way I could get to know my men very well, and so strengthen the bond between the leader and the troops.[31]

After an enjoyable Christmas on Austrian rations the WMB soon found themselves on a troop train, not as some had hoped en route to Italy, but to the Vosges sector of the Western Front. Although the most mountainous part of the Western Front, rising up to heights of 1000 to 1400m, the ground was in no sense of alpine character, rather high wooded hills. Moreover, here as all along the Western Front the two sides faced each other in strongly entrenched lines, and for the next nine months no major offensive was made in this sector, and the only action described by Rommel is a successful raid on the night of 4 October. It would seem that the WMB's main effort during this period was to take the opportunity to carry out further training.

Soon after the raid on 4 October the WMB was called to a new front. On 27 August Rumania had declared war on Austria, thus extending the length of the Eastern Front by at least 250 miles. Details of the consequent fighting are given by Cruttwell, Hammerton, and Stone,[32] and do not concern us here, except to note that by 15 September German forces were arriving in Rumania to support the Austrians. The WMB arrived at the end of October, and were initially attached to the 41st Division, and subsequently to the 11th Division and to the Alpine Corps. Then for the next two months the WMB were involved in a war of movement against a redoubtable enemy among mountains rising up to 1700 metres, often in very wintry weather, when cold, rain and frost-bite were severe enemies of both sides.

Details of the largely successful actions of the WMB are given by Sproesser and Rommel,[33] and we note here only that the Battalion was now gaining much experience at working together under hard moun-tain conditions. Rommel too was gaining experience, as for much of the time he was in command of a detachment of two rifle and one machine-gun company.

Following the arrival of the Germans the tide turned against Rumania, and by December much of the country had been occupied including Bucharest, but by the middle of January 1917 it was clear that German hopes of overrunning all Rumania were now stalled. Hence, in January the WMB spent ten days in unheated trains travel-ling back to the Vosges. After a few weeks in the Army Reserve, two thirds of the Battalion took over a stretch of the front line, while a detachment of two rifle and an MG company under Rommel ran a course of combat and training exercises, attended over a period of weeks by all companies in the Battalion, no doubt studying the lessons to be drawn from their time in Rumania.

The WMB were now in a quiet sector, and Rommel makes no mention of any actions between January and July. However, during the summer the political instability in Russia suggested that Rumania was unlikely to receive further Russian support. Therefore, the German High Command decided to complete the occupation of Rumania by an offensive into Moldavia on a sixty-mile front from the south-east corner of the Carpathian mountains north of Bucharest.[34] Hence, the WMB spent a week on a train in extremely hot weather, and were back in Rumania by 7 August.

For the next two weeks the WMB found themselves engaged in a fierce to-and-fro struggle for the ground around the summit of Mont Cosna (788m), one of the strategic bastions of the front.[35] The Rumanians were a formidable enemy. The summit was first captured by the WMB, then withdrawn from, and finally retaken. But no general advance was made, either here or further south at Masaresti, where the Germans encountered epic Rumanian resistance.[36] Reviewing the situation at the end of August the German High Command decided that as Russia was now gripped by revolution, Rumania was now on her own, and would soon have no alternative but to seek an armistice.

Therefore the offensive was abandoned, and the WMB withdrawn from the front.

The WMB had shown themselves to be a most effective fighting force against a brave and determined enemy, but not without cost. In only two weeks the Battalion had casualties of 88 dead, 299 wounded and 6 missing, greater losses than those suffered during their whole time on the Vosges front, or later in Italy. The Battalion had gained considerable battle experience, and no-one more so than Rommel, who had found himself carrying increasing responsibility. On 8 August his detachment comprised one company and three MG companies, but on 11 August comprised four companies and two MG companies (including one company from a reserve regiment).[37] Then for the defensive action on 13 August he was in command of six companies plus two MG companies.[38]

The attack to retake Cosna on 17 August was made by two groups, the Madlung Group (22nd Infantry Reserve regiment) and the Sproesser Group (WMB and the 1st Battalion 18 Infantry).[39] Rommel was ordered to oversee the preparations for all the front-line units of the Sproesser Group, and to take the regimental and battalion commanders of the Madlung Group to see the nature of the ground. Hence, on 18 August he was out all day from dawn to dusk. Then in the attack next day he led a detachment of three companies and two MG companies, plus an army assault detachment, and an engineer platoon.

Rommel was now becoming an experienced battalion commander; he was also becoming extremely exhausted. He had been wounded in the elbow, with loss of blood as early as 10 August, but had carried on with his arm heavily bandaged. Nevertheless he still showed his remarkable capacity to drive himself to the limit, and continued in his command for another ten days, until on 20 August he was overcome by a high fever and forced to hand over his command to the next senior officer, Captain Gössler.

The fighting now died down, and the WMB was withdrawn from the front on 25 August, and then for some reason not stated was sent to Macedonia. However, they were soon sent to Carinthia in Austria to join General von Below's XIVth Army preparing to strike against Italy. Here in early October they were joined by Rommel, now fully restored by a few weeks leave by the sea in northern Germany.

Italian Strategy and Tactics

2.1 War Weariness

All the combatants in the autumn of 1917 faced a grim outlook. They were now engaged in costly battles with great casualties but without any obvious gains. The stresses of war had led to the communist revolution in Russia and its withdrawal from the war. The French Army, sorely tried in 1916 at Verdun, had been launched into General Nivelle's April offensive to break the deadlock on the Western Front. But the principal effect of this ill-conceived operation was to produce mutinies in the French armies on such a scale that the French were unable to mount any substantial actions for the rest of the year. (Fortunately for the Allies, the Germans failed to realize how little the French generals could rely on their units.)

In Italy, as elsewhere, the war had turned out very differently than expected. After heavy losses in 1915 and 1916 the operations in 1917 had by the end of September claimed another 330,000 dead, wounded or missing.[1] The home front was suffering from shortages of food and fuel particularly because of the successes of the German U-boat campaign. On innumerable peasant farms the womenfolk had to struggle on as best as they could in the absence of their men. At times crops of fruit were left to rot because there were no ships to export them.[2]

Shortages and general dissatisfaction with the war gave fertile ground for anti-war propaganda by a mixed bag of pacifists, socialists, communists, and clerics. Their arguments were the more effective because, as had been shown by the debate preceding Italy's declaration of war, the country as a whole had no very clear idea of its war aims. Many of the infantry soldiers bearing the brunt of the fighting came from small farms and holdings in central and southern Italy, and had little idea of what the war was about, see for example Trevelyan.[3] Certainly the sentences of military tribunals indicate that a high proportion of offenders were illiterate,[4] and according to Silvestri up to 50 per cent of some units were illiterate.

The British Ambassador to Italy during the war has described how illiterate families had to rely on professional or friendly assistance when they wished to send a letter to a son or husband. Apparently benevolent individuals moved from village to village and offered to write letters from parents to sons, gratuitously, even adding the additional inducement of free postage. However, it seemed that some of these writers were using the opportunity to paint a most gloomy picture of life at home so as to depress the men at the front.[5]

Perhaps the most influential of the various subversive activities were those sponsored by the Roman Church. It was only in 1870 that the Vatican had lost control of the Papal State including Rome and the States of the Church which together formed a wide band of territory stretching right across the Italian peninsula. If Catholic Austria won the war the Vatican might hope for greater influence and perhaps once again take possession of these lands. In fact the Treaty of London included a clause at Italy's request in which France, Britain and Russia agreed to support any objection by Italy against a Vatican representative at any of the peace negotiations or settlements.[6]

The Church was also considerably concerned by the spread of socialism and communism. Here again the best solution to the problem appeared to be the victory of Catholic Austria. The Church was well placed to pursue a policy supportive of Austria with a priest in every parish, and also access to diplomacy at the highest levels. Since 1914 the Vatican had made clear its abhorence of war and had continued to make representations to the warring nations to find a peaceful solution to the conflict. Unfortunately the terms suggested by the Vatican as a basis for peace proposals always appeared unduly favourable to Austria and Germany, and were never acceptable to the Allies.

The combination of the hardships of the war and the influence of anti-war propaganda produced various reactions during 1917. On the home front there were many sizeable demonstrations, often by the women going each Monday to collect their subsistence allowances.[7] These demonstrations appear to have spread over the whole country and from the end of April to the beginning of November the 4th Cavalry Division was stationed in Piedmont and Lombardy for purposes of public security.[8]

By far the most serious incident occurred in Turin where 125,000 workers in the factories gave scope for agitators and dissatisfaction. At the beginning of August a shortage of flour led to queues at the bread shops. On 21 August several shops were forced to close and after the midday break many workers did not return to the factory. Further demonstrations and disorder followed on 23, 24 and 25 August which ended with thirty-five demonstrators dead and three police and military dead.[9]

Not surprisingly General Cadorna was concerned that this

propaganda and unrest in the country was affecting the state of the army, and that troops were returning from leave with lowered morale. Throughout the summer of 1917 he urged the government to clamp down on the publication of seditious material and other activities. However, the government chose to claim that it was not the country subverting the army but soldiers subverting the country. Even so it was in Parliament on 12 July that deputy Treves made his famous call '*I prossimo inverno non piu in trincea*' (No one in the trenches this winter).[10]

A peace initiative by the Pope in August 1917 was regarded with particular disfavour by the Army Command. On 9 August, after lengthy consultations with Germany and Austria, the Pope had presented a note to the Allied governments which set out proposals for a peace, and called for an end to this 'useless slaughter'.[11] News of the note was only published in the Italian press on 16 August which happened to be the day before the start of the 11th Battle of the Isonzo. The generals were furious, and Cadorna concerned for morale, put an embargo on all the newspapers which had given the reports. (However, the offensive turned out to be relatively successful, and Cadorna was forced to lift his ban on the press in order to scotch ill-founded rumours that some revolution had broken out in Italy.[12])

2.2   Stresses in the Army

Cadorna had always been very conscious that the war would impose severe stresses on the army and that a successful outcome would depend on maintaining a good morale. In addition he believed that the principal source of this good morale would be an '*iron discipline*' as described in Circular No.1 from the Comando Supremo issued on the first day of the war, 24 May 1915. This long order stated, inter alia, that 'the main source, the most pernicious, of a declining discipline is the '*culpable* and sometimes *criminal tolerance* by those who should instead be its most vigilant guardians . . . One proceeds with sharp sighted observation and suppresses with inflexible rigour . . . Punishment must follow swiftly, the immediateness of the response succeeds by salutatory example, destroys at birth the germs of indiscipline.'[13]

As in other countries the modes of discipline were set out in Army Acts promulgated by Parliament, according to which those guilty of serious offences were tried by courts martial. In all 170,000 sentences were pronounced by Italian tribunals during the war.[14] This is a high number but not surprisingly so in view of the very large number of men in the army for several years. The British military tribunals delivered some 226,000 sentences for a somewhat larger army over a somewhat longer period.[15]

The Italian total included 4,028 death sentences but the greater part of these were on men who had been too easily taken prisoner, and were only available to the authorities at the end of the war when amnesties were introduced. Of those present and condemned, 1,006 in all, 729 were shot and 277 were reprieved.[16] These figures make an uncomfortable impression on the modern reader, but are not greatly different from those for other countries. For example British tribunals pronounced 3,080 death sentences, mainly for desertion, of which 346 were confirmed.[17]

During the twenty years following 1918 the medical aspects of the stresses of war became better understood and better methods devised for coping with these stresses. In the Second World War death sentences were extremely rare, and British courts martial pronounced only four death sentences for military offences.[18] Yet there is no doubt that the higher officers in the First World War, corps and army commanders, both British and Italian, believed that the death penalty was essential to maintain the efficiency of the armies, particularly by giving a stark warning to others of the consequences of failing in their duty. In the Italian Army, units were on occasion paraded to witness the execution of some of their members,[19] and executions in the British Army were announced in General Routine Orders.[20]

The Australians were unique among the Allies in that their government always commuted any death penalty that might be pronounced by a tribunal. They regarded it as totally out of place in an army of volunteers as they were (and indeed as the British Army was until 1916). Their official historian, C.E.W. Bean, remarks on 'the constant reading out, on parade, by order throughout the British Army, of reports of the infliction of the death penalty upon British soldiers – a ceremony which aroused in the Australians, officers and men, only a sullen sympathy and a fierce pride that their own people was strong enough to refuse this instrument to its rulers'.[21] On the other hand Bean also gives figures which show that for the first six months of 1917 the rates of desertion in France were three times greater for the Australian forces than for the British.[22]

The systems of discipline outlined above may now appear outdated and draconian, but they were not fierce enough for Cadorna. Already in his order for 24 May 1915 there appeared the warning that 'the Comando Supremo will hold responsible those in high commands who did not, at the proper time, know [how] to apply the powers which the regulations for discipline and the military penal code confer on them, or who show hesitation to take, without delay, the initiative to enforce, when the situation demands, the extreme measures of coercion and repression.'[23] This was followed by even more explicit statements in Circular n.3525 on 28 September 1915 which laid down, inter alia, that anyone who attempts to ignominiously surrender or

27

retreat will meet with 'the summary justice of lead from the lines behind them or from the military police behind the troops'. Moreover, 'anyone who succeeds in escaping this salutatory summary justice will encounter – inexorably, exemplarily, immediately – that of the military tribunal; for the infamy of the guilty, and as an example to others, the capital sentence will be carried out in the presence of adequate representatives of the corps'.[24]

On occasion the safety of a unit or the success of an entire operation may be jeopardized by failures of duty. In such cases reference to a tribunal is hardly an adequate response and summary action in the form of a pistol shot may be the only alternative. Yet, reading Cadorna's orders, it is clear that the Comando Supremo believed that the condition of the army called for a much wider application of the methods of so-called summary justice.

In fact Cadorna favoured an even rougher form of summary discipline, the old Roman punishment of decimation of units that failed in their duty. The original term implied the execution of one man in ten selected at random, but was now used to include the execution of a number of men selected at random. Cadorna much regretted that the law did not permit decimation and pressed his views on the government. Not surprisingly the government did not respond, but nevertheless his views must have been known to senior commanders.

The first well-documented case of decimation occurred during the Strafexpedition on 26 May 1916 following the flight of members of 141 Regiment during an Austrian attack. A 2nd Lieutenant, 3 sergeants and 8 men were shot, and subsequently 74 others sent to tribunals. Subsequently on 22 June Cadorna's order of the day included a commendation of Colonel Thermes for dealing so well with the situation, and according to Simone this was the first time in the war that an individual officer had been formally recognized in the Army Orders of the Day.[25]

On 1 July 1916 a company of the Salerno Brigade, completely cut off in no-man's-land for two days, attempted to surrender to the Austrians. They were shot down by their own machine guns and artillery. The Corps Commander then ordered the execution of eight men, one said to be guilty, three on suspicion, and four selected at random.[26]

On 30 October 1916 stones were thrown at the commander of the 75th Regiment and on 1 November Cadorna telegraphed a circular congratulating the Corps Commander for executing two men chosen at random from the suspects, and insisting that such action was the duty of all commanders.[27] However, on 20 November he thought fit to cover himself by writing a long letter to the Prime Minister, Signor Boselli, in which he justified decimations, particularly that on 1 July, and claimed inaccurately that decimation was practised in all armies.

28

Subsequently Boselli talked with Cadorna but apparently without being firm enough to produce any appreciable change of policy.

Various similar incidents followed in 1917. On 6 March the Ravenna Brigade were withdrawn from the front line for a rest period and found their time fully occupied with training and fatigues. Hence when ordered to return to the front on 21 March men of the 38 Regiment protested, but were restored to order when addressed by their Brigadier. Subsequently after the men had all moved off to the front the Divisional General, who had then finished his dinner, came to enquire how many men had been shot for this indiscipline. After some equivocation by the Brigadier, the General ordered the immediate execution of two soldiers found sleeping in barracks (one an older man with seven children) even though all the other troops had left two hours earlier. The next day the Brigadier was dismissed from his post and replaced by an officer who executed five men selected at random from the company principally concerned.[28]

The months from May to September, a period including the 10th and 11th Battles of the Isonzo, appear to have been particularly stressful in that the number of death sentences by courts martial reached an all-time high: 239 of which 199 were carried out.[29] The number of reported summary executions also rose. From 1 May to 1 June, twenty-seven men were shot following six different incidents. (Also during this period the notorious General Graziani spent hours during battle, not at his command post but in the front line, with a hand gun ready to give chase to threaten any shirker.[30]) In August a further nine men were summarily shot following two incidents.

A still more serious incident occurred on 15 July in the Catanzaro Brigade. This unit had fought well on the Carso but had justifiable grievances concerning lack of leave and being kept in the front line longer than other units. On 15 July the Brigade Commander ordered the arrest of nine men identified as trouble makers by under-cover carabinieri posing as infantry. He brought up parties of carabinieri and cavalry and referred to the rules of decimation. These events set off an organized mutiny that evening principally by the 6th Company of the 142 Regiment.

Order was soon restored but 2 officers and 9 men were left dead, and another 2 officers and 25 men injured. In the early hours of the following day 28 men were summarily shot on the orders of the Corps Commander, General Tettoni; 16 had been found with smoking guns and 12 were taken at random from the 6th Company. During the following days another 4 soldiers were shot, 135 others sent to military tribunals, and some 500 others (officers, cadets and soldiers) transferred to other units.[31]

A further source of great concern to Cadorna was the large number of prisoners, 25,000 in all, captured by the Austrians during the 10th Battle of the Isonzo. A first-hand account of Cadorna's reaction to these events is given by Colonel Gatti who was attached to the Italian High Command in the role of Official Historian from March 1917 until December 1917 and had free access to the GHQ at Udine. His personal diary for this period published only in 1964 gives a detailed account of his privileged view of events.

On 7 June Cadorna told Gatti that he was much worried that during the fighting on the Carso near Monte Hermada 10,000 men from three regiments (in the Ancona, Verona and Puglie Brigades) had dishonourably deserted to the enemy without cause. This was such a disgrace, said Cadorna, that one could write in the name of military camaraderie to the Austrian Commander, General Boroevic, and ask him to flog the villains.[32]

A more complete account of the events at Hermada was only given in 1938 by General Bencivenga who had worked as Cadorna's military secretary. According to Bencivenga the troops involved had been halted during an assault up the slopes of Monte Hermada and found themselves in very poor defensive positions. Then an Austrian counter attack from above had been able to penetrate their line and encircle units from the rear. Hence Bencivenga states that the units had fought well until their generals were killed and they were completely cut off.[33]

Whatever the details of the events on Hermada, the debacle itself pointed to serious weaknesses in the army, including inadequate direction and inadequate training to deal with infiltration techniques. As usual, however, Cadorna saw only a need for more discipline, and for more action against seditious propaganda both in the army and in the country. Gatti's diary shows that he had a high opinion of Cadorna, but also thought that Cadorna's essentially negative response inadequate to meet the situation.[34] (An example of a more positive approach was given in a document 'Outline of a scheme of patriotic education for the troops' issued by the Chief of Staff of the German Army in July 1917.[35])

Gatti's diary also makes clear the hard and dangerous life of the infantry soldier as in his description of an attack on Monte Santo in May.[36] Too often troops were thrown into ill-prepared operations with inadequate artillery preparation which left enemy wire unbroken. The rotation of troops between the front line, the reserve line, and rest quarters was often very badly organized, with the result that troops might be kept in the front line for long periods without relief. For example, the Bergamo Brigade were called on for an attack after having been in the trenches for 35 days. Likewise the rotas of leave were often poorly arranged with the result that the best troops might spend most time in the trenches and have least leave.[37]

Gatti was well aware that Cadorna, a Piedmont aristocrat, had little appreciation of the character and way of life of his often illiterate soldiers and little idea of how to motivate them.[38] Moreover a similar gap between officers and men was not uncommon as was noted for example by Villari[39] and Geoffrey Young.[40] The latter worked with a British ambulance unit and much enjoyed sharing the mess and company of the doctors and surgeons of an army medical unit, but described their surgery which seldom used anaesthetics as 'brilliant but without compassion' and 'needlessly cruel'. It seemed to him that 'the cultivated officer-mind had no touch at all with the soldier or peasant, and no imagination of what he thought or felt'. Gatti and others were well aware of these and other problems, but their views had little influence.

2.3   The Move to the Defensive

After the conclusion of the Bainsizza offensive in September General Capello, commanding the 2nd Army, was eager to advance further into the Bainsizza as soon as possible, but Cadorna was more cautious. It was necessary to prepare for the campaigns of 1918 and he was well aware of the need to recuperate from the heavy losses in men and material on the Carso, the Bainsizza and Ortigara. He was also aware of stresses produced by anti-war propaganda tugging at the morale of the army, and of failures in the army, as at Hermada earlier in the year. In addition, Cadorna was concerned at the possibility that the Austrians would transfer troops from the Russian front for an offensive perhaps from the Trentino, the Asiago plateau, or towards the Isonzo. He therefore decided to husband his resources and to take up the best positions to resist any attack.

At this time the position of the Italian Armies on the Isonzo front was similar to that shown in Maps 1 and 2 which are based on Carta 3 of the IOH giving the positions on 1 October. The front from Monte Rombon and Bovec in the north to about three miles south of Gorizia was held by the very large 2nd Army with eight Corps (IV, XXVII, XXIV, II, VI, VIII, XIV, XXVIII). Then from below Gorizia to the sea the line was held by the 3rd Army commanded by the Duke of Aosta with four Corps (XI, XXV, XIII, XXIII). The whole front was everywhere to the east of the Isonzo except for Monte Rombon and a small bridge-head at the north end held by the Austrians near the small town of Tolmin.

Cadorna's order f.4470 of 18 September[41] laid down his defensive strategy for the 2nd and 3rd Armies. A photograph of the original autograph order in the Official History shows Cadorna's own underlining of three main points: the renunciation of offensive operations along the whole front; a concentration on defence; and the importance of

31

working immediately on the various tasks necessary to establish good defensive positions, including the relocation of the artillery. The Italian phrase for 'immediately' at the end of the order was doubly underlined. The next day, 19 September, the Duke of Aosta commanding the 3rd Army issued clear and concise orders for a planned realignment to positions best suited for defence, and stating that the necessary work was to be started at once (*non se perda un sol minuto*).[42]

General Capello commanding the 2nd Army acted rather differently. His 2nd Army had just made a relatively large advance of up to five miles on the Bainsizza. He favoured the doctrine of attack and had no interest in a purely defensive strategy. He appears to have believed that he could crush any Austrian attack launched from Tolmin by attacking its flank from the Bainsizza, even though the well prepared 2nd Army offensives on the Bainsizza in August and September had failed to gain ground towards Tolmin.

On receiving Cadorna's order of 18 September, Capello did not issue orders as Aosta had done, but on 19 September held a conference with his Corps Commanders. A report of this conference sent to the Comando Supremo ended with a paragraph which stated: 'Remember finally that even if the defensive concept must guide us at the moment, in all of us there must always be present the spirit of the counter-offensive.'[43] The use of the term counter-offensive was particularly significant. Any defensive operation may, and very probably will, include counter-attacks but Capello chose to use the word counter-offensive which refers to an operation on a much greater scale and out of line with Cadorna's instructions.

There was clearly a considerable gap between the views of Cadorna and his Army commander. Capello's response was not what Cadorna had expected, but Cadorna himself was partly responsible. His order is described by the IOH as 'extremely laconic', not sufficiently stressing the importance of a defensive strategy, and not setting out principles for the conduct of the defence.[44] Nor was the position much clarified by Cadorna's subsequent order N.4484 on 19 September concerning the defence of the Bainsizza.[45] This stated inter alia that the 2nd Army had more guns than were needed for its defensive role; that the guns were required for other (unspecified) armies; and ordered Capello to 'foresee immediately a possible reduction of 270 medium and heavy guns'.

These serious differences between Cadorna and Capello should have been resolved. Yet Cadorna made no move, and Capello continued to blur the issue by confounding the concept of a counter-offensive with that of a normal counter-attack in a defensive battle. After the war these differences were to give rise to discussion and argument, here we merely outline some of the more important conse-

32

quences during the following weeks, using mainly the orders and documents published in the IOH. First, however, we need to outline some details of the Italian defensive system on the upper Isonzo.

2.4   The Italian Defence System

The standard Italian practice for laying out lines of defence was set out in two directives issued on 28 January and 29 April 1917, which replaced an earlier directive of 10 February 1915, in order to take account of subsequent developments and experience. The normal scheme for a defensive system where the topography of the ground was not unduly complicated was based on three lines of defence. The 1st line was usually an advanced line, essentially the limit of previous advances, often not well placed, and generally lightly held. The 2nd line was usually the line of resistance, or main line, chosen to give good defensive positions, with shelters, supported by artillery and other units to the flank. The 3rd line was usually the 'Army' line chosen to be very strong by making the best use of natural features.[46]

The plan of the defence lines on the Isonzo front is set out in Carta 8 of the IOH, which shows that the lines on the ground were more numerous and less clearly related to each other than in the scheme laid down in the directives. Nowhere was this difference more marked than in the very mountainous sector selected for the XIVth Army's offensive. The asperity and complexity of this ground is such that the Italian positions at the commencement of the battle do not readily fall into a system of three separate lines. Therefore, rather than attempt to show these lines Map 3, based on the IOH[47] and Faldella,[48] shows the approximate positions of the Italian infantry divisions and battalions which faced the enemy in the main defensive line on 24 October.

When viewing Map 3 one must remember that the ups and downs of the ground are considerable. The north end of the front began high up on the slopes of Monte Rombon (2208m) and Monte Canin (2587m), descended to the river near Bovec (460m), and then rose to the summit of Monte Vrsic (1898m) and followed the main ridge to the summits of Monte Nero (2245m) and Monte Rosso (2052m). Immediately beyond Monte Rosso the sheer south-facing cliffs below the ridge made defensive positions both impractical and unnecessary. After this gap the line continued at altitudes between 1300m and 1100m, on steep slopes below the summit ridge of Sleme and Mrzli, and eventually fell to cross the Isonzo between Gabrje and Dolje.

The section of the front between Monte Rombon and Gabrje was held by the Italian IV Corps comprising the 50th, 43rd and 46th divisions, and most of the troops were close to the line of contact, in positions with very little depth. The IOH comments that the defence

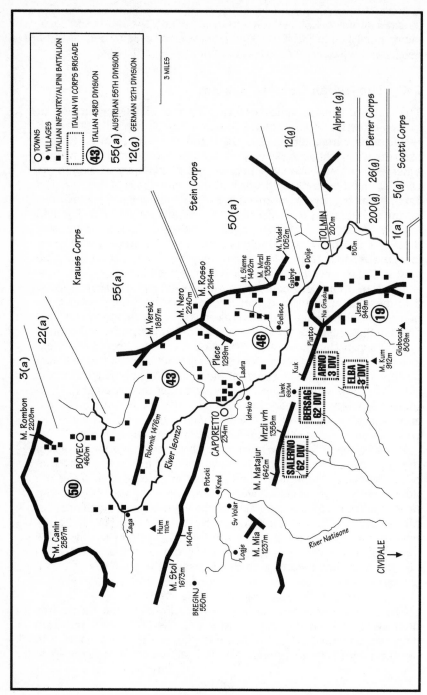

Key:
- ○ TOWNS
- ● VILLAGES
- ■ ITALIAN INFANTRY/ALPINI BATTALION
- [43] ITALIAN VII CORPS BRIGADE
- (43) ITALIAN 43RD DIVISION
- 55(a) AUSTRIAN 55TH DIVISION
- 12(g) GERMAN 12TH DIVISION

3 MILES

3. The initial Italian deployment. (Positions of battalions after Faldella Vol. 2.)

system of three lines shown in Carta 8 of the IOH could have been the basis for a good defensive system with some depth, and with its main strength in the 2nd and 3rd lines. Yet, as the IOH continues, the majority of the troops were stationed on the weakest 1st line, and if no time were available to activate the 2nd and 3rd lines then those positions would be useless.[49]

The deployment of the troops was far from ideal in the sectors held by the 43rd and 46th Divisions. In the 43rd Division the greater part were concentrated high up on the long ridges of Monte Nero. Although in some ways this front line provided good positions it had two very considerable disadvantages. The positions lacked depth and, as most of them were high up, were ill placed for bringing forward reserves from the valley floor between 1000m and 2000m below.[50]

The situation was even less satisfactory in the 46th Division's sector. The 1st line, running along the slopes of Sleme, Mrzli and Vodel, was very largely the line which marked the limit of the move forward in 1915, and had in no way been chosen to provide good defensive positions. The IOH describes the line as being on very steep and impractical ground, and dominated by nearby enemy trenches higher up the mountain side.[51] Despite the disadvantages of this line, set out in detail in the IOH, it was garrisoned as the principal line of defence, while a spur running down from Monte Nero to Monte Pleca and Salisce which offered good defensive positions was held less strongly (by the 43rd Division above M.Pleca and by the 46th Division below).

Beyond Gabrje the front line crossed to the right bank of the river, and was held by the 19th Division and the Vth Alpini Group of XXVII Corps, deployed to defend the line of the heights Hlevnik, Na Gradu, Jeza, Cicer, Grad (Maps 3 and 4). The first defence line lay low down in wet ground just above the level of the river and was used primarily only for forward observation. Next a principal line ran along the lower slopes of the hills at about the 500m contour level, about 200m above the valley floor. According to the IOH this was a good line recently constructed in the light of current experience and was held in a state of efficiency. Then the third and strongest line followed the heights of the main ridge from beyond Na Gradu to Jeza and Globocak, with good defensive positions around Na Gradu, Hlevnik, Jeza and Globocak.

The IOH also states that the works had been built some time previously and their design was not fully up to contemporary standards,[52] probably because the mountains from Tolmin onwards are higher and rougher than those further downstream. Probably for the same reason this part of the front was manned by a relatively small number of troops. The three divisions of IV Corps and one division of XXVII Corps covered a front of about twenty miles,

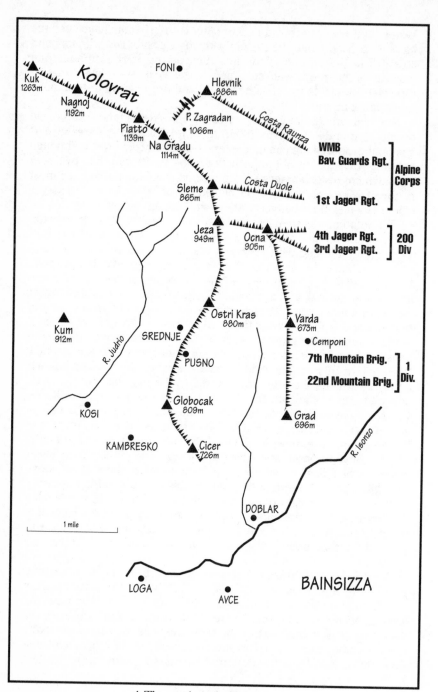

4. The attack on the Kolovrat.

whereas to their right the next twenty miles of the 2nd Army front were held by ten divisions. Moreover, of the four divisions of XXVII Corps, one was allocated to a five-mile sector on the right bank opposite the Tolmin bridgehead, and three to a three-mile sector on the Bainsizza. (The 19th Division was a large one with three brigades, and was augmented by three alpini battalions, but even so there was still a considerable disparity.) Nor was this low level of support compensated by the presence of nearby reserves, for Carta 15 of the IOH reveals a striking absence of reserve units in the region to the north of Cividale. Indeed, according to the historian G.M. Trevelyan who directed a British Red Cross ambulance unit working with the 2nd Army, Caporetto was a quiet area where drivers who had served under particularly severe conditions at Plava or Gorizia 'could serve a term under peace conditions'.[53]

2.5 Cadorna's Orders

General Cadorna's order N.4470 of 18 September had stated unambiguously that the 2nd and 3rd Armies were to renounce offensive operations and concentrate on establishing good defensive positions. Yet General Capello appeared reluctant to inform his commanders of this change in policy. His order N.5268 to his corps commanders on 22 September stated that it was necessary to convince the enemy of 'our offensive intentions',[54] and the IOH states that Cadorna's order had 'no immediate repercussions in XXVII Corps'.[55]

At the end of September intelligence reports suggested a build-up of Austrian forces by up to 30 battalions during the previous two weeks, and also the presence of some German troops behind the lines.[56] However, on 30 September the daily bulletin from the situation office at the Comando Supremo concluded that the enemy was doing no more than taking precautions against any renewal of the Italian offensive.[57] Hence on the following day, Capello proposed to Cadorna that until the situation became clearer the 2nd Army should suspend its movements for both attack and defence, including presumably those ordered by Cadorna.[58]

On 2 October a captured Polish officer told of the likelihood of a large-scale attack from behind Tolmin.[59] On 4 October Capello, who was not in good health spent the day in bed, and on 5 October Cadorna left for two weeks leave in Vicenza (including inspections of defences in the Trentino and on Monte Grappa).[60] It was unfortunate that at this critical time Capello was not at full efficiency, and that Cadorna was unaware of how little had been done to carry out his orders of 18 September. In fact Cadorna's instruction that a maximum effort be given to defensive preparations was eventually passed on to the 19th

Division by General Badoglio, commanding XXVII Corps, only on 6 October.[61]

On 7 October Capello gave General Cavaciocchi commanding IV Corps permission to go on leave.[62] However, the next day Capello received a report of a possible attack by German troops,[63] so he recalled Cavaciocchi, and on 8 October issued directive N.5757 to his corps commanders, which stated not only that the defence of the first line must be undertaken with energy and by means of counter-attacks, but also that when an enemy offensive is halted and paralysed there is an opportunity for a great counter-offensive. This, so the order continued, was particularly relevant at the present time when the Italian morale was notably superior to that of the enemy.[64]

Soon, however, the continuing reports of enemy preparations appear to have produced at least some change in Capello's views. On 9 October he held a conference with his corps commanders, a summary of which was set out in directive N.5796.[65] The dispositions of the 2nd Army were now described as 'excessively offensive', and it was stated that they should be 'partly modified'. On the following day the 3rd Division of XXVIII Corps was ordered to organize defences behind the 19th Division of XXVII Corps on the line M.Piatto – M.Kum – M.Globocak.[66] At the same time Capello reinforced the reserve of IV Corps (the 2nd Regiment Bersaglieri) with the 9th Regiment Bersaglieri, but as the IOH comments, this was still 'a modest reserve for a 40 km front'.[67]

Cadorna was now on leave in the Trentino but on 10 October, probably after learning of Capello's order of 8 October, he issued a general directive to Capello, order N.4741, listing measures necessary for a defensive posture, including an instruction that the greater part of XXVII Corps move to the right bank of the Isonzo.[68] But, as the IOH comments, Cadorna failed to take this opportunity to sort out the various conceptual differences between himself and Capello.[69]

In fact Capello had now been ill for several days. On 10 October he was obliged to take a course of medical treatment, and General Montuori assumed the Command of the Army as *Comandante Interinale* (acting commander).[70] The next day General Porro, Cadorna's Chief of Staff, visited 2nd Army HQ and talked with the Director of Medical Services. Capello was apparently suffering from an intestinal infection with renal repercussions, was responding to a milk diet, and was expected to be fit in three or four days. In the meantime Porro confirmed Montuori as *Comandante Interinale* and ordered him 'to exercise complete command of the Army, and have the entire responsibility for it'.[71]

Capello, lacking his usual health and energy, was now on sick leave, relieved of all responsibility, but he was still present at Army HQ. Even when confined to his bedroom, he expected to be kept informed of what was being done by his subordinates, by the Comandante, and by the Comando Supremo. This obviously unsatisfactory arrangement, discussed in more detail by Faldella, was to have a debilitating effect at 2nd Army HQ for the next twelve days.[72] For example, Porro's report on his visit to 2nd Army HQ states that he visited Capello but did not discuss the move of XXVII Corps towards the right bank of the Isonzo because he 'was reluctant to aggravate Capello's illness'.[73] Also, Montuori's order N.5845 of 11 October to his Corps Commanders, essentially a gloss on Capello's order 5757 of 8 October, made no mention of Cadorna's specific instruction that the greater part of XXVII Corps move to the right bank.[74]

On 13 October Montuori requested the Comando Supremo to allot an alpini group to IV Corps for the defence of Bovec, explaining that he did not want to use any alpini from XXVII Corps as that corps was committed for the counter-offensive. The Comando Supremo failed to make any objection to the stated intention of a counter-offensive by XXVII Corps, and transferred the IInd Alpini Group to the 2nd Army the same day.[75] By 15 October Capello was apparently somewhat better, and requested another visit by Porro. As Porro was busy, and perhaps because Capello was still not yet back in command, Colonel Cavallero was sent in his place, and subsequently Porro reported to Cadorna on the information obtained by Cavallero. On 16 October Montuori gave further support to IV Corps by the transfer of alpini battalions from XXVII and XXVIII Corps. (The Vth Alpini Group of three battalions went to the 43rd Division, and the IInd Alpini Group of three battalions to the 50th Division.[76])

Cavallero's report on his visit to Capello included a request by Capello for an additional army corps of three divisions under General Bongiovanni, which would be stationed in the region behind Monte Jeza 'ready to deliver at the right moment the thunderbolt of the counter-offensive'.[77] Such a counter-offensive was clearly contrary to Cadorna's orders, but he avoided any comment on this point in his order issued on 17 October to 'General Capello Comandante della 2nd Armata', even though Montuori was now the acting commander.[78] This somewhat diffuse order transferred the Command of VII Corps (General Bongiovanni) from the 3rd Army to the 2nd Army, in response to Capello's request. The same day, the Duke of Aosta, commanding the 3rd Army, issued order 9688 which noted that the Command of VII Corps was now with the 2nd Army, and transferred the units of the Corps to XXX Corps of the 3rd Army.[79] This was certainly not what Capello had asked for, and the 2nd Army was therefore obliged to set up VII Corps with its own troops.

Both Cadorna and Capello had so far failed to recognize a serious flaw in the Italian defence system. Any enemy forces attacking across the Isonzo would have to scale the line of mountains Matajur – Kuk – Piatto – Na Gradu – Jezu – Globocak (Map 4). From Piatto to Globocak these mountains were strongly protected against an attack from Tolmin by prepared positions and troops. However, should the enemy ever arrive on the right bank of the Isonzo above the Tolmin bridge-head he would then be at the foot of the ridge from Piatto to Matajur, and here there were no troops and no prepared positions. (Although the 3rd Division had been allocated to XXVII Corps to strengthen the defences, it had been ordered to study and organize the line Piatto – Kum – Globocak, behind the already strong positions east of Piatto.[80])

News continued to arrive of increasing enemy activity on and behind the front, as in an intelligence report on 18 October which stated that 'without doubt' preparations were being made with strong forces of German troops for a 'grandiosa' offensive.[81] Capello now gave further attention to his defence system, and on 17 and 18 October (still on sick leave) took part in a conference with his corps commanders.[82] It was laid down that the new VII Corps would consist of the 3rd Division (Arno, Elba and Firenze Brigades), and the Napoli Brigade and the 2nd and 9th Bersaglieri Regiments[83] (presumably to form the 34th Division). Its tasks were: to support the advance defences; to garrison the most important positions on the line Matajur – Kolovrat; to act as a reserve behind IV and XXVII Corps; to manoeuvre counter-offensively at the opportune moment.[84] The IOH comments that the Corps was hardly more than sufficient to garrison the line Matajur – Kolovrat, and that these four tasks were partly irreconcilable, and very difficult to carry out with only five brigades.[85]

On 19 October General Bongiovanni set up Corps HQ at Carraria near Cividale, and issued a detailed order N.10803[86] to his unit commanders. This laid down that the command of the Napoli Brigade would study the positions in the region around Piatto and Na Gradu (1114m); the command of the 3rd Division the positions between Piatto and Livek; the command of the 9th Bersaglieri the positions between Livek (exclusive) and Matajur; and the 2nd Bersaglieri the positions to block the Natisone road between Matajur and Mia. The order also instructed the unit commanders to study the areas of their fronts, from the point of view of both defence and counter-offensive. But the troops were still on their way. General Basso with the command of the 34th Division was the first to arrive, on 20 October, presumably to take charge of the Napoli Brigade and the two Bersaglieri Regiments. [87]

By the time Cadorna returned to Udine on 19 October there was clear evidence of some imminent attack, although its location was still uncertain. He held a discussion ('*un colloquio diretto*') with Capello who was still on sick leave, and then sent for copies of all orders after Capello's conference on 9 October, including 'all deployments set out, sketches showing the deployment of guns and mortars, illustrations and descriptions of defence works'.[88] The next day, 20 October, Cadorna issued order N.4889 to General Capello as *Comandante della 2ª Armata*, stating that the project of a great counter-offensive with distant objectives must be abandoned because 'it has become impracticable'.[89] Also on 20 October Capello's health deteriorated still further and he was admitted to a hospital in Padua.[90] The same day a deserting Czech officer gave another report of a projected attack from Tolmin, and the following day deserting Rumanian officers told of an attack being prepared from Bovec.

Cadorna was by now increasingly concerned that his order N.4741 of 10 October[91] to concentrate the greater part of XXVII Corps towards the right bank had not been implemented. In fact it was only on 22 October that the first infantry units, four alpini battalions, were ordered to the right bank.[92] If we take the order of battle on 24 October,[93] and assume three battalions in a regiment unless otherwise stated, it appears that the Corps had approximately 20 battalions on the right bank holding about 5 miles of line, and 22 battalions on the left bank holding about 3 miles of line. Thus a disproportionate fraction of the strength still remained on the left bank. There was also much delay in responding to Cadorna's order in N.4741 to withdraw all but the most mobile guns from the Bainsizza. By 23 October only 120 medium and large guns had been withdrawn out of a total of 730, a response which the IOH describes as 'very modest'.[94] Moreover the lateness of all the movements produced traffic blocks and delays on the roads at a critical time.

On 22 October Cadorna visited IV Corps HQ at Kred (Map 3) to discuss the state of the defences between Caporetto and Bovec. The Corps Commander, General Cavaciocchi, was suffering from the after effects of some dental treatment and made a poor impression.[95] Cadorna decided that it was essential to strengthen IV Corps as a matter of urgency, and that the only readily available unit was the 34th Division in the newly created VII Corps. As described in the following section, the Division had only been established on 18 October, but had already lost all its initial units, and now consisted only of the Foggia Brigade, recently arrived near Savogna (Map 5) and still awaiting its artillery. The Division was now transferred to IV Corps to provide reinforcements at Zaga, Livek and Caporetto.[96] Then, to maintain the strength of VII Corps, the 62nd Division in the 4th Army was sent from Bassano del Grappa (on the River Brenta) to substitute for the 34th Division.[97]

Meanwhile Capello, on learning that an enemy attack appeared imminent, had left the hospital at Padua and arrived back at his head-quarters at Cormons at 02.30 on 23 October. At 07.00 he conferred with Cadorna at Udine and in the afternoon attended a meeting with Cadorna, Badoglio and his other corps commanders. According to Faldella, Cadorna is said to have expostulated 'My orders, my orders! My father took Rome and it falls to me to lose it!'[98] Later at 16.00 Capello held a conference with his corps commanders and for the first time definitely ruled out the option of a large-scale counter-offensive.[99] Thus it appears that Cadorna's final and most categoric order to abandon any idea of a counter-offensive (N.4889 of 20 October) was only passed on to the 2nd Army Corps Commanders at 16.00 on 23 October.

2.6 The Final Preparations

As described above, the days immediately before the start of the battle saw much activity in the Italian 2nd Army. However, according to the IOH, the 'work of orientation and preparation, as much conceptual as material, became disorganized by the frequent modifications of struc-tural organizations which were characteristic of all the units of the left wing of the 2nd Army'.[100] In this section we summarize how these rearrangements affected some of the units which would be involved in the coming battle.

After VII Corps was set up on 18 October, General Bongiovanni established his Corps HQ at Carraria near Cividale, and issued a detailed order N.10803 to his unit commanders instructing them to study their fronts, from the point of view of both defence and counter-offensive.[101] But the Corps troops had yet to arrive.

On 21 October further information from Austrian deserters led to more rearrangements in an atmosphere described by the IOH as 'tumultuous'.[102] By 22 October the new VII Corps had lost all the units in its embryo 34th Division; the 2nd and 9th Bersaglieri Regiments had been transferred to IV Corps;[103] and the Napoli Brigade to the 19th Division of XXVII Corps.[104] To replace this loss, VII Corps was to receive the reserve 62nd Division, but the first troops from these units only began to reach Savogna between Cividale and Livek on 23 October (Map 5).

At the beginning of October the 62nd Division (Salerno and IV Bersaglieri Brigades) was a reserve division of the 4th Army in the Dolomites, but on the 22nd was posted to VII Corps to replace the 2nd and 9th Bersaglieri Regiments and the Napoli Brigade.[105] The Division left Bassano del Grappa the same day with orders to proceed to Livek. They reached Udine by the evening and the next day were taken on by lorries, but progress was very slow beyond Cividale because the road was blocked by guns and waggons of all kinds, moving in opposite directions, with no obvious march discipline. Therefore, beyond Savogna they proceeded on foot to reach Livek in the dark, and then continued to the Kolovrat and Matajur (1641m), the first units arriving at dawn on 24 October, and the final units on Matajur on the morning of 25 October.

An account of the arrival of the Salerno brigade on the bare mountain top of Matajur is given by Caviglia.[106] The officers were new to the zone. Their orders were to defend the ridge running from the summit of Matajur to near Livek by establishing two lines each between three and four miles long, one at about the 700m contour and the other near the crest of the ridge. According to Caviglia, there were no traces of any defensive works and the troops had to prepare positions as best they could. The mountain was in cloud and the weather stormy. There was no contact with any troops on the left and almost none with the rest of the division on either side of Livek.

Numerous last-minute changes produced a particularly unfortunate situation in the sector of the front which ran down from the Kolovrat and Hlevnik to cross the Isonzo between Gabrje and Dolje. As described above, the most advanced line on the left bank of the river was also the principal line of defence, but on the right bank the 1st line was an advanced line of no great consequence. A 2nd line climbed up to the village of Foni (Map 4), and then followed the 500m contour line as a principal line. The 3rd line (of little significance on the left bank of the river) continued to the ridge of the Kolovrat as a vital part of the defences opposite Tolmin. Hence there was a very marked disjunction as the defence lines passed across the Isonzo from the 46th to the 19th Division, a disjunction described by the IOH as an 'estrema delicatezza'.[107]

Until July 1917 the 19th Division had been part of IV Corps whose front had extended from Rombon to Doblar south of Tolmin. It was then decided to transfer the Division to XXVII Corps, but in order to ensure some unity of command across the river, IV Corps remained responsible for the stretch of line on the right bank of the Isonzo from the river to Foni and Hlevnik. The defence of this line was discussed during a conference at IV Corps on 14 October.[108] The line was said to be well constructed but short of caves and it was suggested that this shortage might be overcome by making use of numerous folds in the wooded ground.[109]

The conference also decided that the reserve for IV Corps would consist of the 2nd and 9th Bersaglieri Regiments except for that part of the 9th Regiment 'strictly necessary' for the defence of the line Isonzo – Hlevnik.[110] The commanders of both the 2nd and 9th Regiments were then ordered to reconnoitre the ground between the Isonzo and

Hlevnik, and garrison the line through Foni with the 'minimum necessary' number of troops.[111] Orders were also given for two companies of the 9th Bersaglieri and two companies of engineers to work on this line.

After the above conference, General Cavaciocchi, commanding IV Corps, issued orders on 17 October, stating that the 2nd and 9th Regiments were to come under the 46th Division for administration but tactically were to remain directly under Corps.[112] However, the next day General Montuori's order N.6046 transferred both regiments to the new VII Corps, commanded by General Bongiovanni, with a front from Matajur to Passo Zagradan.[113] On 19 October Bongiovanni directed the 9th Bersaglieri to 'study' the front from Matajur to Livek (exclusive), and the 2nd Bersaglieri to study the defence of the Natisone valley above Pulfero between Mia and Matajur.[114] The report of a IV Corps conference the same day noted the loss of the 2nd and 9th Regiments but made no mention of which units were now to be responsible for the line between the river and Foni and Hlevnik.[115]

On 21 October General Montuori transferred the 2nd and 9th Regiments back to IV Corps,[116] and the 2nd Regiment was then located near the village of Livek on the Kolovrat, and the 9th Regiment at Idrsko on the Isonzo to defend the line from the river to Foni and Hlevnik.[117] At the same time General Cavaciocchi was asked to assess the state of the defences on Hlevnik. Cavaciocchi's reply N.6128 on 22 October dealt mainly with the summit area, and his only reference to the line from Hlevnik down to the Isonzo was a request that the 19th Division and VII Corps help with work on the defences there, so that he could withdraw the 9th Regiment for other purposes.[118]

Probably in response to Cavaciocchi's request Montuori issued order N.6155, at 14.30 on 22 October, which transferred the Napoli Brigade from the 34th Division to the 19th Division of XXVII Corps, and ordered this corps to garrison and work on the line Hlevnik – Foni – Isonzo. But the order also stated that 'the defence of the river is entrusted to IV Corps'.[119] This last instruction concerning the defence of the river was remarkably vague, but the intention of the rest was clear enough: XXVII Corps was to use the Napoli Brigade to garrison the line Hlevnik – Foni – Isonzo. Yet General Badoglio's order N.3268, of the same day at 17.35, recommended the Napoli Brigade to deploy the least possible force on the line in order to be able to act as a reserve force.[120]

Badoglio's orders to the 19th Division included the charge 'to occupy Hlevnik with the strictly indispensable force and watch [sic] the stretch of the Isonzo to the north of Foni'.[121] That is the 19th Division was to use the absolute minimum numbers on this line and then only 'watch' the river from above. General Villani commanding the 19th Division talked with Badoglio who confirmed that he wanted most of the Napoli Brigade high up as a force of manoeuvre to hold Passo Zagradan. Apparently Villani was sufficiently unhappy about these arrangements that his chief of staff phoned Badoglio's chief of staff who confirmed that one battalion between Hlevnik and the Isonzo would be sufficient.[122] Eventually, of the six battalions of the Napoli Brigade, one was deployed near Foni and two between Piatto and Na Gradu. The Brigade Commander and the three other battalions were located below the ridge of the Kolovrat on the reverse south slopes, far away from any action near the river.[123]

These frantic last-minute changes as well as causing further delay must surely have produced a poor effect on the morale of all concerned. For example, on 20 October General Basso was expecting to take command of the 34th Division consisting of the Napoli Brigade and the 2nd and 9th Bersaglieri Regiments. Two days later all these units had been sent elsewhere. He himself was transferred to IV Corps, where the 34th Divison was reconstituted, by Cavaciocchi's order of 23 October, with the Foggia Brigade (280, 281, 282 Regiments) and the 2nd and 9th Bersaglieri Regiments.[124] But this order also laid down that the 280 Regiment was to be at the disposal of the 50th Division, and that while the Bersaglieri regiments were to be dependent on the 34th Division 'for discipline and tactical purposes', the 2nd Bersaglieri was to be located in the zone of the 46th Division and the 9th Bersaglieri in the zone of the 43rd Division. Hence, when General Basso arrived at Kred (Creda) west of Caporetto on 23 October, his command had been reduced to only the 281 and 282 Regiments. Finally during the morning of 24 October 281 Regiment was assigned to the dependence of the 43rd Division and 282 to that of the 46th Division,[125] so that at that moment General Basso was left with no troops at all.

Finally to sum up a somewhat confused situation we note that the front-line defences of the 50th, 43rd, 46th and 19th Divisions at midnight on 23 October were held by battalions located as shown in Map 3. Behind them, the units of VII Corps had arrived, or were arriving, on the line Matajur – Piatto. The IOH states that

the VII Army Corps approached the battle with the deployment: 62 Division, on the left, with the Salerno Brigade in the zone of Matajur and the IV Bersaglieri Brigade from Livek to M.Kuk; 3 Division on the right, with the Arno brigade on the Kolovrat, and the Elba Brigade on a line between M.Piatto and M.Kum; with the Firenze Brigade as the Corps reserve.

45

It was a deployment of potential: only nuclei out in front and the body of the troops on rear positions which would permit, according to the intentions of the Corps Command, their rapid assembly for engagement in whatever eventuality, either for defence or for counter attack.[126]

3

The Breakthrough at Caporetto

3.1 The Austro-German Attack (24 October)

The attack on the Italian positions was made primarily by the XIVth Austro-German Army under the command of General Otto von Below and his Chief of Staff, General Krafft. The XIVth Army was divided into four groups or corps named after their commanders and comprising Austro-Hungarian (a) and German (g) divisions as shown below:

Krauss (a)	3(a), 22(a), 55(a), Jäger(g)
Stein (g)	50(a), 12(g), Alpine Corps(g), 117(g)
Berrer (g)	26(g), 200(g)
Scotti (a)	1(a), 5(g)
Reserves:	4(a), 13(a), 33(a), 35(a), 94(a)

The 3rd Austrian, or Edelweiss Division, and the 22(a) Division were experienced mountain units. The German Alpine Corps, another specialist mountain unit, was comparable in size to a division rather than a corps, and consisted primarily of the Bavarian Guards Regiment, the 1st and 2nd Bavarian Jäger Regiments, and the Wurttemberg Mountain Battalion (WMB).[1] Although Caporetto was essentially a XIVth Army operation the Austrian armies on either side were ordered to exert pressure on their fronts, but the effects of any such pressure were at first insignificant except on the Bainsizza immediately to the south of the XIVth Army.

On 23 October the front-line divisions of the two armies were deployed as shown in Map 3. The night was cloudy, cold and wet. The Italians waited for the attack in often badly sited positions, and sometimes having been deployed there only very recently. The offensive began at 02.00 with an intense bombardment including the use of gas.

There was little response from the Italian guns. The troops of the XIVth Army began to move forward in mist and rain about 07.30 along the whole length of line from Monte Rombon in the north to Avce on the Isonzo eight miles below Tolmin (Maps 2 and 4).

The principal initial objective at the south end of the front was to gain the high ground west of the river on either side of Tolmin, including the summits of Piatto, Na Gradu, Jeza, and Globocak (Maps 3 and 4). The way would then be open down to Cividale and the plain, but these heights were well defended. First by a lightly held advance line on the valley floor, then by an important line about 300 metres above the valley floor, and finally by a line on the summit ridge. This ridge was generally broad and grassy with numerous small knolls, and gave ample space for the principal defence line furnished with strong points, caves and gun positions all served by good military roads coming up from the rear.

The valley of the Isonzo makes a right-angle turn opposite Tolmin in the region of Na Gradu and Jeza, and Krafft regarded these two summits as the kingpins of the whole Italian defence system, and probably the most strongly defended points of the whole region. Any attackers seeking to breach these defences would be faced with climbs of up to 900 metres on steep mountain slopes rising from the river to the summits. Hence he deployed here a very considerable concentration of force. The German Alpine Corps was assigned to Na Gradu, the German 200th Division to Jeza, and the ridge south of Jeza to the Austrian 1st Division (Map 4). Thus, three selected divisions were to attack the line from Na Gradu to beyond Globocak, held by one Italian division, the 19th of three brigades and an alpini group.

At daybreak the Alpine Corps and the 200(g) Division began to move up the wooded spurs rising from the river to Na Gradu and Jeza, while the 1(a) Division made towards Varda and Grad. Notwithstanding the strength of the defensive positions around Na Gradu, a unit of the Guards Regiment in the Alpine Corps led by Lieutenant Schoerner, a future Field Marshal, captured enemy positions on the summit of Na Gradu on the evening of 24 October, although other Italian positions on the ridge nearby were still holding out (Section 5.1).[2] Meanwhile, the adjacent 200(g) Division had been advancing towards Jeza, where the Italians had turned the summit into 'a veritable fortress'.[3] Even so, by the evening the 3rd Jäger Regiment had taken the summit together with 'thousands of prisoners, 99 guns of which 43 were of 105mm calibre and 2 of 280mm; over 75 machine guns, 45 mortars, 3 large searchlights' and stores of all kind. Further south, units of the 1(a) Division occupied the heights of Varda and Grad (Krad Vehr) overlooking the river, taking some 4,600 prisoners, 77 guns and much other material, and then moved on towards the Italian line high up on the slopes of Globocak.[4]

Notwithstanding such excellent progress on the Kolovrat, the most striking success of the day was on the central sector between Tolmin and Caporetto. The Austrian 50th Division high up on the slopes of Sleme and Mrzli (Map 3) bore down successfully on to the poorly sited positions held by the Italian 46th Division (Section 2.4). Meanwhile, far below, six battalions of the German 12th Division set off from Tolmin to move upstream along the valley floor, towards the point between Gabrje and Dolje where the front line crossed the river. Four battalions followed the road on the Tolmin side of the river, and two followed the main road on the other side.

The four battalions moving up the Tolmin side encountered appreciable opposition, but with the support of their artillery fought their way through two lines of defence, and by 14.00 had crossed the river at Idrsko and joined up with the two battalions on the right bank. Then by 16.00, after only eight hours, the Germans had taken Caporetto, at the rear of the 46th Division, and had captured some 2,000 prisoners. The two battalions which had marched up the right bank of the Isonzo had encountered surprisingly little opposition. One battalion continued to Caporetto, and the other reached Golobi, close to the village of Livek (690m), the lowest point on the ridge of the Kolovrat, where it was halted by units of the Bersaglieri Brigade of VII Corps.[5]

At the north end of the front, defended by the Italian 50th Division, the CCXVI Brigade of the Austrian Edelweiss Division and the LIX Mountain Brigade of the Austrian Xth Army attacked Italian positions high up on Monte Rombon (Map 3) and were rebuffed. But on the valley floor near Bovec, units of the 22(a) Division supported by a massive gas bombardment attacked the three battalions of the 87th Italian Infantry Regiment on the right bank of the Isonzo and two battalions of the 88th Regiment on the left bank. The details of this action are not at all clear but it is known that the Italian gas masks were inadequate, and Caviglia refers to 600 killed by gas in positions south of Bovec.[6] Krafft states that the advancing troops found trenches and gun positions empty. Hence, three battalions of the 22(a) Division were able to advance down the right bank of the Isonzo and by 12.00 had reached Pluzna about a mile beyond Bovec.

During the afternoon, units of the Italian 50th Division were forced back on each side of the river towards Zaga. At this time there was still the possibility of stemming the advance, because upstream from Zaga the narrow Zaga defile offered good defensive positions, well sited to block the road to Uccea. Moreover, most of the 43rd Division had not come under much attack, and were holding their positions on the ridge running up to Monte Nero, and on Monte Polovnik over-looking the road to Zaga. But this division was soon to be in trouble.

It appears that in the early afternoon General Farisoglio, commanding the 43rd Division, received orders from IV Corps HQ to organize a counter-attack on the enemy troops below him on the valley floor around Caporetto.[7] There is no exact record of this conversation, and the IOH says that perhaps it was badly understood and inter-preted.[8] Be that as it may, at about 15.00 General Farisoglio gave orders not only for an attack on the enemy on the valley floor by those troops available, but also for the retirement of all the troops on the front line from Vrsic to Nero! This done, Farisoglio thought he should report on the situation to his Corps Commander, so he went down by car to Caporetto to telephone. There he was captured by the enemy. Faldella remarks that Farisoglio was thus the first general to be captured in the battle, and also the first member of his division to be captured.[9]

Meanwhile the commander of the Etna Brigade in the 43rd Division, who was also Farisoglio's deputy, remained unaware that Farisoglio had been taken prisoner. Hence, left without any direction, and with orders for the front-line troops to retreat, the Division appears to have dissolved into a state of chaos. By the end of the day the whole Italian salient east of the Isonzo running up to Monte Nero had been cut off, most of the troops of the 43rd and 46th Divisions captured, and many of the remainder in some disorder.

In spite of the failure of the 43rd and 46th Divisions it was still possible to hope that those battalions of the 50th and 43rd Divisions still sited on either side of the Zaga defile, could block the road to Uccea, but already the enemy was at Caporetto and could soon threaten the rear of the Italian defences at Zaga. Hence when General Montuori visited Cavaciocchi at Breginj at 16.00 he gave orders 'not to persist' in the defence of Zaga, but to retire 'without fail' to positions across Val Uccea to deny the enemy this road to the west; and the move was made during the night.[10] Hence, on the next day the CCXVII Brigade of the Edelweiss Division and the Austrian 22 Division from Bovec were poised to advance to Uccea and beyond.

Apart from positions held by alpini on Rombon and Nero, now of little consequence, the whole of the Italian main line consisting of supposedly well-prepared positions had been taken by the end of the day. The Italian resistance was sometimes fierce and effective, and the Austrian 1st Division suffered 14 per cent losses in the first two days. But too often the resistance was not sustained. Krafft refers to weak resistance, units surrendering easily, guns not manned, and large numbers of prisoners.[11] The 43rd and 46th Divisions had largely ceased to exist, while the 50th and 19th Divisions had suffered serious losses.

50

Already the Italians had lost between 20,000 and 30,000 men together with most of their guns.

The troops which had avoided capture were now withdrawing, either as disordered units moving to take up new positions, or as individuals making their way rearward as best they could. Geoffrey Young first realized that something was seriously amiss on 24 October when, going up towards the front, he saw troops 'pouring irregularly down the hill sides'.[12] Caviglia refers to columns of deserters from XXVII Corps moving down the road along the right bank of the Isonzo.[13] The diary of the 2nd Army records how General Montuori was held up by crowds at Stupizza on the road from Cividale to Caporetto at 15.30 and had to proceed on foot.[14] The IOH describes how General Badoglio of XXVII Corps encountered a group of artillery retreating in disorder, and at gunpoint ordered the group back to its post.[15]

The only significant Italian success of the day came at the southern end of the front where the Austrian IInd Isonzo Army, on the left of the XIVth Army, had taken part in the offensive. The Austrian 60th and 35th Divisions had attacked the 65th, 22nd and 64th Divisions of the Italian XXVII Corps, but were held by the 65th and 64th Divisions, the 64th taking about 500 prisoners.[16] The attack on the 22nd Division had some initial success, but was then driven back by a counter-attack which left over 800 Austrians dead or wounded, and took 200 prisoners.[17]

3.2   At Italian GHQ (24 October)

News of the enemy attacks filtered back quite slowly to the Command of the 2nd Army, and to the Comando Supremo. The 2nd Army summary of events written at 10.00 recorded some intense artillery fire during the night, and that it was still continuing. Yet, as the IOH comments, 'there was no shadow of preoccupation in this communication with the fact that there was no news from the line of combat'.[18]

Cadorna, having no news, was still uncertain where the main attack would fall: on the lower Isonzo, on the upper Isonzo, or the Trentino. At 09.30 he had sent a message to 2nd Army stressing the importance of holding the line Jeza – Globocak,[19] but this was followed by other messages at 10.35 and 12.15 asking how many guns the 2nd Army could send to the 3rd Army in case of an enemy attack there.[20] After 10.00 news began to arrive at Capello's HQ, and at about 10.30 he telephoned General Caviglia, commanding XXIV Corps to say that the line of XXVII Corps on his left had been broken, and the enemy had reached Cemponi and Costa Duole (Map 4).[21]

At 11.40 Capello began bringing up his reserves by ordering a brigade of the 47th Division to join VII Corps in the defence of the line

Matajur to Globocak. Then at 12.00 he ordered the 53rd Division to move to Stupizza (Map 5) in the valley of the Natisone north of Cividale.[22] Also, at about the same time he put IV Corps and VII Corps, the left wing of the 2nd Army, under the command of General Montuori, whose first move was to visit the commander of IV Corps, General Cavaciocchi.

Meanwhile General Cadorna at Udine remained uncertain whether he was dealing with the main offensive or with the prelude to a greater attack elsewhere. It was only at 13.00 that Capello received some detailed news of the situation in IV Corps, namely that the enemy facing the 50th Division had occupied Bovec, and were now a mile or two beyond, moving towards Zaga. The line of the 46th Division had been overcome, and the enemy was advancing up the Isonzo beyond Selisce.[23] The diary of the Ufficio Storico at the Comando Supremo records that only a little more news had arrived by 14.30: there was no change in the situation in IV Corps; XXVII Corps had reported that the enemy bombardment was continuing, and that communications were interrupted. On the east side of the Isonzo XXIV Corps were organizing a counter-attack to recover a small length of lost trench.[24]

The first detailed information of the fighting on the front of the 19th Division came from General Badoglio, the Commander of XXVII Corps, in his message N.1920 sent at 15.20 to 2nd Army HQ. This stated that the enemy had taken the spur of Cemponi below Varda (Map 4). He himself was on Globocak with the commander of the Puglie Brigade (the Corps reserve brigade) seeking to halt the enemy advance by deploying the Brigade on the line Pusno to Jazna (just to the east of Globocak). The message ended with a request for a further brigade to support this effort.[25]

In a second message at 16.00 Badoglio reported that the enemy had been seen moving towards Vogrinki south of Jeza, and that the Puglie Brigade had been deployed with one regiment barring the Judrio stream and the other in positions between Srednje and Cicer (726m, Map 4). However, he had no news either from his 19th Division or from the 46th Division of IV Corps on his left. Badoglio said he intended to resist the advance of the enemy by bringing up reinforcements, and (if possible) by the 3rd and 19th Divisions acting together to defend Jeza. His message ended 'I am at Cave Kambresko. I have no facility to communicate with anybody.'[26]

The scale of the disaster was now becoming apparent. Although the Italians had a considerable number of reserve divisions, they had thought the ground to the west of the upper Isonzo so mountainous that there was little danger of any rapid enemy advance in this area. Hence, of the thirteen reserve infantry divisions in the zone of the 2nd

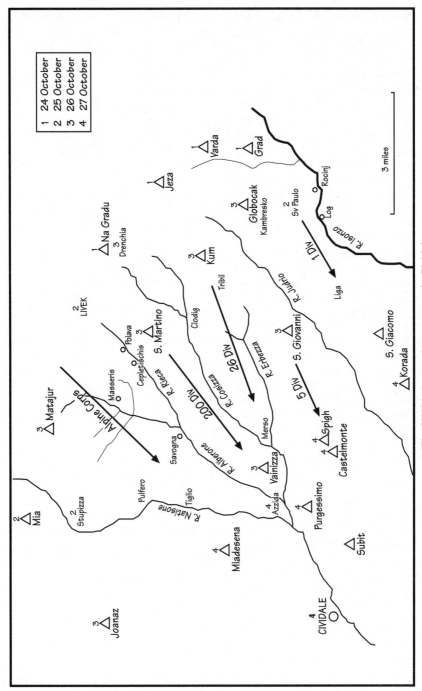

5. The XIVth Army advance towards Cividale.

and 3rd Armies, none had been stationed north of Cividale, and most were considerably further to the south.[27]

During the afternoon Cadorna left the Comando Supremo at Udine to consult with Capello at his HQ at Cividale, and afterwards the greater part of the reserves were called up. The 60th Division and the VII Alpini Group were directed to Breginj to block the route leading from Caporetto to Tarcento and the upper Tagliamento.[28] Other reserves were ordered to the edge of the mountains to move against any enemy troops emerging on to the plain. The 16th and 21st Divisions were directed to a zone south of Tarcento (Map 2);[29] the Jonio, Avellino and Messina Brigades of the 13th and 23rd Divisions to a zone south of Cividale;[30] and a brigade of the 30th Division to block the lower end of the Judrio valley between Castelmonte and Korada (Map 5).[31] At the same time a regiment of field artillery and twenty-eight batteries of medium calibre guns were transferred from the 3rd to the 2nd Army.[32]

The Italian Armies were now in a very difficult position, with the possibility of both the 2nd and 3rd Armies being forced to withdraw behind the Tagliamento river. At 19.50 Cadorna sent messages to Capello and the Duke of Aosta, the Commander of the 3rd Army, saying that the Austrians and the Germans were seeking to seize the land that had been conquered and to invade the sacred soil of the motherland. 'A great mission is entrusted to every soldier. Today one must conquer or die.'[33]

At 21.50 Cadorna ordered Capello to prepare for the withdrawal of all his troops from the Bainsizza to the right bank of the Isonzo. At 22.45 he ordered the 2nd and 3rd Armies to act with urgency and all possible speed to bring the defence line behind the Tagliamento to a state of efficiency, particularly by making use of civilian labour.[34]

These orders given, Cadorna turned to deal with the immediate situation. At 23.00 he sent Order N.4964 to Capello in which he appears to have visualized Montemaggiore (Map 2) as the hinge of three defence lines: the current line of contact, Montemaggiore – Stol – Matajur – Kolovrat – Globocak; an intermediate line; and a third line: Montemaggiore – Carnizza (Map 6) – Mladesena – Korada (Map 5).[35] Given time, it would have been possible to establish such lines amidst the mountains, but the Italians faced the problem of moving back over this difficult ground, closely pursued by the XIVth Army, while at the same time attempting to establish good enough positions on which to stand and halt the enemy advance.

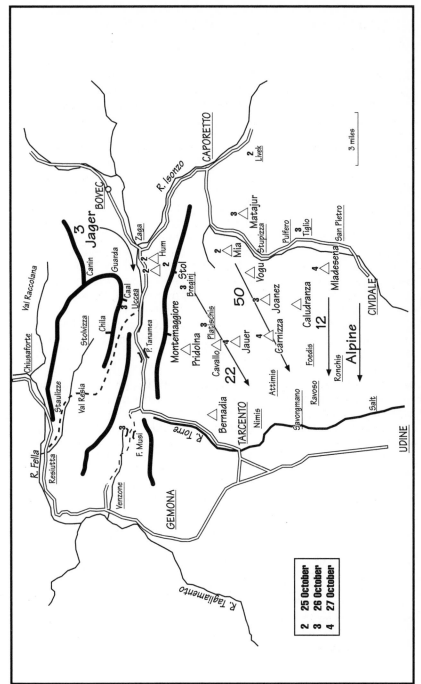

6. The advance to the Torre.

3.3   The Austro-German Attack (25 October)

After the miserable weather of the previous day, 25 October was fine and clear with the snow glittering on Monte Nero, but the outlook for the Italians was grim. The XIVth Army was now in possession of both banks of the Isonzo above Tolmin, had gained parts of the summit ridge of the Kolovrat, and were preparing to seize the whole ridge, and then to descend the valleys leading down to the plain. At the northern end of the front, the Krauss Corps was beginning to push westwards, towards the upper reaches of the Tagliamento river.

During 25 October the 50(a) Division reached Monte Mia, opposite Matajur across the River Natisone, and went on to prepare for an attack on Monte Joannaz the next day (Map 5). Units of the 12(g) Division, followed by the 117(g) Division, moved along the road from Caporetto down the Natisone valley towards Cividale, and reached Stupizza. Other units of the 12 Division advanced from Golobi into the village of Livek, where they were joined by units of the Alpine Corps which had fought their way along the Kolovrat from Na Gradu to Monte Kuk. As on the previous day the number of prisoners continued to mount. Krafft refers to 10,000 captured by the 12(g) Division on 24 October, and 15,000 by Stein's Corps on 25 October.[36]

On the left of the Alpine Corps the 200(g) Division advanced against stiff resistance from Italian positions still holding out on the ridge of the Kolovrat between Na Gradu and Jeza (Maps 4 and 5). Then, following the roads high up on the south side of the Kolovrat, the right wing of the Division made towards Monte San Martino, and the left wing towards Monte Kum, a heavily fortified position with a commanding view over the heads of the valleys running up to the Kolovrat.[37]

Further to the left, the 1(a) Division occupied the heavily fortified summit of Globocak by 11.00, and after some further hard fighting took Cicer (726m) and the hill of Sv. Pavel south of Globocak (Map 4). The division had now captured 4,000 prisoners and about 60 guns, albeit at a cost of 1,600 casualties, dead and wounded, about 14 per cent of its strength.[38] The 5(g) Division, following behind the 1(a) Division, moved over Varda (673m) to the ridge running from Globocak to Jeza with the intention of occupying the strongly fortified Monte Kum the next day. But the Division was held up near Pusno by fire from Kum on the far side of the Judrio river, and prisoners reported the presence of three Italian regiments and many guns.

The advance of the 1(a) Division across the Isonzo had already opened up the possibility of seizing the bridges at Loga and beyond, and thus cutting the supply lines and escape routes of the Italian divisions on the Bainsizza, already under attack by the Austrian IInd Army. Immediately at risk were the 65th, 22nd and 64th Divisions of

XXVII Corps (General Badoglio), and then on their right the 49th, 68th and 10th Divisions of XXIV Corps (General Caviglia).

As mentioned above, on 24 October the 65th, 22nd and 64th Divisions of XXVII Corps had held their ground against attacks by the 60th and 35th Divisions of the Austrian IInd Army, but General Badoglio had been so preoccupied with the breakthrough on the right bank of the Isonzo that his first orders to his three divisions on the left bank arrived only at 19.15. They were addressed to General Fiorone, commanding the 64th Division, and stated that he (Badoglio) was intending to stop the enemy advance on a line from Monte Kum to Globocak. Fiorone was to assume command of the three divisions on the left bank, with instructions no more detailed than 'to seek to impede the enemy proceeding to the west of Subiuk'.[39] (Presumably Major Freguglia who had brought the orders explained that Subiuk was the south ridge of Globocak on the other side of the river.) The orders made no reference to the Austrian IInd Army divisions facing and attacking Fiorone's divisions.

Following Badoglio's instructions, Fiorone issued orders at 21.20 for the 22nd and 64th Divisions to move to the right bank, but the situation changed before these moves could be made. At 21.20 Cadorna ordered the 2nd Army to withdraw all its troops from the front line on the Bainsizza to new positions, preparatory to a retirement across the Isonzo,[40] and at 22.15 the command of the 2nd Army transferred the three divisions to the dependence of XXIV Corps.[41]

During the night of 24/25 October XXIV Corps moved back to a new defence line closer to the river. The three divisions of XXVII Corps started later, as their orders from XXIV Corps had to be passed first to the 64th Division and then to the 22nd and 65th Divisions, but all were on their way by dawn. At first these retirements went according to plan, but during the morning the Austrians struck at the three divisions of XXVII Corps. These divisions 'found themselves practically surrounded: in some cases captured, in other cases were obliged to fight in very difficult conditions, separated, and not on their intended positions'.[42] Subsequent references in the IOH to all three divisions speak only of remnants (*resti* or *remanenti*).[43] At 14.30, XXIV Corps was ordered to cross to the right bank of the Isonzo; Caviglia describes how his troops retired in good order; and the bridges were blown either that evening or in the early morning of 26 October.[44]

At the other end of the XIVth Army front the Krauss Corps also made good progress, advancing from Zaga towards the upper reaches of the Tagliamento; the CCXVII Brigade of the Edelweiss Division and units of the 22(a) Division moved up the road leading from Zaga through Val Uccea to Uccea and Tarcento (Maps 2 and 6). Meanwhile other units of 22(a) Division climbed the slopes of Monte Stol towards the summit of this long, high ridge on the south side of Val Uccea. The advance of these troops was opposed by the Italian 50th Division (General Arrighi) which had suffered severe losses at Bovec but still had 'a certain efficiency',[45] and during the night of 24 October had taken up positions on a line running across Val Uccea from high up on the north side of the valley down to the valley floor and then up the slopes of Monte Hum (1113m) and the adjacent Prvi Hum (1079m) towards the ridge of Monte Stol. Early on the 25th this line was attacked by the Edelweiss Division with the 22(a) Division on its left. During the day, despite Italian opposition, the Edelweiss Division reached Uccea, where it found that the expected road to Val Resia was no more than a rough and broken track. However, the advance guard continued towards Monte Caal (1297m) and Monte Chila (1419m) at the head of Val Resia (Map 6).

The principal objective for the 22(a) Division was the long, high ridge Monte Stol – Montemaggiore. Access to the ridge was provided by two roads, one from Uccea on the north side, and one from Breginj on the south side, both reaching the ridge just below Hill 1404m (Map 3). From this point another road ran eastwards along the ridge for about four miles giving access to strong points and gun positions.[46] However, these positions had long been regarded as being far behind the front, and they were now virtually empty of troops and guns. The 22(a) Division started up the steep slopes towards the outliers Hum and Privi Hum on the Italian defence line; the two summits were taken by 13.00; and by nightfall two or three battalions of Kaiserschützen had reached positions high up on the north side of the main ridge.

On the south side of the Stol ridge, units of the 50(a) Division advanced along the road from Caporetto towards Breginj, and were opposed by the Italian 34th Division (General Basso), last mentioned as having no troops (Section 2.6) but now augmented by the three regiments (271, 272 and 273) of the reserve Potenza Brigade. At daybreak these units were holding a line running from high up on the Stol ridge down to positions at Potoki and Sv Volar on the valley floor of the upper Natisone river, with orders to bar the way to Breginj and the lower Natisone (Map 3). The IOH states without comment that this depleted division of not more than 3,000 men, without artillery and machine guns, was responsible for 'an extensive front of about 7km'.[47]

To oppose the advance of the XIVth Army Cadorna had laid down that IV Corps should hold the line Montemaggiore – Stol – Mont Mia. General Cavaciocchi had now set up his HQ at Breginj below Monte Stol, but his Corps consisted principally of only the much reduced 50th Division and the Potenza Brigade of the 34th Division. Moreover, it was difficult to make an accurate assessment of the situation. During the morning General Basso reported that two battalions of Austrians had been seen on the summit of the Stol, but it was soon realized that they were in fact two battalions of Bersaglieri who had come up from the far side to join other units of the 50th Division already on the ridge. Shortly after, news arrived that the units of the 50th Division holding Privi Hum had been forced back and were retiring to the Stol. Whereupon Cavaciocchi decided to move his Corps HQ from Breginj, first to Platischis and then to Nimis near Tarcento (Map 6), and then was told by the Army Command to stay at Breginj.[48]

As Cavaciocchi waited at Breginj for supplies of more ammunition, and the promised arrival of a reserve brigade, he received another report saying that the Austrians were descending from Stol towards Breginj. Therefore at 13.00 he ordered the 34th Division to withdraw its battalions from Potoki and Sv Volar to Monte Mia on Cadorna's 2nd Line of Defence, and stated that Corps HQ would withdraw first to Platischis and then to Nimis. He then went out to view the Stol from a small hill above Breginj and realized that the report of Austrians descending was another false alarm.[49] However, the battalions of the 34th Division at Sv Volar and Potoki had already received his order of 13.00, abandoned their positions, and set off for Monte Mia. Arriving there by 15.30, they saw no sign of the food and ammunition they were expecting, so decided to retreat down to Logje on the upper Natisone (Map 3) where they arrived about 21.00.[50]

General Cavaciocchi next received a report from the battalions of the 50th Division on the Stol, saying that the enemy appeared to be making an encircling movement around them towards Monte-maggiore. The report also stated that the units were tired, short of ammunition, doubtful of their ability to hold Stol, and on the point of retreating. Cavaciocchi's Chief of Staff telephoned Stol and was answered in German. An officer from the adjacent 36th Division, in the Carnia Group on the left of IV Corps, arrived at Breginj and reported that he had been sent to contact the 50th Division on Stol but had been unable to find the Division, and that positions on Stol had been occupied by the Austrians.[51] Therefore at 15.20 Cavaciocchi sent out somewhat vague orders to the 50th and 34th Divisions saying that should the 50th Division be forced to retreat from the Stol, both divisions should retreat via Platischis to positions on Montemaggiore and Monte Carnizza (Map 6; on Cadorna's 3rd Line of Defence). The retreat was to be conducted in stages and 'in an orderly manner'.[52]

The account in the IOH of subsequent events at IV Corps HQ relies mainly on extracts from the Corps Diary which does not present an entirely clear picture. For example, it states that 'At 16.20 the Corps Commander set out towards Platischis . . . and telephoned the 2nd Army Commander.' This suggests that Cavaciocchi spoke to Capello after leaving Breginj, but from where is not stated, and it is unclear where the Corps command was located from 16.20 until almost midnight.

However, it does appear that Cavaciocchi talked to both Capello and to the Chief of Staff of the left wing of the 2nd Army, to say that the IV Corps troops were now insufficient to garrison the length of its assigned front from Montemaggiore to Monte Mia. Even after the arrival of the reserve 60th Division now on its way to Breginj, the Corps would only be able to hold a line between Montemaggiore and Monte Cavallo (Map 6). At 18.40, presumably to avoid any encirclement of the right flank of the Corps, the 34th Division was ordered to send 600 rifles to the saddle between Monte Joanaz and Monte Carnizza, on Cadorna's 3rd Line of Defence, to guard against incursions from the north, north-east and north-west (Map 6).[53]

Meanwhile, the 1st Battalion of the 271 Regiment of the Potenza Brigade (34th Division) and a battalion of Bersaglieri (50th Division) were still maintaining positions on the Stol ridge 850 metres above Breginj, but more confusion arose when the 1st Battalion was ordered to descend to support other units of the Potenza Brigade in Val Natisone. As this move would expose the flank of the adjacent battalion of Bersaglieri, General Arrighi (50th Division) thought it necessary to order all the troops on Stol to retreat down the military road to Breginj, beginning at 18.00.[54] However, Arrighi learned subsequently that Corps had cancelled the move of the 1st Battalion, so those troops that had started to descend were ordered back up again. Hence, on the evening of 25 October the Italians were still holding positions on the ridge of the Stol, and troops of the Austrian 22 Division, high up on the north side of the ridge, although tired were pressing on through the night.

At 21.00 General Arrighi received Cavaciocchi's order, issued at 15.20, which said that should the 50th Division be forced to retreat from the Stol it should retire via Platischis to positions on Montemaggiore and Monte Carnizza. In view of this order and the current situation General Arrighi took the decision to retreat down to Breginj.[55] Eventually, after some fighting, the Italians were able to disengage and make their way down to the valley, and a battalion of Kaiserschützen arrived at the road junction at 1404m on the ridge of Stol.[56]

Finally, the day's entry in the Corps Diary ends by saying, without comment or explanation, that at 23.30 General Cavaciocchi was walking on the road towards Nimis, and was met by General Gandolfo carrying an order from the Comando Supremo that he, Gandolfo, was to assume command of IV Corps.[57] Later, in the early hours of 26 October, two battalions of Kaiserschützen on Stol raced down to

Breginj, surprised a great number of half-dressed and fearful Italians, and so 'captured a Brigade Commander and 5,000 men'.[58]

To sum up, after two days fighting the Italians found themselves in a grim position all along their front facing the XIV Army. Three Divisions, the 43rd, 46th, and 19th, and parts of the 3rd, 34th, 50th, 65th, 22nd and 64th had largely ceased to exist as fighting units. Krafft gives many examples of units being surprised and surrounded, and the subsequent capture of large numbers of prisoners. Von Below in his diary for 26 October notes that 50,000 prisoners were streaming back down his lines of communication. News had come to the Comando Supremo only slowly but some of the accounts were alarming in the extreme. There were reports of poor morale, of early surrenders, and of roads choked with troops moving up to the front and with troops retreating from it.

To counter the enemy advance Cadorna had ordered up eight Italian Reserve Divisions on 24 October and three more (the 63rd, 23rd and 25th) on 25 October. This was a sizable force but the units had some distance to move and as they approached the front they found the roads encumbered and blocked by the volume of traffic and by the masses of retreating and often dispirited troops. Moreover, the proper employment of the reserves was the responsibility of the 2nd Army Commander, and it was unfortunate that General Capello who had been unfit for some time was now quite ill, and was ordered to hospital at 18.00.[59]

Capello was again replaced by General Montuori who assigned the command of the left wing of the 2nd Army (the remnants of IV, VII, XXVII Corps together with the XXVIII reserve Corps) to General Etna, and of the right wing to General Ferrero. In addition, foreseeing that the XIVth Army might soon emerge from the mountains, Montuori set up another command to form a defence along the line of the Torre river (Map 6) with the 13th, 16th, 21st, 23rd, 30th, and 60th reserve Divisions under the command of General Sagramoso.[60] However, the 16th, 21st and 60th Divisions had already been transferred to IV Corps parts of the front, and by the following day the pressure of events resulted in the 13th, 23rd and 30th Divisions being diverted to the XXVII, XXVIII and XXIV Corps respectively. Thus General Sagramoso soon found that he had no troops at all.[61]

3.4   At Italian GHQ (25 October)

Throughout the day reports continued to arrive at the Comando Supremo with news of enemy attacks thrusting forwards against the main Italian defences along the whole of the front held by IV Corps and by the 19th Division of XXVII Corps. There was already the prospect that the XIVth Army might push right through the Italian 2nd Army to reach Cividale, and then arrive at the rear of the southern part of the 2nd Army, and perhaps eventually behind the rear of the 3rd Army. Moreover, at the north end of the front, the Edelweiss Division had reached Uccea, from where Passo Tanamea led to the River Torre and Tarcento, and a track down Val Resia led to Val Fella and the upper reaches of the Tagliamento (Map 6). Hence, there was here a threat to the rear of the Carnia Group, as well as to the rear of the 2nd Army to the south.

To avoid complete disaster the only course open to Cadorna was to retire to a line of defensive positions which could halt the enemy and permit time to regroup and reorganize. The first two classic defence lines in north-east Italy against invaders from the east have always been the Rivers Tagliamento and Piave, about 40 and 70 miles west of the Isonzo. However, a retirement even to the Tagliamento would involve the retreat of all the Italian troops between Carnia and the sea in order to avoid exposing lines of communication to flank attacks. This was a bitter prospect, involving the loss not only of all the territory won during the war, but also most of the Italian province of Fruili-Venezia Guilia.

The Piave was clearly a better defence line than the Tagliamento. After flowing through narrow mountain valleys it emerges on to the plain near Pederobba, at the south-east corner of the Monte Grappa massif, and then follows a course of only about 40 miles to the sea (Map 1). Hence a line on the Piave would link up with the defence works on Grappa (constructed after the Strafexpedition in 1916), which in turn joined up with the positions at Asiago. Most significantly, this line would be much shorter than one based on the Tagliamento. On the other hand a retreat to the Piave would mean the loss of parts of the Veneto and bring the enemy to within 20 miles of Venice.

During 25 October Cadorna consulted the Commanders of the 2nd and 3rd Armies. The record is not entirely clear but it seems that Cadorna talked with General Capello of the 2nd Army both in the morning and early afternoon, and that Capello subsequently wrote to Cadorna recommending an immediate withdrawal at least to the Torre river (Map 6) and perhaps to the Tagliamento.[62] Cadorna also talked with the Duke of Aosta of the 3rd Army and subsequently issued order N.4973[63] saying that medium and heavy guns on the Carso should be withdrawn nearer to the Isonzo, that all necessary preparations should be made for a retreat over the Tagliamento, and that the 3rd Army's least mobile guns should retire behind the Piave. As already mentioned, Capello was unwell and at 16.00 left for the hospital at Padua, the command of the 2nd Army being taken over by General Montuori at 18.00.

As the day wore on it became increasingly obvious that the XIVth Army had reached the summits of most of the high ground on the right bank of the Isonzo below Caporetto and was moving towards the valleys and ridges which lead down into the plain along the line Gemona, Tarcento, Cividale and Gorizia. Thus Cadorna was faced with the drastic situation that unless action was taken the XIVth Army would soon be on the plain where they could turn south against the rear and the lines of communication of the still intact 3rd Army. It was also clear that the Italian resistance was sometimes very patchy with some units too ready to surrender.

The only possible response for Cadorna was to order the retirement of the 2nd and 3rd Armies at least to the Tagliamento, where he might stand and reorganize his shattered divisions. By the late afternoon he had prepared the orders for a general retreat to the Tagliamento, but then he hesitated. The 3rd Army was still fully efficient and it was vital that its lines of communication were not exposed by the retirement of the 2nd Army. Therefore it was essential for the 3rd Army to move as rapidly as possible. Yet the Italian Armies had little experience of retreat, so it was equally important that the move was not so rapid that the 3rd Army lost cohesion and began to disintegrate.

Cadorna, clearly aware of these possibilities sent a staff officer, Colonel Cavallero, on the evening of the 25th to ask Montuori if an immediate retreat was absolutely necessary. At 19.47 he sent a bulletin to the War Ministry saying that he had prepared but not yet issued the orders to retreat, and that the decision had not yet been taken. Montuori consulted his Corps Commanders and then, somewhat surprisingly, notified Cadorna that it was thought possible to prolong the resistance, and eventually to make a halt on the River Torre.[64] Cadorna then decided to hold back the order to retreat.

3.5   The Austro-German Attack (26 October)

Early on 26 October Cadorna issued Order N.4988 to the commands of the 2nd and 3rd Armies to hold the line Montemaggiore to Salcano (two miles above Gorizia), 'One must conquer or die.'[65], but the XIVth Army continued to advance.

At the north end of the front, the CCXVI Brigade of the Edelweiss Division reached the main ridge of Monte Canin after hard fighting and captured 40 officers and 800 men.[66] A column of the CCXVII Brigade occupied Monte Guarda (1720m) and Monte Chila (1419m) at the head of Val Resia (Map 6), while an infantry battalion made a long and exhausting descent into Val Resia to reach the village of Stolvizza. Other units of the Brigade were held up by strong resistance at the Pass of Tanamea leading to the upper reaches of the

Torre river, and to Val Venzone over Forcella Musi (Maps 2 and 6).[67]

After two battalions of the 22(a) Division had captured an Italian brigade in the early morning at Breginj,[68] the major part of the Division arrived by midday and then proceeded towards the line Monte Pridolna (891m), Monte Cavallo (1050m) and Monte Jauer (1093m) (Map 6), and found the latter still firmly held by the Italians. Meanwhile a detachment sent from Breginj along the ridge of Stol saw off two battalions of alpini and occupied the summit of Montemaggiore in the early evening. South of the 22(a) Division, the 50(a) Division in Stein's Corps was transferred to the Krauss Corps, and received orders to prepare for an attack the next day on Monte Carnizza (991m) west of Joanaz (Map 6).

In Stein's Corps, the Alpine Corps and the 12(g) Division were on the move by 04.00, from Livek up the road running along the line of the summits towards Monte Matajur (1641m). This mountain overlooked Caporetto and dominated the road to Cividale, and von Below had promised a high German military award, the '*Pour le Mérite*', to the officer who captured it. The spearhead of the attack turned out to be the Rommel detachment of the Wurttemberg Mountain Battalion with three rifle and three machine-gun companies. Starting in the dark from Javscek at 05.00 (Section 5.4) it arrived at the summit of Matajur at 11.40 after what Faldella describes as a series of 'daring and extra-ordinary manoeuvres'.[69]

Meanwhile the Berrer and Scotti Corps had spent the day of 26 October moving south-west from the Kolovrat down the ridges and valleys leading to Cividale (Map 5). The 26(g) Division reached Merso in the Cossiza valley, and the 200(g) Division Monte Vainizza west of Merso. The 5(g) Division, aided by three battalions of the 26(g) and one battalion of the 200(g) Division, made a dawn attack on the heavily defended area of Monte Kum, which they occupied during the morning. The 1(a) Division followed the ridge running down from Globacak to Monte San Giacomo (Map 5). Also, preparations were made for the 57(a) and 28(a) Divisions of the Austrian IInd Army of the Isonzo to attack Monte Korada the following day, thus leaving the 1(a) Division free to move down the valley of the Judrio.

3.6   The Decision to Retire (October 26)

Cadorna had spent the day of 26 October at the Comando Supremo waiting to decide on the right moment to give the order to retreat. At 16.20 he warned the 4th Army of an eventual retirement, and ordered the least mobile and the more modern of its guns to move immediately to the right bank of the Piave, on the line Pederobba – Asolo – Montebelluna (N.4998).[70] In the evening he sent out a directive

(N.4999) to the 2nd and 3rd Armies setting out further arrangements for an eventual retreat to the Tagliamento,[71] and order N.5010 to the 2nd Army to establish a force of two divisions under General de Giorgio to guard the bridges over the Tagliamento at Pinzano and Trasaghis (Map 8).[72] Following this order the 33rd Division passed to De Giorgio's Command on 26 October, and the 20th Division on 28 October.[73]

At 23.30 a message (F.6370)[74] arrived from Montuori reporting that the enemy had attacked Montemaggiore at 15.00 and that the Italians were holding out. But a further message at midnight[75] announced that the mountain which Cadorna viewed as a great bastion[76] had been lost. Cadorna then sent out the orders for a retreat to the Tagliamento: at 02.30 to the Carnia Group, at 02.50 to the 3rd Army, at 03.50 to the 2nd Army.[77]

(In fact Montemaggiore seems to have been somewhat overrated as a defensive bastion. This high ridge runs east and west, that is parallel to and not across the line of the enemy advance. According to Faldella the bastion was lacking fortifications, the guns had long been taken away for use elsewhere, and on 24 and 25 October there was not a single Italian soldier on the mountain. It was only on the evening of 25 October that the two alpini battalions arrived at the foot of the mountain and climbed to the summit ridge during the night. The alpini found themselves alone and isolated, and on the approach of some Kaiserschützen along the ridge from the east their commander ordered a retreat from the mountain, a decision which Faldella described as 'deplorable and unjustified'.[78])

Contributions to Disaster

In three days the XIVth Army had brought about a disastrous change in the fortunes of the Italian Army. It was to be some time before an official enquiry reported on how this catastrophe had come about, but Cadorna had no doubt. In his communiqué of 28 October he placed the responsibility squarely on the troops of the 2nd Army, saying that they had 'retreated without fighting or had ignominiously surrendered unharmed to the enemy'.[1]

The communiqué was manifestly unjust. As described above, the preparations made by the Comando Supremo and the Commands of the 2nd Army, IV Corps, VII Corps and XXVII Corps were unsatisfactory in many ways. They would have been unsatisfactory if the Italians had faced an Austrian attack, but the XIVth Army had deployed some of the best troops in the German and Austrian Armies, against one of the weakest parts of the Italian line. The Italian government on seeing the communiqué forbad its issue, but not in time to prevent it reaching the press, and making public how Cadorna viewed the situation.

The Italian public was much concerned at this state of affairs, and in January 1918 the government established a Commission of Enquiry to determine the causes of the disaster of Caporetto. The Commission received a great number of submissions, both from the principal participants and elsewhere, and issued its report in 1919. Naturally enough the principal actors sought to justify their own performance, and to blame others for all the various deficiencies. But reading the Commission's report today, it appears as a reasonable attempt to reach equitable conclusions, and not surprisingly decided that the responsibility for the disaster was spread very widely.

Following the Report of the Commission of Enquiry, several of the generals presented their own accounts of the events criticized by the Commission. Capello was first in the field in 1920 with two books *Per la Verita* and *Note di Guerra*, and was followed by Cadorna with substantial volumes in 1923 and 1925. This was but the beginning of a considerable literature analyzing the battle, reviewing the accounts given by the generals, and seeking to resolve the conflicting opinions of earlier authors. One of the earliest of such reviews, by Papafava, appeared in 1923, and others have continued to appear, one of the latest being that of Ungari in 1999.

Much basic information was given in the Report of the Commission, and in the accounts by various generals, but it remained difficult to arrive at the truth behind sometimes contradictory reports, despite detailed studies such as those by Bencivenga (1932), and Faldella (1965). Then in 1967 the *Ufficio Storico* of the Italian Ministry of Defence published the volume of the Italian Official History dealing with Caporetto, which presented a great deal of valuable factual information and comment not hitherto readily available. Various studies have since been made incorporating information from the IOH, particularly the excellent books by Silvestri, Melograni and Pieropan, but the IOH remains the one essential account of these past events. We shall therefore usually rely on its factual and documentary contents rather than attempting to analyze all the arguments set out in the various polemical accounts now available.

We start by briefly summarizing some of the actions of the Comando Supremo, the Army Command and the Corps and Divisional Commands which made substantial contributions to the debacle. First, however, it should be noted that so many different circumstances coalesced against the Italians that both chance and fortune seem to have deserted them altogether. Even the weather gave its support to the XIVth Army.

4.1 The Weather

From 10 October onwards the weather had been cloudy and damp. The XIVth Army troops marching up to the front were frequently in the rain and often wet through.[2] Even so the weather was to be most helpful to the Austrians and Germans. Firstly during the approach march, cloud and rain helped them to come close up to the front unobserved. (Many were also very wet on 23 October but they were strong and not unused to such conditions.)

The first day of the offensive, 24 October, coincided with continuous drizzle and heavy cloud during the hours of darkness but at dawn some of the summits and upper slopes of the mountains began emerging from the cloud. Later rain set in decreasing the visibility.[3] These conditions were ideal for the attackers who were well briefed and had relatively simple objectives, either to mount the opposing slopes to their summits, or to make their way along the floor of the narrow Isonzo valley.

On the other hand the restricted visibility made it difficult for the Italians to determine the course of events, and made them particularly liable to infiltration techniques. Furthermore, in some areas the Italian troops had only moved to their defensive positions, often on bare summits and hillsides, on the eve of the battle or even later. Many high up on the mountains found themselves in the mist and had little or no idea of the complexities of the terrain. All had difficulty in maintaining contact with adjacent units. (A conference at IV Corps headquarters on 14 October had discussed methods of communication in cloudy weather including the use of pigeons and trumpets, but without reaching any firm conclusions.[4])

The weather the next day, 25 October, was totally different. The sun shone brightly in a clear blue sky, and a layer of fresh snow scintillated on the tops of the higher mountains, Rombon, Nero and Matajur.[5] The advance units of the XIVth Army had now reached the summits of the Kolovrat on the right bank of the Isonzo. From here, through clear air, they obtained a splendid view of the complex systems of spurs and valleys leading down to Cividale at the edge of the plain, with the sea beyond. Behind them, beyond the Isonzo stood Monte Nero (2245m) backed by a range of other peaks presenting to one mountain soldier 'a picture of bewitching beauty in the early morning sunlight'.[6]

The Austrian and German troops saw below them, as on a map, the routes they had already studied in their plans for the attack. Here they must have sensed that 'scent of victory which can set aside the misery of cold and wet and the weight of heavy packs',[7] and which was to carry them on to the Piave.

4.2   Failures of Cadorna and Capello

Before criticizing the generals of the First World War one should take into account the immense difficulties of directing and coordinating armies of hundreds of thousands of troops. Even so, the performance of the Italian higher commands, before and during the battle, fell short of what might reasonably have been expected. Cadorna, in his communiqué of 28 October, placed the blame for the disaster of Caporetto solely on the behaviour of the troops, but the foundations were well and truly laid by the senior commanders (Comando Supremo, Army Commander and Corps Commanders) in the months and weeks prior to the battle.

First of all, the Italians appear to have had little knowledge of the new methods of tactics being developed on the Western Front. Certainly, the French General Weygand and the British General Robertson during a visit to the Italian Front in March 1917 had been concerned at the pre-war pattern of Italian defences with little depth, and by a poor co-operation between the artillery and the infantry.[8] All too often at Caporetto, a line of defence was broken, and units found themselves being encircled, and did not know how to respond.

In addition, before considering the actions of some of the principal commanders, it must be remembered that during the two and a half years of war since May 1915, the Austrians had adopted an essentially defensive strategy, apart from their foray into the Trentino in 1916. Therefore all this time the Italian armies had been predominantly on the offensive, and the Italian 2nd Army had obtained little experience or practice in defence.

Besides these overall deficiencies, several of the principal generals made their own contribution to the disaster. General Cadorna was an officer of considerable capacity who had been responsible for the re-organization and expansion of the army since his appointment as Comando Supremo in July 1914. Although not highly innovative he had presided with some competence over the Italian Army during the two and a half years of war, and had risen to the occasion when faced by the onslaught of the Strafexpedition, the major Austrian offensive in the Trentino in 1916. However, he may reasonably be faulted on at least three aspects of his command: his misjudgement of the efficiency of the Italian positions on the upper Isonzo; his failure to maintain the morale of some parts of the Italian Armies; and his failure to exert his authority over the command of the 2nd Army.

It seems that Cadorna had generally regarded the ground opposite and above Tolmin as so mountainous that the enemy had no possibility of making any sudden breakthrough. Indeed Trevelyan, besides describing the region of Caporetto as a quiet area (Section 2.4), also refers to it as a 'happy valley' and a 'health resort'.[9]

A similar impression is given by two of the maps in the IOH. Carta 15 shows the locations on 24 October of all twenty-nine reserve brigades in the 2nd and 3rd Armies, from Monte Rombon to the sea; and Carta 14 the locations of the heavy and medium artillery. One would naturally expect to find fewer guns and reserve troops for such mountainous ground, but of twenty-nine reserve brigades not one was behind the northern half of the front. Carta 14 shows a great mass of artillery south of Tolmin, appreciable forces between Tolmin and Caporetto, and rather weak forces above Caporetto. Even as late as 23 October the Diary of VII Corps recorded Cadorna saying that an attack would be so hazardous that it might well be a feint to cover an attack elsewhere.[10]

Cadorna was always very aware of the need to maintain morale. He was much concerned by the presence of political activists at work in the army,[11] and was repeatedly urging the government to do more to stamp out communist/socialist/anti-war propaganda. His constant concern was visible, for example, at a meeting at VII Corps on

23 October, when the Corps Diary quotes him as saying that the Austrian menace cannot have any probability of success, provided that 'there is no less vigilance and if the troops do their duty', (our underlining).[12]

Cadorna knew that the morale of an army had to be carefully nurtured, but he believed that this was best achieved by an iron discipline including decimation of recalcitrant units (Section 3.2). In fact he was too remote from the men to appreciate their lives and problems, and too ready to accept assurances from his subordinates that all was well, even on the eve of Caporetto.[13] Particularly, he failed to consider purely military changes in the administration of the army that would have made life more bearable for the troops, and which were introduced by General Diaz after he was substituted for Cadorna as Comando Supremo on 9 November. These included an increase in rations, canteens near the front selling food, drinks and other necessities, an extra ten-day leave in addition to the annual fifteeen-day leave, and most importantly an order that entitlement to leave would be on a regular basis without any suppression except in exceptional circumstances.[14]

Finally, we note that Cadorna's order of 19 September for 'the concentration of all activity on dispositions for defence'[15] could hardly have been more definite, and was immediately acted upon by the Duke of Aosta who issued detailed orders the next day (Section 2.3). On the other hand, Capelio was reluctant to relinquish the offensive and on 1 October suggested to Cadorna that a halt be made on all changes in 2nd Army dispositions.[16] This should have alerted Cadorna to the slow progress being made to implement his orders, and to take some action to expedite matters, but there is no evidence that he did.

On 5 October Cadorna left his HQ at Udine for the Villa Camerini at Vicenza apparently for two weeks of leave,[17] during which he was kept informed of events, and made some visits of inspection in the Trentino.[18] Gatti (the official historian) noted in his own diary that as Cadorna left, he remarked to Gatti that on his return they must take up their winter quarters, and then get down to the work of the history, as if assuming that all the action was now over for the year. But on returning on 19 October he found intelligence reports that an enemy offensive was on the way, and that little had been done by Capello for defence preparations in the 2nd Army.

General Capello was born in 1859 and after a distinguished career had been responsible for two of the most considerable successes during the war. As commander of the VI Corps in 1916 he had been responsible for the capture of Gorizia, and in 1917 he had command of the 2nd Army during the most successful advance on the Bainsizza.

However, he had his limitations. For example, to quote Villari 'his sense of discipline was not absolute, and he did not know how to adapt himself to a plan of operation out of harmony with his own conceptions'.[19]

He was by no means popular with his troops. Many found him overpowering. The Commission of Enquiry received many reports telling of a hard and irascible character, and of violent, angry language creating indignation and loathing, repressed by the bonds of discipline.[20] The Enquiry was told that his regime was based on 'fear, on threats, on oppression' and that he aroused 'not only fear and aversion, but was absolutely hated by the greater part of the officers and men'.[21] All this was in contrast to the 'enlightened spirit of the 3rd Army'.[22]

Cadorna, himself, found General Capello a difficult person to work with. We have already referred to Cadorna's constant insistence on firm discipline and obedience to orders. For example, on 26 October Cadorna sent an order to all commanders down to company level insisting that any disgraceful behaviour of their troops must be 'cleansed by steel and fire' with 'no hesitation, no tolerance'.[23] Yet there had been a grave breach of discipline by Capello, Cadorna's immediate subordinate, in not carrying out Cadorna's order of 18 September.

There seems little doubt that this breakdown in discipline arose from a lack of rapport between two quite different characters, Cadorna, a Piedmontese aristocrat, and Capello from a quite modest Neapolitan background. A perceptive sketch of the differences between these two personalities is given by Gatti in his diary entry for 17 May. Cadorna had the finer character, a greater sense of his duty, and perhaps a greater capacity for constructive thinking (given the opportunity to do so quietly rather than during a debate). Capello was perhaps the more intelligent, and certainly more acute and quick witted in discussion. Hence he would present Cadorna with new ideas and schemes which Cadorna could not readily rebut, and would then leave thinking he had made his point. But Cadorna remained unconvinced, and little by little retreated from what he had agreed.[24]

Undoubtedly Cadorna found himself in an uncomfortable position. He believed in trusting his Army Commanders, and leaving them to get on with their tasks, for any appearance of interference would have weakened their authority.[25] This approach was well justified in the case of the Duke of Aosta and the 3rd Army. But not with Capello. Moreover, since the capture of Gorizia in 1916, there had been suggestions in some political and journalistic circles, probably encouraged by Capello's entourage, that Cadorna should be replaced by Capello. It would appear that Cadorna was somewhat intimidated by Capello, for he failed to deal adequately with three separate issues involving

71

Capello: the move to the defensive; the constitution of the 2nd Army; and the ill health of Capello.

Capello was later to write at considerable length in order to justify his response to Cadorna's order of 18 September. He claimed, essentially, that any enemy attack could be broken by a counter-offensive from the Bainsizza towards Tolmin. But in September a well-prepared attack by the 2nd Army against Tolmin had been halted by the Austrian IInd Army of the Isonzo. Moreover, while Capello largely ignored Cadorna's orders to adopt defensive postures, there is no evidence that he made any effective preparations for counter-offensive action. For example, at the VII Corps Conference on 18 October, the Corps was ordered 'to manoeuvre counter-offensively at an opportune moment', but only as one of four tasks described by the IOH as partly irreconcilable, and beyond the means of the Corps (Section 2.5). One is forced to conclude with Faldella that 'no preparations [for an attack] had been made'.[26]

The 2nd Army was by far the largest of the Italian Armies, with nine corps and twenty-five divisions, whereas the adjacent 3rd Army had only four corps and nine divisions. The co-ordination of nine corps by the Army Command with no intervening level of command must have been a very demanding operation. In fact, by about 12.00 on the first day of the battle, the pressure of events made it necessary to appoint General Montuori to take command of the left section of the front.[27] However, it was now too late for the remedy to have much effect, and one wonders why Capello had failed to order it much earlier, and whether Cadorna had ever reviewed the size of his armies.

Finally, there can be little doubt that the command of the 2nd Army was much affected by Capello's illness. On 4 October Capello was in bed and had been ill for several days. He was seen by a doctor the next day who diagnosed a fever, high temperature, and renal and intestinal disorder. When his condition had not improved by 10 October General Montuori was appointed as 'Comandante Interinale' (temporary commander) with full authority and powers of action. However, his position was very ambiguous. Capello wrote subsequently that he 'was well aware that the Comando Supremo had no great faith in General Montuori'.[28] Hence, although he had been relieved of his command, he remained in his residence, near his HQ at Cormons, taking an active interest in affairs, even when confined to his bed. Indeed, as already mentioned, on 17 October when Montuori was still in command, Cadorna sent a communication addressed to 'His Excellency General Capello – Commander of the 2nd Army' (Section 2.5).

Capello's condition deteriorated on 18 October, and he was admitted to the military hospital in Padua on 20 October. Two days

72

later, hearing that an enemy offensive was imminent he returned to his HQ, arriving at Cormons at 02.30 on 23 October. He then had a busy day visiting the Comando Supremo at Udine, IV Corps at Kred, and holding a conference of Corps Commanders at a new HQ at Cividale.[29] The following day, 24 October, was spent directing operations at his HQ, but by the evening he was seriously ill. The next day, he was authorized to give up his command and proceed to the hospital at Padua, and left the 2nd Army for the last time.[30]

Capello's illness had been most unfortunate. He had been the driving force behind the large and unwieldy 2nd Army, and there appears to have been no obvious successor. Hence during the critical time from the beginning of October, there had been no leadership of the quality the situation required. Indeed, one of his orders, N.6245 issued at 18.05 on 24 October, stated no more than: 'Enemy proceeds along valley of the Isonzo and is near Caporetto. Necessary to make attack on left flank so as to stop them'. The IOH comments that this order shows 'neither the tone, nor the vigour, nor the spirit which the circumstances called for', and that it was 'vague and general: did not assign a task, did not specify an objective'.[31]

(According to the Commission of Enquiry Capello was seriously ill when he left the front. Colonel Doctor Marino stated that by 08.00 on 25 October, Capello's condition had worsened with 'vomiting, cramp, giddiness, and albumen and blood in the urine', amounting to a 'grave urinary condition'.[32] But the Commission's report also gives details of Capello's subsequent movements. Having spent the night of 25 October in the military hospital at Padua, he appears to have discharged himself the next morning, and journeyed the forty or so miles to Verona, where he spent the night at the top hotel ('high charges for extras'[33]). The next morning, 27 October, he was visited by Colonel Doctor Bernucci, the Director of Army Health Services for the region of Verona. The Colonel found Capello 'morally somewhat agitated', and observed 'symptoms only of a small uremia'.[34] Capello was admitted to the military hospital at Verona the same day, and he remained there until 17 November.)

4.3   Failures of the Corps Commanders

We now turn to the part played by the commanders of the three corps, IV, XXVII and VII, which were overwhelmed at Caporetto. Like Cadorna and Capello, their influence on the events of 24 October was primarily in the preparatory arrangements for which they were responsible in the days and weeks before the battle. But, being appreciably nearer to the front line, they were in a position to influence the course of the battle more directly.

(a) IV Corps (Cavaciocchi)

General Cavaciocchi was born in 1862, and at the start of the war was Chief of Staff of the 3rd Army.[35] In April 1916 he commanded the 5th Division at the time of the remarkable Italian advance across the snow and ice of the Adamello glaciers.[36] By June 1916 he had been promoted Lieutenant General and commanded XXVI Corps with the 3rd Army on the Carso.[37] On 15 June 1917 Gatti, the Official Historian attached to the Comando Supremo, noted in his diary that both Cadorna and his secretary Bencivenga saw only three possibilities for appointment to the vacant office of Minister of War: Cavaciocchi, Diaz and Giardino.[38] However, this was not to be, and in July 1917 he was in command of IV Corps.

As already described, IV Corps' sector was so mountainous that it was too much regarded as a safe area unlikely to be attacked (Section 2.4). Indeed, a 2nd Army conference of corps commanders which met on 19 September to discuss the more defensive strategy ordered by Cadorna, was attended by the commanders of only II, XXIV and XXVII Corps, while IV Corps was not involved.[39] According to Gatti the Corps had always been left to itself, and 'was not in the best condition, strategically, tactically or morally'.[40] Nor does it appear that Cavaciocchi had done much to improve the atmosphere after he arrived in July.

There were certainly various long-standing weaknesses in the IV Corps defence lines, such as the defence positions on the steep slopes of Sleme, Mrzli and Vodel overlooked by the Austrian positions twenty to ninety metres higher up the slope (Section 2.4). One might have thought that the arrival of Cavaciocchi with his experience of the mountains would have led to some review and improvements of these weaknesses, but of this there is no record. A first sign of such attention came on 19 September when he issued order N.5551 to his divisions, stating that an attack was to be expected, perhaps the next day and certainly by the end of the month. Unfortunately this order, rather than laying down precise instructions, favoured exhortation and recommendation, as for example in the warning that difficulties can be encountered 'in the apathy and lack of conscience of some lower rank commanders'.[41]

It was only after another four weeks on 14 October that a Corps conference laid down further and more detailed instructions. At that date IV Corps was still responsible for the defence of the line on the right bank from the river up to Hlevnik, and two companies of Bersaglieri and two infantry companies were ordered to work on the line. In addition, the shortage of caves should be overcome by making use of the numerous folds in the wooded ground; and no more troops should be stationed on this line than was 'strictly necessary'.[42]

By now Cadorna was becoming increasingly anxious about the state of preparations, and on 19 October he sent one of his officers, Colonel Testa, to see Cavaciocchi and assess the situation of the Corps. Testa was assured by Cavaciocchi that all the dispositions for the defence were in hand, the morale of the troops was most satisfactory, and he was sure that they could withstand a strong bombardment. Though still concerned for the positions from Sleme down to the Isonzo, he believed that these could be maintained by the support of the artillery. He also assured Testa that he had no need of anything, as all his requests had been met, although the promised artillery had not yet arrived.[43]

Cavaciocchi had so far asserted that he was fully satisfied with the dispositions of IV Corps, but on 22 October he had his doubts. Therefore, he suggested to 2nd Army that he adopt a plan, first proposed in 1916, which aimed to strengthen the north end of the front in the region of Bovec, by drawing back units of the 50th Division to better defensive positions. General Montuori, the Acting Commander of the 2nd Army, agreed with this suggestion even though the Army Command in 1916 had ruled that the move should only be made if at least five days were available before an attack began.[44] However, before a final decision was taken Cavaciocchi was to discuss the proposal with Cadorna when he visited IV Corps HQ later in the day.

The Corps Diary, quoted in the IOH, does not give a very clear picture of events, but it appears that Cadorna arrived at Corps HQ at Kred at about 15.00, and after discussion said that he did not wish to interfere with the operational orders of the 2nd Army, and that General Montuori should decide. Orders for the move were then sent out to the 50th Division. However, later in the afternoon more intelligence from telephone interceptions suggested that the enemy offensive might start that night, so at 18.00 Cadorna cancelled the rearrangements. At 19.35 2nd Army passed this order on to IV Corps, and according to the IOH 'the Corps was caught in a crisis of movement in one of its divisions'.[45]

Cadorna remained concerned that an offensive towards Bovec might reach Zaga and then march up the road through Val Uccea towards the Tagliamento. Therefore, shortly after cancelling the redeployment of the 50th Division, he ordered the immediate reinforcement of IV Corps by the 34th Division, to be taken from VII corps for the urgent occupation of the narrow straights of the Isonzo above Zaga.[46] Though constituted only four days previously, this division had already been completely reconstructed (Section 2.6), and on 22 October comprised only the Foggia Brigade (280, 281, 282 Regiments). The Division reached IV Corps on 23 October, and Cavaciocchi brought it up to full strength by incorporating the 2nd and 9th Regiments Bersaglieri from his reserves. He then allocated the

280 Regiment to the 50th Division, and the 2 and 9 Bersaglieri Regiments to the 46th and the 43rd Divisions respectively.[47] Thus by the end of the day the 34th Division, sent by Cadorna to cover the approach to Zaga and the road beyond, was reduced to just the 281 and 282 Regiments.

By now Capello was again active. When he returned to the command of the 2nd Army on 23 October, he became concerned for the security of IV Corps and assigned the Corps two more brigades (Potenza and Massa Carrara) and two alpini groups from the 2nd Army reserve.[48] The two brigades were to block the road west from Caporetto by defending a line from Matajur to Starijski Vrh on the opposite side of the road; one alpini group was directed to positions around Zaga, and the other to positions on Monte Stol. These forces were to be supported by seventeen batteries of heavy field guns; five of which were assigned to the narrows at Zaga but did not arrive in time to give support when the German attack began the next day.[49]

The stage was now set for various disasters to IV Corps, and for what the IOH describes as 'fortuitous circumstances which created confusion in the activity of the command'.[50] As described previously, the 46th Division was soon overwhelmed from above by the Austrian 50 Division, and from the rear by the German march up the Isonzo, and there was little that the Corps Commander could do to intervene. On the other hand, the 43rd Division was less fiercely attacked and was holding its ground, until General Farisoglio received the telephone call from Corps, described by the IOH as 'perhaps badly interpreted or set out', which led to the premature retirement and capture of most of the 43rd Division (Section 3.1).

The regiment of the 50th Division in the region of Bovec had suffered heavily in the initial gas attack, but other units remained efficient, including those positioned around the narrow straits above Zaga, ready to block an enemy advance into Val Uccea. However, General Cavaciocchi, at his HQ at Kred about three miles west of Caporetto, was well aware that he had placed far fewer forces around Zaga than the division sent by Cadorna,[51] in fact only the 280 Regiment, which was still awaiting the arrival of one of its three battalions and the guns which had been promised. Therefore, at 10.30 Cavaciocchi allocated the two remaining units of the 34th Division (281 and 282 Regiments) to the 50th Division.[52] But this order was cancelled when the Division reported that for the moment it had sufficient forces near Zaga (even though the enemy were already advancing in the neighbourhood of Bovec).[53] The 281 Regiment was then sent to the hard-pressed 43rd Division, and the 282 to the 46th Division.[54] Thus the 34th Division (General Basso) had now no troops at all. The IOH comments that the Division had been used neither strategically nor tactically, but as 'a sort of reservoir of men from which to draw to answer requests for reinforcements, and the Corps Commander was soon left without any possibility of action having nothing more at hand'.[55] (General Basso himself soon found employment by taking charge of a mixed bag of units attempting to defend the outskirts of Caporetto.[56])

Meanwhile the reserve Potenza Brigade, sent by 2nd Army as further support for IV Corps, had arrived near Breginj on the morning of 24 October. However, both the Brigade Commander and General Cavaciocchi had been given clear instructions that the Brigade was to remain at the disposition of 2nd Army.[57] Hence, despite IV Corps' urgent need for reserves, no use was made of Potenza until the arrival of General Montuori at IV Corps HQ at about 15.30. Montuori, now in command of the left wing of the 2nd Army, had walked the last four miles to Kred because of 'the enormous congestion on the road'.[58] He found Cavaciocchi preparing to move his HQ back from Kred as the enemy was now at Caporetto, and the IOH states that on the arrival of Montuori 'the Commander of IV Corps saw much alleviation of his responsibility at a very critical moment'.[59] Montuori asked why no use had been made of the Potenza Brigade, and then telephoned Capello to obtain permission for its deployment.

We should also note that Cavaciocchi was in no way responsible for the withdrawal of the 50th Division from the Straits of Zaga, severely criticized by Bencivenga[60] and Pieri[61]. During Montuori's visit to IV Corps he issued orders that the 50th Division should withdraw from the Straits, and take up positions in Val Uccea (Section 3.1). These orders were sent out at about 16.00 but did not reach General Arrighi, commanding the Division, until midnight.[62] But during the afternoon Arrighi was concerned at the prospect of his troops at Zaga being taken in the rear by the enemy coming up the valley from Caporetto. Therefore (according to Faldella, but not noted by the CI or the IOH), he sent Major Piazzoni to drive by car on the road over the Stol ridge to Corps HQ at Breginj. There he consulted the Chief of Staff, Colonel Boccacci, who naturally confirmed Montuori's order.[63] Therefore, on Piazzoni's return at 17.00 Arrighi ordered the withdrawal to begin at 18.00, and this appears to have been carried out in good order, for during the night the Edelweiss Division was still held up at 21.00 at Podcela just above the Straits and, before leaving, the bridge on the main river was completely demolished.[64] Thus, by the morning, units of the 50th Division had taken up positions in Val Uccea as ordered by Montuori. (Bencivenga's account of this withdrawal criticizes General Arrighi most severely, even though the Commission of Enquiry had decided not to proceed against him, as he was a relatively junior officer and had acted on orders.[65] However, it must be remembered that Bencivenga's book was published in 1932, long before the information in Faldella's book and the IOH became available.)

We have already described events at IV Corps HQ on 25 October at Breginj, and how during the day Cavaciocchi struggled to resist the pressure of the XIVth Army (Section 3.3). He found it very difficult and, like other Italian commanders, did not succeed in imposing his will on the unrelenting succession of events.

(b) XXVII Corps (Badoglio)

In January 1916 a little known Lieutenant Colonel Pietro Badoglio, an artillery officer, was serving as the Chief of Staff of the 5th Division commanded by General Montuori. The latter was considering a plan to obtain possession of the hill of Monte Sabotino, the massive Austrian stronghold overlooking Gorizia, and he decided that Badoglio would take charge of the preparatory work for the attack. Hence, on 27 February, Badoglio was appointed to the temporary command of the 74th Infantry Regiment, which was then preparing for an attack on Gorizia. However, the Regiment was assigned elsewhere in April, and was substituted by the 139th Regiment with Badoglio in command. Then on 29 May, Badoglio was appointed Chief of Staff of VI Corps, and on 4 August was put at the disposal of the 45th Division to command the first column of the attack, which captured Monte Sabotino during the 6th Battle of the Isonzo (4 to 17 August).

Badoglio's reputation was thus established, and by May 1917 he was a major general and Chief of Staff to General Capello commanding the Zone of Gorizia. In the initial stage of the 10th Battle of the Isonzo on the night of 12 May the defences of II Corps were severely damaged by an enemy bombardment. During the next day Capello became much concerned for the security of the Corps, and sent Badoglio to make a report of the situation. It appears that the Corps Commander, General Garioni, expressed doubts as to the eventual outcome, rather than a determination to maintain his positions. Therefore Capello replaced him by Badoglio, who in a few days restored the situation.[66]

In less than a year Lieutenant Colonel Badoglio had risen from his position as Chief of Staff of VI Corps to that of General commanding II Corps. He was undoubtedly an outstanding officer. Capello had justified his promotion by referring to his qualities of a clear mind, well balanced, a deep knowledge of military techniques, a firm sense of reality and the moral courage to assume the heaviest and most dangerous responsibilities.[67] Probably other generals were more impressed by the dismissal of a corps commander, together with his chief of staff, deputy chief of staff, and his general of artillery, in favour of Badoglio, now the youngest corps commander in the Italian army.

(General Fara, one of Badoglio's divisional generals, no doubt recalled his days in Libya when Badoglio was only a captain.[68])

As already described, the enemy offensive on 24 October broke through the whole line of IV Corps, and the whole line of XXVII Corps on the right bank of the Isonzo. This was a very bad day for Badoglio who on 23 August had been promoted Lieutenant General and appointed to the command of XXVII Corps. During Capello's 2nd Army conference on 9 October it was stated that 'General Badoglio has a deep knowledge of the problems posed by the defence of the region of his corps',[69] and he was charged with making provision to stem any enemy attempt to capture Jeza by a thrust from the bridgehead at Tolmin.[70] Yet on 24 October Badoglio found it very difficult to obtain any grasp of the situation, or to influence events.

Badoglio had established the tactical command of XXVII Corps together with the commands of the Artillery and the Engineers on Ostri Kras (880m) about a mile south of Jeza.[71] However, on 22 October, probably because the enemy artillery had been registering on Ostri Kras, he moved his command down to its rear office at Kosi about three miles further back and 350m lower down. But on 24 October Kosi was one of the targets of the initial bombardment which interrupted all the telegraph and telephone lines, so Badoglio received no news from the front until 11.00, when a message arrived by hand from Colonel Cannoniere, the Commander of the Artillery presumably on Ostri Kras. This message, written at 10.10, stated little more than that clouds prevented observation, that the enemy bombardment was intense but appeared 'disordered', and that all communications were interrupted.[72] Messages also arrived from the 22nd and 64th Divisions on the other side of the river; they too had been attacked, but the position here seemed not too serious as they had a good defensive system.[73]

Badoglio decided to go to Ostri Kras intending to contact Cannoniere, and then the HQ of the 19th Division. On his way there he encountered some gunners retreating from the Varda – Grad ridge and ordered them back at gunpoint. Thus 'unexpectedly and incidentally'[74] Badoglio learnt that the enemy had gained this ridge, one of his most important defence positions. Fearing that the enemy would now attempt to encircle Jeza, he decided that it was essential to occupy the area Pusno – Srednje – Avsko (just east of Globocak), to form a barrier behind Jeza. Therefore he returned to Kosi, and at about 14.00 ordered the reserve Puglie Brigade to occupy these positions.

While Badoglio had been away from Kosi messages had come in from his 22nd, 64th and 65th Divisions, indicating that they were mainly holding their own on the other side of the river. But there was still no news from the 19th Division. Then in order 'to ensure personally the rapid execution of his order to Puglie' he moved his HQ to the quarry at Cave Kambresko.[75] Here in the early afternoon he received his first news from the Commander of the 19th Division, sent by a runner at a time not stated. General Villani's message told of severe damage in the final stage of the bombardment. All telephone and telegraph wires were down, and optical communications were prevented by cloud. Attempts to communicate with his dependent troops by runners had failed, and he ended by requesting 'boxes of military pigeons' to transmit messages 'which will eventually be received'.[76]

Badoglio now moved from Cave Kambresko to Globacak, and at 15.20 sent a message to 2nd Army saying that he was with the regimental commanders of the Puglie Brigade, which was to take up positions in the area Pusno, Srednje, Avsko.[77] Another message to 2nd Army at 16.00, gave further details of Puglie but no more news of the 19th Division. Badoglio stated that 'I intend to resist . . . opposing the enemy advance. Reinforcements will be necessary for me, and possibly the support of the 3rd Division [VII Corps] united with the 19th on Jeza'. The message ended: 'I find myself at Cave Kambresko. I have no possibility of communicating with anyone.'[78]

Five minutes later Badoglio sent a message by hand to the 3rd Division informing them of the movements of the Puglie Brigade, and that 'it is necessary that the 3rd Division occupy the line Podklabuc [Na Gradu] – Kum and is able to aid the 19th Division to act offensively on Jeza'.[79] Subsequently various messages arrived from the 64th and 22nd Divisions on the left bank, some requesting reinforcements, but as the situation there appeared to be stable Badoglio decided to keep his reserve Puglie Brigade for the defence of Jeza. However, realizing that he was now very much out of touch with the situation on the far side of the river, he sent an order to General Fiorone, the commander of the 64th Division, to assume the command of all three XXVII Corps divisions on the left bank. Fiorone received this order at 19.15, and at 20.20 ordered the transfer of some units to support the defence on the right bank, but was overruled by 2nd Army who transferred the XXVII Corps divisions on the left bank to XXIV Corps.[80]

At 17.55 Badoglio received more news of the 19th Division in a message from Colonel Cannoniere, sent at 14.20 after receiving a report from a captain sent to him by General Villani. The message stated that the division had been forced to retire and intended to stand on the line Jeza – Ostre Kras – Pusno. 'The bombardment continues most violently. Communications are almost impossible. The rear lines are blocked with traffic. Perhaps it would be advisable to send reinforcements.' Badoglio passed this very out of date information to 2nd Army at 18.20, saying that he was preparing to hold the line Jeza – Pusno, adding that he had given orders to Puglie and the 64th Division (on either side of the Isonzo) to bar the route down the river; and that he needed reinforcements.

Towards 20.00, two battalions of the Puglie Brigade, on their way to support the line Jeza – Pusno, encountered enemy units near Pusno, where one company suffered serious losses and was almost all captured. It now looked as if the 19th Division had been cut off, and the situation appeared extremely serious. Therefore Badoglio decided to go to Lig, about three miles south of Kambresko, where the Vth Bersaglieri Brigade was now at his disposal, and personally give orders to restore the situation.[81]

On arriving at Lig, Badoglio telephoned Capello, and was told that the Ist Bersaglieri Brigade had also been alloted to him (by a message sent at 18.00, which did not arrive until 23.40). Capello asked if a counter-attack could be made towards Jeza and Tolmin with the four regiments of Bersaglieri now available. Badoglio replied that with these good troops he would try next morning at all cost to retake Globacak which had now been lost, but he had no artillery support and would be under strong enemy artillery fire. In fact, Badoglio had been badly informed, as only a spur of Globacak was in enemy hands; the main mass was still held by the Italians, and was only given up the next day when they received orders to retire.[82]

The inadequacies of Badoglio's preparations were now brutally clear. There had been insufficient liaison with both VII and IV Corps, most obviously on the line between Foni and the Isonzo, where two German battalions had followed the road on the right bank of the river, and en route to Caporetto had passed through his front line almost unopposed. Nor was this weakness the result of some oversight, but of a deliberate instruction by Corps, overriding the view of the Divisional Commander (Section 2.6). Moreover, as described below, Badoglio's preparatory orders to his artillery, combined with the subsequent breakdown of communication, led to the failure of his guns to respond effectively to the enemy attack (Section 4.4).

(During 2nd Army conferences in September and October there had been talk of halting an enemy attack by launching a counter-offensive, from the Bainsizza towards Tolmin. But the IOH does not record any preparations for such an offensive, and in the event the three divisions facing Tolmin, the 65th, 22nd and 64th of XXVII Corps, so far from leading an attack, were themselves largely broken up by the Austrians on 25 October (Section 3.3).)

Badoglio has been much criticized for his performance on 24 October, particularly for being out of touch with his divisions. Any Corps Commander who reports to Army that 'I have no possibility of communicating with anyone' must accept some criticism, but Badoglio found himself in a difficult position. Visual observation and signalling were largely ruled out at first by the cloudy weather, while the unexpected violence and accuracy of the initial bombardment had destroyed the telephone communications. Such a situation had been discussed in the IV Corps conference on 14 October, but the only solutions proposed had been pigeons or trumpets.[83]

It was certainly undesirable for a Corps Commander, who may expect to receive reports at his HQ, to spend so much time on the move, from Kosi to Ostry Kras, Kosi, Kambresko, Globocak, Kambresko, and Lig, for how would his units know where to send their reports? On the other hand, Badoglio would have deservedly been censured if he had remained at his HQ and received no more communications, as well might have been the case.

In fact, Badoglio had sent a staff officer, Major Cantatore, to the 19th Division at about 06.30 to obtain some picture of events, and Major Freguglia on a similar mission to the divisions on the left bank of the river. But Cantatore, slightly wounded, returned only about 15.00.[84] Badoglio himself went towards Ostri Kras and saw evidence of the enemy advance, and arranged for the deployment of the reserve Puglie Brigade. He maintained some contacts with the divisions on the left bank, and contacted the adjacent 3rd Division in VII Corps with orders for the defence of Jeza and for a counter-attack the next day.

When any army is overwhelmed by an enemy offensive, corps commanders will find it extremely difficult to keep any grasp on the situation, as for example was the case in the British Fifth Army in France during the German offensive in April 1918.[85] Even so, Badoglio's performance as a Corps Commander is certainly open to severe criticism, particularly for the inadequacies of his plans and preparations before the battle. However, these failings only became apparent at a much later date. Hence, while Cavaciocchi was dismissed from his command on 25 October, and Cadorna was dismissed on 7 November, on 9 November Badoglio was promoted to be one of the two deputies to the new Comando Supremo, General Diaz.

Finally, in January 1919 the Commission of Enquiry set up to determine the reasons for the failure at Caporetto made its report. This lengthy and detailed account concluded that nearly all the principal generals had some responsibility for the debacle. However, it made no criticism or censure of Badoglio whose performance had left much to be desired, probably because by the time that the Commission's Report was published, the war had been won, and Badoglio was a national hero. Therefore, so it appears, thirteen pages of the Report were excised before publication,[86] and Badoglio was set on his military career, which though not entirely successful, was to dominate the Italian Army for the next twenty-four years.

(c) VII Corps (Bongiovanni)

General Bongiovanni was appointed to the command of an entirely reconstituted VII Corps only seven days before the enemy attack, and seems to have been placed in an almost impossible position. To appreciate the problems he faced, we briefly recap some of the various orders already mentioned in Sections 2.5 and 2.6. The first move to reinforce the Italian front was taken on 10 October, when the 3rd Division of the reserve XXVIII Corps was ordered to prepare defensive positions on the line Monte Piatto – Kum – Globocak, behind the 19th Division of XXVII Corps.[87] A week later, on 17 October, Capello further strengthened this arrangement by setting up a new VII Corps, consisting of the 3rd Division, the Napoli Brigade (from the 19th Division), and the 2nd and 9th Regiments Bersaglieri.[88] However, at the same time the responsibilities of the new Corps were greatly increased beyond those previously assigned to the 3rd Division. The Corps had four tasks: to guard the 'most important line Matajur – Kolovrat; to support the advanced defences; to act as a reserve behind the adjacent wings of IV and XXVII Corps; and to manoeuvre counter-offensively at an appropriate moment'. As the IOH comments, these aims were far beyond the Corps' resources, and to some extent contradictory.[89]

General Bongiovanni issued further orders on 19 October saying that until new orders were received, both the 3rd Division and the Napoli Brigade were to continue their work on the line of defence behind XXVII Corps. At the same time, the command of the Napoli Brigade was to study the region around Piatto and Na Gradu; the command of the 3rd Division to study the positions on the Kolovrat (facing north) from Monte Piatto (exclusive) to the saddle of Livek (inclusive), both for defence and for counter-offensive action; and the command of the 2nd Bersaglieri to study the defence of the road down the Natisone valley between Matajur and Monte Mia.[90]

Bongiovanni issued further orders on 22 October, by which time his two Bersaglieri regiments had been transferred to IV Corps, and were to be substituted by the 34th Division which had yet to arrive.[91] The 3rd Division (Arno, Elba, Firenze, Napoli Brigades) was now assigned to a line running first from Monte Kuk (inclusive) to Passo Zagradan, and then behind the 19th Division from Passo Zagradan to Kum and Pusno. In addition, the Napoli Brigade was to continue the work of reinforcing the strong point around Jeza, as requested by XXVII Corps.[92] The rest of the Corps sector, from Matajur to Kuk would be the responsibility of the 34th Division.

During 22 October further changes by the Army Command transferred the 34 Division to IV Corps, and Bongiovanni was advised that the 62nd Division would substitute for it, and was on the way. At 24.00

he issued orders to the 3rd Division that during the night the Arno Brigade would occupy the line Kuk – Piatto, the Elba Brigade the line Piatto – Kum, and that the Firenze Brigade would act as reserve. The rest of the line from Matajur to Kuk was to be guarded by units of the 62nd Division 'as they arrived'. The latter were ordered 'to take steps in order to be able to establish a defence of Livek', described as located 'between the strong points of Kuk and Matajur', a rather optimistic description of two bare mountain tops, one nearly four miles away.[93]

During the few days that General Bongiovanni had been in command of VII Corps, his preparations for the coming battle must have been greatly compromised by the continual changes in the constitution of the Corps imposed by higher commands. On 24 October, however, his problems arose from enemy action, and not from his superiors. It is neither necessary nor possible to follow all the details of the day, and we mention here some items from the IOH which suggest that Bongiovanni, like Cavaciocchi and Badoglio, had some difficulty in responding to the enemy attack.

An extract from the VII Corps Diary printed in the IOH makes no mention of Corps HQ receiving any information on the morning of 24 October prior to a visit at 11.00 by the King of Italy. The King was nominally the Commander-in-Chief, but since the appointment of Cadorna as Chief of Staff of the Comando Supremo in 1914, it was accepted that all military decisions were the responsibility of the Chief of Staff. The King fully respected this convention, but took an informed interest in the Army, and spent most of the war in uniform with the Army, perhaps to the detriment of his other duties.[94]

Years later in conversation with Caviglia the King recalled that, on the above visit, Bongiovanni and all his staff appeared not only unaware of the battle, but in a state of mind far away from the war.[95] Be that as it may, the Corps Diary records that during this visit the King thought it necessary to order 'that one telephoned the Command of XXVII Corps to ask for news of the situation'.[96] (The reply was that there had been intense artillery fire during the night, but up till then no news of any infantry attacks had come through.)

It was only at 12.00 that VII Corps HQ received news from IV Corps that enemy units had taken Selisce on the left bank of the Isonzo. Then in response to this news, and to orders received from the Army Command, Bongiovanni sent a brief order to the 62nd Division to take action 'not only for the effective defence of the saddle of Livek but also for the eventual occupation of the line from Golobi down to Idrsko, already prescribed'.[97] A reply from General Viora was received at 14.30, acknowledging the message, and saying that 'The occupation of the line Golobi – Idrsko requires a battalion. I have replaced it with one of the reserves.'[98] These somewhat vague and indecisive messages show remarkably little sense of urgency. Indeed it was not until 19.00 that Bongiovanni sent a more unambiguous order (N.11176) to the 62nd Division to 'attack . . . the left flank of the enemy proceeding to Caporetto whenever one sees the possibility'. But by now any opportunity of a useful intervention had been lost.[99]

All through 24 October the 2nd Army suffered much because of the destruction of telegraph and telephone lines, but even when General Bongiovanni was in touch with 2nd Army he failed to realize the importance of presenting an accurate picture of events. For example, when the 62nd Division (General Viora) acknowledged Bongiovanni's order N. 11176 his message stated that the Bersaglieri would operate immediately to regain Golobi and the eleven abandoned 105mm guns, and that they would then advance on either side of the road 'to disturb the enemy on the valley floor'. However, when this news was passed on to 2nd Army as part of Phonogram 11290 the phrase 'to disturb the enemy' was replaced by 'to proceed counter-offensively'.[100]

General Viora had also reported that 'I firmly hold the positions but cartridges and munitions for the guns are needed with great urgency', and this news was not passed on at all. Even more importantly General Viora had reported to Corps that 'Telephonist Livek about 16.30 has left his post without orders removing some material and ruining the telephone.' This information also was not passed on to 2nd Army, and the IOH suggests that General Bongiovanni failed to realize the importance of this item.[101]

4.4   Failures of the Guns

It is generally agreed that the Italian artillery failed in its response to the attack. The Official History states that there are good grounds for evaluations such as 'our batteries remained silent though in full efficiency', 'our artillery failed in their duty', and 'the defensive fire did not take place'.[102] General Sagramoso who was sent to make enquiries on 25 October reported that 'the conduct of the groups whose officers I questioned was certainly not that expected from the previous ability and valour shown by our artillery'.[103] In fact, although the Italians were used to handling guns in attack, they were much less experienced in handling them effectively in defence. At Caporetto the Italian artillery was put to the test and found wanting due to a variety of circumstances.

We have already described the disagreements between Cadorna and Capello, and Capello's reluctance to obey Cadorna's orders and take up defensive positions. Many guns were still in the course of moving to their defensive positions on the eve of the battle. According to the IOH, seventeen batteries had been posted to Zaga and Monte Stol,[104] but only two were in position on 24 October, and they had no ammu-nition.[105] Other batteries had arrived in position only recently, without time to set up lines of fire.

On 24 October, from 02.00 onwards those guns that were in place were the targets of a massive and well-prepared artillery assault, using both high-explosive and gas shells, which appears to have been very successful, both against the guns and in disrupting communications. Moreover, those crews which did survive found that their view was often limited by mist and cloud, and were apparently not trained to fire on fixed lines. The Diary of IV Corps records a message sent at 11.30 from Cavaciocchi to Capello saying that cloud was hindering obser-vation, reducing the efficiency of the artillery, and favouring surprise action by the enemy.[106]

Over and above these difficulties there was also uncertainty on when the artillery was to open fire, because the relevant orders had been thoroughly obfuscated by the Corps and Army staffs. As early as 10 October Cadorna had issued Order N.4741 to the 2nd Army saying that in the event of an enemy bombardment on Italian positions violent *contropreparazione* action was to be made in reply. That is, the Italian artillery should fire on the enemy's trenches and their rear services so as to disorganize and crush an attack before it commenced. Taking this order in its general context it seems clear that Cadorna intended that the *contropreparazione* should begin when the enemy commenced his bombardment, but what he actually wrote in his order was that it should take place <u>during</u> the enemy fire, a somewhat im-precise instruction.[107]

The substance of Cadorna's order was passed on by 2nd Army (Montuori then deputizing for Capello) to Corps Commanders in similar but not quite the same terms, and with not entirely the same meaning. For although it was clearly stated that the guns should fire 'from the start of the enemy bombardment', it also said that other batteries (unspecified) should open fire of *contropreparazione* when the enemy infantry left their lines to attack![108] The Official History gives details of other subsequent orders by Montuori, Badoglio and Capello. These express somewhat similar intentions but again suffer from a lack of precision and clarity, and also introduce new terms to describe the different types of fire. In fact not all of these various orders were fully consistent with each other (see for example Faldella[109]). Thus it was unlikely that the gunners on the ground would have any clear idea of what was expected of them if they were isolated by a breakdown in communications.

According to Faldella, Badoglio believed in keeping a close personal control of all his operations. For example, Faldella claims that when the Commander of the Corps Artillery moved to another unit, Badoglio

1. Lieutenant Rommel, December 1917. *(Collection Kainz)*

2. Troopers of the Wurttemberg Mountain Battalion. *(Collection Kainz)*

3. The Isonzo valley near Tolmin. Monte Ocna left centre with Na Gradu behind and to the right.

4. The slopes of Mrzli above Tolmin.

5. Monte Nero across the Isonzo valley.

6. The Isonzo valley above Caporetto. The slopes of Monte Polovnik on the right.

7. General Cadorna. *(Ufficio Storico)*

8. General Capello. *(Ufficio Storico)*

9. The Isonzo valley above Bovec.

10. The subsidary ridges of Matajur viewed from the south.

11. General Krafft von Dellmensingen.

12. Major Sproesser. *(Collection Kainz)*

13. View from the Kolovrat looking south.

14. Defences on Passo Zagradan. Na Gradu behind, left of centre. *(Ufficio Storico)*

15. Hill 1192 on the Kolovrat viewed from the east.

16. Italian prisoners on Monte Kuk. *(Collection Kainz)*

17. Transport section of the Wurttemberg Mountain Battalion. *(Collection Kainz)*

18. On the march. *(Collection Kainz)*

19. The Tagliamento at Codroipo; seen in dry conditions.

20. The broken bridge at Cornino. *(Collection Kainz)*

21. Abandoned equipment after the retreat from Caporetto. *(Collection Kainz)*

22. Refugees. *(Ufficio Storico)*

23. View across the Meduna valley looking towards the mountains to the west.

24. View towards Passo San Osvaldo from Cimolais.

25. Major Sproesser, his troops and two Italian prisoners on the Clautana Pass. *(Collection Kainz)*

26. The valley of the Piave at Longarone looking north.

27. Troops of the Wurttemberg Mountain Battalion on the bridge over the Vajont Gorge, 11 November 1917. (Collection Kainz)

28. The Vajont dam viewed from near Longarone.

29. The ridges of Monte Grappa viewed from the south.

30. The cliffs of Spinoncia viewed from near Monte Pallon; Fontanasecca behind.

31. Troopers of the Wurttemberg Mountain Battalion on Spinoncia. *(Collection Kainz)*

32. The cliffs of Fontanasecca viewed across Val Stizzon.

appealed to Capello against the two names of two major generals put forward for the appointment, in favour of his own preference for a Colonel Cannoniere. Faldella suggests that this more junior and less experienced officer was appointed because Badoglio wished to have someone who would be deferential to his own views.

When the enemy bombardment commenced at 02.00 on 24 October Cannoniere needed Badoglio's permission to respond, and Caviglia states that all communications between Ostri Kras and Kosi were interrupted.[110] On the other hand, the IOH quotes a submission to the Commission of Enquiry by XXVII Corps which states that after the enemy bombardment intensified after 06.30, Badoglio did telephone Cannoniere, and ordered the heavy and medium guns to open fire on the enemy front line and rear areas.[111] For a further discussion of this obscure situation, and of the part played by previous orders from 2nd Army, see Pieri and Rochat.[112]

The IOH also refers to an account given later by the colonel commanding the 6th Group of Artillery, stating that his batteries were silent until he received orders from XXVII Corps at about 08.00 to fire on the bridge at Tolmin.[113] The inference must be that for several hours the guns of the XIVth Army were allowed to prepare for their offensive with little or no opposition from the guns of XXVII Corps. Although somewhat reticent on how this came about, the IOH makes the general comment that the Italian fire was 'was completely ineffectual and extremely modest both in an absolute sense and in relation to the mass of guns in the sector'.[114]

So far we have discussed the direction of the artillery at the highest levels of command. We now turn to the performance of the troops manning the guns. It is clear both from the accounts of Krafft and Rommel, and from the IOH, that the behaviour of the gunners was very variable. Krafft describes how several batteries of heavy guns were caught by surprise while they were actually firing, and although taken aback to see German helmets they defended themselves courageously with their revolvers until overcome.[115] But other crews behaved differently.

Krafft records that at 11.30 on the morning of 24 October the crew of a heavy battery on Hlevnik were surprised while playing cards in a bunker, and the officers while eating lunch in a nearby bunker.[116] Even allowing for the breakdown in communications, it is hard to imagine how they could have been so unaware of the battle that they had not organized sentries and outposts. Besides surprising and capturing gun crews, the XIVth Army found batteries of guns deserted even though in working order with supplies of ammunition. At 14.00 on 24 October General Badoglio going up from Kambresko towards Pusno (Map 4) encountered deserters from batteries at Srednje and elsewhere. They claimed that the Germans were at Kambresko; this was obviously untrue and Badoglio ordered them back at gun point. (This episode, reported by Faldella,[117] is probably the same one mentioned in the IOH where the gunners are said to have come from Krad Vrh (Monte Grad).[118])

According to the report by General Sagramoso, sent to interview gunner officers on 25 October, many of the batteries on 24 October did not receive any orders to fire. None of the batteries had been trained to protect their guns. Indeed Sagramoso stated that some gun crews had left their guns without haste and with the officers at their head, not thinking it was their duty to fight or defend the guns.[119] According to Faldella, batteries at the village of San Paolo (Sv Pavel) were abandoned on the evening of 24 October even though the site was only captured on the late afternoon of 25 October.[120] The IOH quotes a message, presumably relating to the same episode, from General Badoglio to the Comando Supremo on 25 October saying that he had ordered the commander of the batteries at San Paola, Lieutenant Colonel Maffei, who the day before abandoned them without reason, to get them back into working order as soon as possible.[121]

4.5   Failures of the Troops

The German tactics had been remarkably successful. So much so that by 26 October General von Below was recording in his diary that his troops had already taken some 50,000 prisoners,[122] and Faldella states that by the same date about 20,000 *sbandati* or stragglers had been gathered together in a camp near Udine.[123] In addition on 25 October Cadorna was informing the War Minister that 'ten regiments have surrendered in mass without fighting. I see the outline of a disaster against which I shall fight to the end.'[124] In fact the Italian Army had not been prepared or trained to resist such an attack, particularly one opening with an unexpectedly ferocious artillery and gas bombardment. Yet on 28 October the Comando Supremo issued the communiqué in which Cadorna threw the whole blame for the disaster on the front-line troops.

Although the communiqué of 28 October referred to the brave resistance of some troops it began: 'the lack of resistance by units of the 2nd Army, cowardly retreating without fighting or ignominiously surrendering to the enemy, has allowed the Austro-German forces to break our left wing on the Julian front'. As soon as the government saw this communiqué it realized the grave consequences that might ensue, and insisted on an amendment: 'the violence of the attack and the deficient resistance of some units of the 2nd Army has allowed the Austro-German forces . . .', but the original version had already been sent abroad and soon became public knowledge. In fact the debacle of Caporetto arose from failures in the Italian army both within the Comando Supremo and the higher commands, as well as in the performance of many troops on the ground. It is also clear that Cadorna's one-sided communiqué was ill-advised, coming as it did from the general who for the past three years had himself been in total charge of the training and deployment of the Italian army.

Some detailed accounts of the behaviour of the front-line troops are given by Krafft and Rommel. Several of these accounts, referred to above, give examples of substantial resistance. The 1st Austrian Division suffered 14 per cent losses during the first two days fighting (Section 3.1). According to Gatti the 4th Regiment of Bersaglieri defending Globocak counter-attacked and took 400 prisoners, but Gatti also remarks that 'other troops surrendered as soon as the shooting began'.[125]

Both Krafft and Rommel give examples of deserted positions, particularly gun positions and of gun crews totally surprised. There are also various accounts of units resisting well until senior officers were killed, then resistance collapsed and the units surrendered. Certainly premature surrenders and 'clearings-out' were on a considerable scale and began soon, as is described by General Montuori's evidence to the Commission of Enquiry. In the early afternoon of 24 October he left Cividale to visit IV Corps HQ at Kred. His car was held up north of Stupizza by 'an enormous crowd' so he was forced to walk to Kred where he arrived about 15.30. After consulting with General Cavaciocchi he returned to Cividale by an alternative route through Nimis in order to consult VII Corps HQ at Carraria near Cividale. Later that evening visiting the 2nd Army Command at Cividale he observed several thousand troops, mainly gunners and bombardiers, without rifles or helmets but with their gas masks.[126]

It seems from many reports that the first to 'clear out' were the gunners and the support troops immediately behind the front line, whereas Gatti was to remark later that the front-line infantry were either dead or had been taken prisoner.[127] With hindsight these failings were part of the debacle waiting to happen on the upper Isonzo. The sector above Tolmin was a quiet area where little fighting had occurred since 1915, and hence was not manned by the best Italian troops. Moreover, disaffected workers involved in the Turin riots had been conscripted into the army and there is some evidence that they had been sent to this sector.[128] If so it was an unfortunate decision.

It should also be noted that the reports coming back from the confusion at the front were sometimes misleading, as in the case of the Brigata Roma. This unit formed part of the 65th Division in XXVII Corps, had a high reputution, and had fought well on 24 October. Then on the morning of 25 October, while the Brigade (now transferred to XXIV Corps) was withdrawing according to orders, the Italian line was penetrated on either side of them, and they were surrounded and obliged to surrender. On receiving this news the Corps Commander, General Caviglia, passed it on without comment to 2nd Army. Unfortunately a 2nd Army bulletin which mentioned the surrender gave the impression that the Brigade had not fought at all either on 24 or 25 October. Caviglia was much embarrassed by not having made the position more clear to 2nd Army, and he gives a detailed account of this episode in his book *Caporetto*.[129]

As another example of misleading information received by the Army Command, messages sent by IV Corps to Army and adjacent Corps in the early hours of 24 October referred to 'the modest efficiency of chemical attacks'. In the 50th Division the gas masks were said to have acted 'most efficiently', and in the 46th Division they functioned 'well'. Yet other reports refer to the finding of 500 to 600 dead Italians in trenches near Bovec killed by gas.[130]

Finally, just as success breeds success, so failure bred failure. At an early stage, masses of troops were moving towards the rear in various states of disorder, some still in units, many as stragglers separated from their units, some deserters. Filling the narrow roads running down from the Kolovrat to Cividale and the plain, the disordered columns would have produced an unsettling effect on the troops of the reserve units still making their way up to the front.

There were undoubtedly scenes of confusion and incidents of flight and panic, but perhaps one should recall a comment on Caporetto in the British official account, *Military Operations in Italy 1917 – 1918*: 'Much is written after all retreats of the confusion and the panics and the loosening of the bonds of discipline . . . such incidents undoubtedly occur on a major or minor scale during retirements and are seen of many and are reported; but little is said of the units and bodies of brave men who remain, even move up to the front, counter-attack and do all they can to delay the enemy, for they are seen by fewer spectators'.[131]

Rommel on the Kolovrat and Matajur

5.1 Prelude (18–23 October)

We now turn to Rommel's part in the first stage of the battle of Caporetto. On the night of 18 October the Wurttemberg Mountain Battalion (WMB) left their concentration area near Kranj in the Sava valley to move up to the front, Rommel usually marching at the head of his detachment. It was a miserable journey, always in the dark, often raining, sometimes heavily. During daylight men and animals were concealed in uncomfortable and inadequate accommodation with below standard rations. But morale was high for 'in three years of war the troops had learnt to endure hard conditions without losing their vigour'.[1] After three nights and 40 miles the Battalion arrived at Kneza about five miles short of the Isonzo, as far as they could go without coming into range of the Italian guns.

The next afternoon, on 21 October, Major Sproesser and his detachment commanders reconnoitred their assembly area for the initial attack. It was sited on the north slope of Hill 510, a small summit on the right bank of the river, south of Tolmin, rising about 300m above the valley floor (Map 3). The area is shown wooded by Krafft,[2] and is described by Rommel as rugged, nearly impassable terrain, with little space for marshalling the troops except for some scree slopes and precipitous gulleys. It presented a dismal prospect but there was no alternative as so many troops were now crowded together near Tolmin. Indeed this was probably the most critical time of all for the XIVth Army, for as Krafft wrote later a systematic destructive fire from the Italian batteries would have caused grave losses.[3]

The WMB moved into their assembly positions on the night of 22 October, and for the first time encountered Italian opposition. Powerful searchlights on the Kolovrat and Jeza forced them to lie motionless for minutes on end, some artillery fire struck around them, and it appeared that they were facing 'an unusually active and well equipped enemy'.[4] Leaving their animals at the foot of the hill, Rommel's detachment of two rifle and an MG Company, heavily laden with machine guns and ammunition, made an exhausting climb to their position. The detachment arrived unharmed, and set about digging in where they could, and camouflaging their positions with shrubbery and branches.

The WMB was now in position to play their part in the assault on Na Gradu (1114m), on the extreme right of the Alpine Corps, with the Bavarian Life Guards on their left. The day of 23 October passed slowly. Attempts to sleep were interrupted by Italian heavy batteries firing intermittently on the roads and installations around Tolmin, and on one occasion sending rocks tumbling down past the detachment. The weather was murky so all that could be seen of the enemy was the apparently well-constructed and well-wired positions of the front line on the valley floor.

5.2   Hlevnik and Hill 1066 (24 October)

At 02.00 on 24 October, the hitherto silent guns of the XIVth Army opened a bombardment of the Italian positions particularly around Tolmin and Bovec. Flashes from a thousand guns on the hillsides lit up the dark and stormy night. Although not so great a concentration as sometimes on the Western Front, the uninterrupted sound of the guns and exploding shells were reflected back and forth between the hills. The WMB saw and heard the bombardment with amazement, and were relieved that only a few Italian batteries answered the German fire, and that these became weaker.

Between 04.30 and 05.30 the bombardment died away. Then at 06.30 it resumed at full strength concentrating on the front line defences, and reached a crescendo in the final fifteen minutes before the infantry assault at 08.00.[5] Meanwhile, shortly after daybreak, the WMB had moved off down the boulder-strewn slope of Hill 510, into positions close behind the right wing of the Life Guards, for the assault on Na Gradu (Map 4). At 08.00 the guns fell silent. The Life Guards and the WMB came up to the first defence line, and saw that the defences had been almost annihilated, with survivors hurrying out to surrender.

The first objective of the WMB was the north side of the ridge running up to Monte Hlevnik, including enemy positions around the little village of Foni. The Rommel detachment (the 1st and 2nd Rifle and 1st Machine-Gun Companies) took the lead, along a rising path on the north side of the ridge running up first to Foni, and then towards the summit of Hlevnik. The whole area was wooded, with the ground rising or falling steeply on either side of the path, which in places was overgrown with bushes. The detachment proceeded cautiously with a point section in front, followed by a machine-gun platoon, then by Rommel and his staff, and finally the three companies at 150 yard intervals. The autumn leaves were still on the trees, the weather cloudy and misty, and visibility was often only a few yards, so there was no possibility of artillery support. Everything was very quiet and the detachment proceeded cautiously, careful to make no noise. Suddenly the silence was broken by the sound of machine-gun fire at close quarters, and news came back to Rommel that the point section had encountered barbed-wire defences, and that five men had been wounded.

Rommel had little idea of the enemy's strength, but it was obvious that a direct attack on this position, across overgrown and steeply sloping ground, was unlikely to succeed. Leaving the point section in contact with the enemy, he drew back about 200 yards to a rough open gully running up the hillside, and reported back to Major Sproesser that he intended to outflank the enemy from above on the left. A new point section climbed the gully, followed by Rommel and Lieutenant Streicher, and then 40 yards behind by a heavy machine-gun crew.

The gully was steep and rough, and very hard going for the machine-gunners carrying their heavy loads. A rolling boulder struck Rommel's foot and nearly put him out of action. As the point section climbed upwards, in pouring rain, the stony gully gave way to dense under-growth, and they eventually emerged from the woods about 200 metres or so below the crest of the ridge running up towards the summit of Hlevnik, about a mile away. To the right of the detachment a continuous line of wire defences ran down from the ridge across open ground and then entered the woods, presumably to connect with the defences on the path to Foni. Beyond the wire, they could see a few men moving about apparently unaware of their presence.

If the enemy were at all alert a direct assault on the wired line, across 60 yards or so of scrub-covered hillside, could be very costly. Rommel saw another possibility. Along the front edge of the wood there was a camouflaged path, obviously a supply route to the Italian positions higher up the mountain, and sufficiently camouflaged that any troops using it would be scarcely visible. Hence, Rommel selected Lance Corporal Kiefner and sent him, with a squad of eight men, to move along the path to the right, hoping that if they were seen they would be thought to be Italians. His order to Kiefner was to follow the path through the wire defences, and then capture the garrison on either side, if possible with no noise of guns or grenades which would give a general alarm. At the same time the rest of the detachment would be in place ready to support him if a fight should ensue.

Lance Corporal Kiefner led his men up the path; Rommel and his three companies waited anxiously, ready to respond at the first sound of a shot, but heard nothing except the drip of steady rain falling on the trees. Eventually a message came back from Kiefner saying that he had captured a dug-out, seventeen Italians, and a machine gun, and that the rest of the garrison had not been alarmed. Assault teams then succeeded in widening the breach in the defence line to about fifty yards on either side of the path, and by their skilful approach quietly captured several dozen Italians found in dug-outs sheltering from the rain. All this without any sign of reaction from the enemy.

Just prior to this success, Rommel had been joined by Lieutenant Schiellein's detachment (3rd, 6th Rifles; 2nd MG), and he was now in command of both detachments. Meanwhile Major Sproesser and the third detachment (Lieutenant Wahrenberger), lower down, were moving towards Foni. Rommel states that he had now to choose between either rolling up the Italian positions along the defence line, or pushing on directly towards the summit of Hlevnik. Being Rommel, he decided that the further he penetrated into the enemy front, the more likely he was to achieve surprise, and that once the peak was secured it would be easy to mop up the remaining enemy positions.

The Rommel group, now of six companies, spaced along a thousand-yard column, worked its way up towards the ridge, taking what cover it could from bush to bush, and in concealed hollows and gullies. By 11.00 the group had reached the ridge, where they made contact with the 3rd Battalion the Bavarian Life Guards, and accompanied them up the ridge towards the summit of Hlevnik. The German artillery was still firing at the summit so the Guards paused to rest until the artillery shifted its fire. Rommel did not pause, but led his companies off the ridge on to the north face of Hlevnik, where they were in dead ground, and thus reached the peak at 12.00 without encountering any opposition. The German artillery fire had now ceased and the weather was improving. The rain had stopped, and breaks in the cloud gave glimpses of Na Gradu and the line of the Kolovrat on the right (Map 4).

From the summit of Hlevnik the way to Na Gradu was down the south-west ridge to the col known as Passo Zagradan (Plate 14), and then up the side of Na Gradu to the summit about 200 metres above. The improving visibility was soon followed by heavy Italian artillery fire directed at Rommel's group on Hlevnik. Therefore Rommel moved both detachments into dead ground on the north face, and gave orders to mop up any enemy artillery positions between there and Foni. By 15.30 the Rommel group had captured seventeen guns, twelve of them heavy, while units of the 3rd Battalion of the Life Guards had arrived at Passo Zagradan.

To obtain some picture of the subsequent events on the Kolovrat we must keep in mind that the top of this ridge is not a narrow edge, but rather a grassy plateau, of the order of a hundred yards wide, interspersed with hummocks, rocky outcrops and hollows, and mainly bare of trees. On either side of this plateau the ground falls away quite steeply, so an enemy on the slopes below the ridge, as at Passo Zagradan, was unable to obtain any good view of the plateau. Equally, the defenders on the plateau could see very little of an attack coming up from below, out of the line of sight and often hidden by trees. On the plateau, the height differences between the various summits Nagnoj, Piatto (Trinski vrh), and Na Gradu are only of the order of 50 metres, and none of the summits are as recognizable on the ground as their corresponding points on a map. Any cloud or mist can make route finding difficult, and even on a clear day the hummocky nature of the plateau can obscure events even a short distance away.

About 16.00 the Life Guards moved off from Passo Zagradan along a camouflaged road leading to Na Gradu via Hill 1066. (Hill 1066 is shown on one of Rommel's sketch maps,[6] and is probably the point shown by Krafft as Hill 1041.[7]) The task of the WMB was to protect the right flank of the Life Guards, so the Rommel detachment moved off behind them. At about 17.00 the Life Guards came under fire as they approached Hill 1066 (now described as a rocky outcrop) and took cover. Rommel brought his six companies up under cover to positions on the right of the Life Guards, and went to consult with their officers.

The Life Guards had already sent out scouts to test the enemy positions on Na Gradu (generally referred to by the Germans as Hill 1114), and found that they were facing a strong and resolute enemy in good defensive positions, which could only be taken by an attack supported by the artillery. By dusk, however, the 12th Company of the Life Guards, under Lieutenant Schoerner, had worked its way up the south side of Na Gradu while the attention of the defenders was engaged by patrols on the north-east slopes. Arriving at the wire defences, these Life Guards found a yard and a half gap, stormed in, and created such surprise that there was little effective resistance. Schoerner then launched a three-pronged attack on the summit itself. Although the first two attacks were repelled, the third broke through, and by 17.30 'the almost impossible had been achieved thanks to the audacious action led by Lieutenant Schoerner'.[8] Over 300 prisoners, a large number of machine guns, and much ammunition was captured, but the Italians were still in firm possession of an extensive system of wired trenches and strong points, both nearby and on the ridge of the Kolovrat towards Monte Piatto about half a mile to the west.

At about 19.00 Major Count von Bothmer, the Commander of the Life Guards, arrived at Rommel's command post near Hill 1066. Rommel reported on his group and positions, and was told by Bothmer that the whole group would now come under his command. Rommel

95

respectfully replied that he took his orders from Major Sproesser, who he believed was senior to Bothmer, and that he was expecting Sproesser to arrive at any moment. Bothmer then told Rommel that the Life Guards had been given the objective of capturing Na Gradu and the rest of the Kolovrat to the west, and he forbad the Rommel detachment from moving either against Na Gradu or further to the west. Rommel could, however, either occupy and secure Na Gradu after its capture by the Life Guards, or follow behind the Guards as they advanced to the west. Rommel returned to his command post 'not at all happy'.

At 21.00 the WMB quartermaster, Lieutenant Autenrieth arrived at Rommel's command post with the news that Major Sproesser and Lieutenant Wahrenberger's detachment had broken the defences around Foni in the late afternoon, capturing prisoners and guns, and that the 12(g) Division had made excellent progress in the Isonzo valley. Autenrieth also informed Rommel that he had encountered the Life Guards on his way up, and learnt an attack with artillery support against Na Gradu and the Kolovrat was planned for the next morning. Rommel informed Autenrieth of the present situation of his group, and asked him to return to Foni, with all speed through the dark night, and request Major Sproesser to come to Hill 1066 as soon as possible, preferably accompanied by the Wahrenberger detachment.

The Rommel group in their wet clothes spent another wet night with a cold wind. Patrols probed the enemy defences looking for weak spots, but found the Italian sentries alert and ready to use hand-grenades and machine-gun fire. Half asleep, Rommel continued to think how the WMB could play a more substantial role than following behind its old rival the Life Guards. He was anxious to push forward as fast as possible, but the attack on Na Gradu would have to await a thorough artillery preparation, and in any case he had been forbidden to take part. Suppose, however, that the WMB were to traverse out of sight along the north side of the Kolovrat, and then make a surprise attack into the Italian positions on the ridge well to the west of Na Gradu. But any such move had been vetoed by Major Bothmer, so for the moment Rommel had to await the arrival of Major Sproesser.

5.3   The Kolovrat (25 October)

At 05.00 on 25 October, while the night was still very dark, Major Sproesser arrived at Rommel's command post with the other three companies of the WMB, and Rommel explained his plan of by-passing Na Gradu with four rifle and two machine-gun companies. Sproesser agreed that he should make the attempt, but initially with only two rifle and one machine-gun company. However, he would remain in contact

96

with Rommel by a telephone line, and promised Rommel full support if he were successful.

Rommel states that, as he was preparing to set out, Major Bothmer arrived at the WMB positions, and that Major Sproesser succeeded in reaching an understanding with him. Sproesser gives rather more detail of this understanding. On arriving at the WMB positions Bothmer informed Sproesser that, as Rommel had stated, the Life Guards had been given the task of capturing the whole ridge from Hill 1114 to Monte Kuk, and the task of the WMB was to act as a reserve and as flank protection to the Life Guards. Sproesser did not agree with this. He saw the WMB with its six rifle companies and three machine-gun companies as too valuable a resource to be left in reserve at this critical stage of the offensive. He replied 'I must thank you. I am fully occupied with my battalion. Moreover, I have no intention of remaining with your 3rd Battalion. I will advance towards Kuk, Luico [Livek] and Matajur. The Rommel detachment is now well on its way, and I can see them in my field glasses moving through the bushes up towards Kuk.'[9]

Rommel with the 2nd and 3rd Rifle Companies and the 1st Machine-Gun Company had left their positions on Hill 1066 at first light, and in improving weather were now traversing westward along the steep north side of the Kolovrat (Maps 4 and 7) some 200 metres or so below the line of wired obstacles visible near the top of the ridge. All now depended on achieving surprise. At first, folds in the ground, and bushes and undergrowth made it possible to traverse unseen below the ridge. But bare ground and the sight of enemy obstacles sited on various knolls on the twisting ridge called for time-consuming detours towards the valley. From time to time Rommel called a halt to decide the best route to maintain cover, and to ponder the critical decision of where to turn up the hillside to break through the enemy defences. After rather more than an hour the detachment was about a mile and a half beyond Hill 1066, and all was quiet except for the sound of machine-gun fire from the direction of Na Gradu behind them.

Rommel paused for a moment in a hollow in the hillside to decide how best to reach the bare ridge above them, and then noticed some disturbance behind him. The lead squad of the 2nd Company had noticed some Italians asleep in the bushes, and then captured fifty men and two machine guns, while a few sentries fled down the hillside; all this being done silently with no shots fired. Having achieved this surprise Rommel immediately made up his mind 'here to attempt the breakthough'.[10]

The point section was ordered to move up the hollow to within a hundred yards of the wire, while the rest of the detachment deployed with extreme caution in a small area giving cover from view.

97

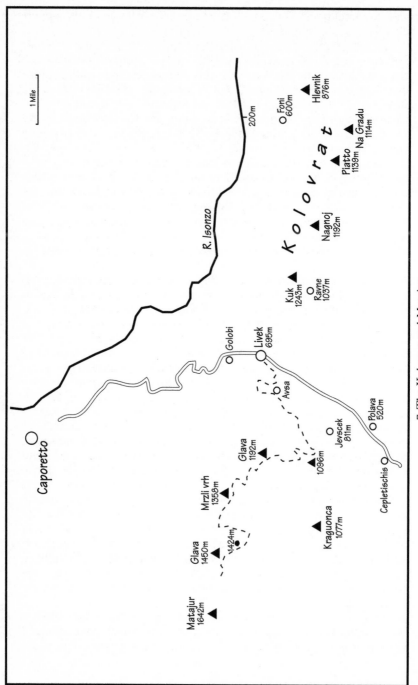

7. The Kolovrat and Matajur.

Lieutenant Streicher with five men and a light machine gun went forward to reconnoitre the defences, and if necessary to cut a gap. The telephone squad had now established a line to Hill 1066, so Rommel spoke to Major Sproesser to report progress and request further support. Sproesser, who had been observing Rommel from Hill 1066, agreed to this request, and also informed Rommel that the projected attack on Na Gradu had been forestalled by a strong Italian counter-attack. Shortly afterwards a message arrived from Lieutenant Streicher, saying that his squad had broken through and taken guns and prisoners.

The entire detachment raced up the steep slopes at full speed to arrive at a shallow saddle on the Kolovrat dotted with dug-outs, heavy guns, and a few dozen prisoners some of whom had been surprised while washing. It was now a clear, bright, autumn day. Rommel's first objective, Hill 1192, was no more than half a mile along the ridge to the west. It appeared to be well fortified with defence lines running trans-versely across the line of the ridge, and was probably held by a substantial garrison. But could they be surprised? Rommel summed up the position and gave his orders. The two rifle companies were to advance on either side of the ridge in order to attack the Italian positions from each flank. At the same time, Sergeant Spadinger with a machine-gun squad would remain at the saddle as a rear guard against any enemy troops advancing along the ridge from the east.

On the right-hand side of the ridge, the 2nd Company led by Lieutenant Ludwig traversed the north slope of the Kolovrat, towards Hill 1192, and found most of the garrison in their dug-outs. According to Rommel, the sudden and unexpected appearance of the Wurttem-bergers so paralysed the garrison that only one or two sentries were needed to marshal the prisoners. Meanwhile, on the south side of the Kolovrat, Rommel, with the 3rd Company and the Machine-Gun Company, had been hurrying along the camouflaged military road running just below the summit ridge. At first all went well and several gun positions were captured. Then the scout squad in front turned up to the final saddle in the ridge before Hill 1192. At this point heavy machine-gun fire from 1192 forced the squad, and Rommel and the 3rd Company, to halt on the road. Shortly afterwards, Rommel heard noise of firing and hand grenades coming from the other side of the ridge, suggesting that all the 2nd Company was now engaged.

Events had suddenly turned against the Rommel detachment. The 2nd Company had a strength of only eighty rifles and six machine guns, and if they were overrun, the enemy might regain all the positions on the Kolovrat so recently captured. It was imperative for the 3rd Company to support the 2nd Company, and the nearest way to them was across the adjacent saddle on the ridge. But this route was

99

so dominated by enemy fire, that Rommel judged it quite impractical, even though the alternative was to go back to the saddle they had started from, and take the 2nd Company's route on the north side of the ridge.

Rommel hurried the 3rd Company back along the camouflaged road to their starting point, pausing only to reinforce Spadinger's squad with two additional squads to protect the detachment's rear. Hastening along the north side of the ridge, they passed the Italian positions taken by the 2nd Company, and then saw 'two mountain soldiers guarding about a thousand prisoners gathered together above the wire entanglements'.[11] After ordering the prisoners to be put below the wire, and as the sounds of the battle greatly increased, Rommel moved on to survey the scene from a knoll about a hundred yards east of 1192.

The 2nd Company had captured some sections of a trench near the foot of the slope rising up to 1192, but were encircled on the west, south and east by what appeared to be an entire battalion. Any retirement to the north was ruled out by the high wire entanglement to their rear, and only their rapid fire was holding back the Italians, massing no more than fifty yards or so away. Sooner or later they would be overwhelmed, and Rommel at once decided that the only way out of this desperate situation was to launch a surprise attack of his own.

Orders were rapidly given, two heavy machine guns were set up in concealed positions, and the 3rd Company concentrated in a shallow depression to the left of the trench. As the machine guns opened fire, the 3rd Company rushed forward in a ferocious assault on the rear and flank of the enemy. Surprised, the Italians halted their attack on the 2nd Company, and turned to face the 3rd Company. Given this opportunity, the 2nd Company leapt from their trench to join the attack on the now disoriented Italians. Taken aback, about a whole battalion surrendered, 8 officers and 500 men. Thus by 09.15 the WMB had captured half a mile of the Kolovrat, including the summit of 1192, and some 1,500 prisoners from the 213rd Regiment of the Arno Brigade.[12]

(Later Rommel was to write of this capture, 'our satisfaction over our success achieved against difficulty was tempered by grief over individual losses. Besides several wounded, two exceptionally brave young fighters lost their lives; Lance Corporal Kiefner who the day before had so superbly led the assault detachment on Hlevnik, and the young Sergeant Kneule who died in hand to hand fighting.'[13] He also describes a typical Rommel episode when the Italian battalion surrendered. The men had laid down their arms, the officers apparently acquiescing, but when the Wurttembergers were only a few yards away some officers drew their pistols. They were soon overpowered, and 'it needed my intervention to save them from the fury of the mountain troops'.)[14]

The detachment took up positions to consolidate their hold on 1192.

The 2nd Company and half the machine-gun company faced west; the 3rd Company and the other half of the machine-gun company were in more sheltered positions on the north-east slope, and a platoon acted as a rearguard on the ridge half a mile to the east. A counter-attack by local reserves was beaten off, but the detachment was under machine-gun fire coming from the west, south-east and east, while artillery on Monte Kum (Maps 4 and 5) to the south was sending down heavy shells. Looking towards Kuk, Rommel could see considerable numbers of the enemy, perhaps one or two battalions, descending the terrace-like slopes of the south-east face in extended lines. To the south, on the road high up on Monte Kum, there was automotive traffic and many troops moving up from Cividale to the Kolovrat. Also, a mile or two further back the Italians appeared to be attacking the recently gained German positions around Na Gradu. All the indications were that the Italians were preparing to regain 1192 by a full-scale attack from their appreciably higher positions on Kuk. Rommel knew that the rest of the WMB were on their way, but they had yet to arrive. So he was much relieved when the Italians began to dig themselves in along three lines on the eastern slope of Kuk, and he began to sketch out a plan for attack when the reinforcements arrived.

A telephone call to the Alpine Corps HQ arranged for artillery fire by heavy batteries on the east and north-east slopes of Kuk between 11.15 and 11.45. The 2nd Rifle Company with a detachment of six light machine-guns, and the 1st Machine-Gun Company would be concealed on either side of 1192 to provide covering fire for the advance. Assault squads would first probe the defences on either side of the east face to determine the site for the main assault. At 10.30 Major Sproesser arrived with the 4th and 6th Rifle Companies and the 2nd and 3rd Machine-Gun Companies, and allotted the 4th Rifle and both Machine-Gun Companies to Rommel, ordering the 6th Company to mop up the ridge to the east of 1192, and to protect their rear. In addition, just before the attack was due to begin, the leading elements of the 2nd Life Guards arrived in support, having followed Rommel's route below the ridge while fighting was still continuing around Na Gradu and Piatto.

The bombardment began at 11.15, while the main body of Rommel's detachment waited in dead ground in the saddle. As the shells burst on the east face of Kuk, sending stones rumbling down the hillside, sixteen-man squads from the 2nd and 3rd Companies went forward to probe the defences on the north and south sides of the ridge. The squad on the north side encountered tenacious resistance, but the squad from the 3rd Company, on the south side, reached the saddle between 1192 and Kuk without being fired on. Disregarding the stone avalanches produced by the German artillery, they began to climb towards the summit and were soon within hand-grenade range. Many of the Italians were exposed to the artillery fire with almost no cover, so some of the Wurttembergers began to wave white handkerchiefs, and soon the first deserters were running down the hill. As soon as this news was reported back to Rommel by his observers, he decided that the main assault would be on that side, and ordered the 3rd and 4th Companies and the two machine-gun companies to follow the detachment staff along the camouflaged road on the south side of the Kolovrat just below the summit plateau.

The attention of the Italians defending Kuk appears to have been fully occupied by the fire coming from 1192, and by the squad on the north side of the ridge, so that by the time that Rommel arrived below the col between 1192 and Kuk, the assault squad on this side had already taken about a hundred prisoners. During the next quarter of an hour the squad collected more prisoners, and Rommel received news that elements of the Life Guards were following him along the ridge road. There was now ample strength to force the east face of Kuk, so Rommel decided on a more ambitious plan. Leaving the rest of the WMB and the Life Guards to take Kuk from the east, his detachment would continue along the camouflaged road on the south side of Kuk, and work round and surprise any enemy positions on the slopes of Kuk west of the summit. He later wrote that he was well aware that there might have been a large enemy reserve force on the reverse west slope of Kuk, but that 'no task was too difficult for the mountain troops who had already proved themselves in so many battles . . . so without further thought I decided to attempt the advance.'[15]

From Rommel's present position below the col the camouflaged road began to descend on the side of Kuk towards the villages of Ravne (1037m) and Livek (695m). He charged down the road with his point section, followed by a machine-gun company sweating and gasping in the hot sunshine, under the heavy loads they had been carrying since leaving Tolmin. It was about noon when they arrived at Ravne where they surprised Italian troops who had thought themselves well away from the front. Taken aback the Italians turned and fled, and their pack animals stampeded, without a shot being fired.

Just beyond the village a knoll gave Rommel a good view of the general scene. To his right the slopes of Kuk rose towards the summit, and to his surprise he saw no sign of any enemy. In front of him the slopes of Kuk descended towards Livek, where both the village and its neighbourhood appeared to be full of Italian troops, while the minor road to the south from Livek to Savogna was crowded with vehicular traffic going in both directions, including a heavy horse-drawn battery leaving Livek. To the north of the village he heard sounds of fighting, presumably where three battalions of the 12(g) Division had come up against the Italian positions near Golobi. Then to the left, beyond the road to Cepletischis and Cividale the ground rose up towards Mrzli vrh (1358m) and Matajur (1642m) (Map 7) about four miles away.

Rommel reviewed the situation. The garrison on Kuk would certainly be captured by either the rest of the WMB, the Life Guards or units of the 12(g) Division. What then should he do next? One possibility would be a surprise attack on the troops at Livek, but most of them might escape by taking to the wooded eastern slopes below Mrzli vrh. Therefore he would attempt to cut off the Italian forces at Livek and Golobi, by descending to block the Savogna road near the village of Polava, and then move up the opposite hillside to the road leading to the Italian positions on Mrzli vrh and Matajur.

At this moment it seems that only the 4th Rifle and 3rd Machine-Gun Companies were right up with Rommel; the other companies were behind and out of sight. So runners were sent back with orders that they make for Polava. Meanwhile, speed was essential. The troops with Rommel raced down the hillside, sometimes across open meadows, sometimes finding cover amid bushes and trees. (The boundaries of these woods and meadows have doubtless changed over the past eighty years.) On reaching the road at about 12.30 Rommel cut the Italian telephone lines and set up a road block where the road made two sharp turns. The 4th Company and the 3rd Machine-Gun Company were deployed on the hillside, on either side of the road, concealed in bushes and undergrowth, with good fields of view up and down the valley. Unfortunately Rommel had lost contact with his other companies, so Lieutenant Walz was sent back to bring up the other units as soon as possible, and to report Rommel's progress to Major Sproesser.[16] (He later explained that the breakdown in communications had arisen because a machine-gun company commander stopped to round up some of the captured Italian pack animals.)

Very soon Italian soldiers, singly or in small groups with horses and mules, moving either up or down the road, arrived at the block and were taken prisoner. Before long sentries were guarding a hundred prisoners and fifty vehicles, and the Wurttembergers were enjoying Italian chocolate, eggs, preserves, grapes, wine and white bread. (In a characteristic aside Rommel comments that the worthy troopers on the slopes on either side were served first.) While the troops were enjoying their lunch, an Italian motor car appeared from the south at high speed, and a waggon was quickly dragged across the road. A shot was fired (against Rommel's orders), the car stopped abruptly and the driver and three officers surrendered leaving a fourth fatally wounded in the car. They were apparently staff officers from Savogna who, after the telephone line had failed, had come to find out what was happening at the front.

After Rommel had been at the road block for an hour, there was still no sign of his other companies, and he began to wonder if he had been isolated by an enemy infiltration to his rear. Shortly afterwards a long column of Italian infantry was seen marching down the road from Livek, with no sign of any advance guards, as if they thought themselves quite safe two miles behind the front. There were obviously many more of them than Rommel's 150 Wurttembergers, but he had selected a strong position with good machine-gun support.

As the head of the column reached a point about 300 yards away, Rommel sent one of his officers forward with a white arm band as an intermediary, in an attempt to avoid further bloodshed. The officer was taken prisoner, a hail of German fire swept the road, and the Italians rapidly sought cover. For the next twenty minutes there were some fierce exchanges of fire as the Italians tried to charge the German positions. However, the German fire from well-concealed positions was so effective that the Italians conceded defeat. Fifty officers and 2,000 men of the IVth Bersaglieri Brigade laid down their weapons on the road, and were sent back to Ravne in charge of a few riflemen.

For some time Rommel had been hearing sounds of violent fighting coming from the direction of Livek, so he armed a captured vehicle with a heavy machine gun and drove up the road to take stock of the situation. On the outskirts of Livek he met up with Major Sproesser, the rest of the WMB, and the 2nd Battalion of the Life Guards who had now taken Kuk. By this time Rommel had seen strong Italian units moving in fairly good order up the road from Avsa towards Mrzli vrh and Matajur, presumably to prepare defensive positions with a rearguard blocking the road above Avsa. Therefore he suggested to Sproesser that the Rommel detachment, with all available units, should go directly from Polava to capture Hill 1096 dominating the Matajur road. This would block the only supply route to Mrzli and Matajur, and the enemy could then be attacked before he had completed his defences. (Rommel refers to Hill 1096 as Monte Cragonza, but according to his sketches and text, Hill 1096 lies close to the military road from Livek to Mrzli and Matajur, whereas the 50,000 Slovene map shows Kraguonca (sic) with a height of 1077m a mile to the west of 1096 and the road.)

Sproesser agreed to Rommel's plan, and gave him the 2nd, 3rd and 4th Companies, the 1st, 2nd and 3rd Machine-Gun Companies, plus the Signal Company. Rommel rushed back to Polava with his three extra companies, and after sharing out the captured pack animals, the whole detachment started up the south-east slope of Hill 1096. The first objective was the small village of Jevscek, about half-way to the summit, and probably part of any enemy defence line. Jevscek is about three quarters of a mile from Polava and about 300 metres higher, but there was no path to follow, and rough gullies and impenetrable hedges forced innumerable descents and deviations. The detachment had been on the move since the early morning of the previous day, and now as the sun went down found themselves on steep ground, with heavy packs, seeking the elusive Jevscek. One senses that this was the low point of the whole march. Rommel states that he 'had to demand from his exhausted troops a great deal of superhuman effort, so that the attack did not get bogged down'.[17]

After several hours the moon was shining and the point section came up to a grassy meadow beyond which they could see a well-lit position behind high obstacles, and could hear Italian voices. The detachment was now in no position to advance further, so Rommel drew back silently about 300 yards to a bivouac site and decided on several hours of rest until midnight. At the same time, however, he sent out several officers to make a reconnaissance of the neighbourhood.

Lieutenant Aldinger returned before midnight to report that he had found a route to Jevscek which was still about half a mile away to the north-west. The village was strongly fortified and surrounded by wire, and was not yet occupied by the enemy, but he had seen enemy troops marching downhill to the west of the village. Hearing this, Rommel decided to break camp and make immediately for Jevscek to forestall any occupation by the enemy.

Led by Lieutenant Aldinger, the detachment made its way forward towards Jevscek, and despite a few shots they entered the north part of the village, and those not on sentry duty rested in the still inhabited Slovene houses. As no sounds could be heard from the south part of the village Rommel concluded that the garrison due to defend the village had not yet arrived, so there was probably a gap in the Italian line of defences. He therefore sent 2nd Lieutenant Leuze to reconnoitre, while the bulk of the unit sat about before the hearths in the solidly built houses consuming coffee and dried fruit provided by friendly Slovenes.

5.4   Matajur (26 October)

(a) Hill 1096

Rommel states that on the night of 25 October 'I knew very little about our neigbours. I knew nothing of where they were, or what actions they planned to take . . . But it was clear to me, that all must be risked, and that on 26 October the assault must again be under way'.[18] Hence, when Lieutenant Leuze returned from his reconnaissance at 04.30, Rommel quickly decided on his plans, and at 05.30 the detachment moved off to attack Hill 1096, while it was still dark.

Not surprisingly, Rommel's account of the capture of 1096 is not as clear and precise as his descriptions of other actions. The only identifiable points on the ground appear to have been the village of Jevscek and the summit of 1096 (which Rommel incorrectly refers to as Kragonza (Section 5.3)). All other positions are described in terms of distances and directions from these two landmarks. Yet the picture he draws is somewhat confused. For example, he refers to directing an attack from a point 'six hundred yards north-west of Jevscek',[19] which locates Rommel at the summit of 1096. Yet it is clear from his account that Hill 1096 was then still in enemy hands. However, these points of detail do not obscure the main broad features of the action.

On the previous night the detachment had encountered defence positions and heard troop movements close to Jevscek, and Rommel thought it likely that he was near an enemy defence line, probably running from the Cepletischis – Livek road to Jevscek, and then on to 1096, Mrzli and Matajur. Therefore, eager to reach Matajur, he ordered the 2nd and 4th Rifle and the 1st and 2nd Machine-Gun Companies to capture Hill 1096, while the 3rd Rifle Company and the 3rd Machine-Gun Company under Lieutenant Grau gave supporting fire and acted as a rearguard against any enemy units near Jevscek.

As it became light, the main force was crossing rough ground on the slopes of 1096, and Rommel saw that it would be dangerously exposed to any fire from enemy positions higher up. He hurried forward and sent out runners with orders to the companies to spread out and find cover. Very soon the Italians opened fire, and despite fire support from the rear company, losses mounted and Lieutenant Ludwig commanding the 2nd Company was seriously wounded.

At this point, much concerned for the security of his main force now pinned down by the enemy fire, Rommel heard the noise of battle behind him from the direction of Jevscek. (In fact an Italian force facing into the village was engaged with Lieutenant Grau's force in the village). Rommel quickly gathered three light machine-gun squads from his front-line companies and led them down to the rear of the unsuspecting Italians, who were so surprised that a force 'about three companies strong'[20] surrendered without a shot being fired.

Meanwhile the 2nd and 4th Companies were still engaged in an exchange of fire higher up on the broad south-west slope of Hill 1096, so Rommel with the greater part of the 3rd Company and the 3rd Machine-Gun Company hurried to their support. He quickly decided that there was no possibility of turning the enemy's flanks, and ordered a frontal assault with the 4th, 2nd and 3rd Companies widely spread out on the bare slopes of 1096. He himself moved up with the 2nd Company in the centre of the line, making directly towards the summit. The assault was supported by fire from the machine-gun companies,

106

but this did not seem to produce much effect on the fierce enemy fire. Lieutenant Aldinger who had replaced Lieutenant Ludwig as commander of the 2nd Company was severely wounded. It was a tough fight, 'but as our losses increased so did the battle fury of the mountain troops'.[21] The Wurttembergers worked their way up, trench by trench, machine-gun post by machine-gun post, and by 07.15 were in posession of Hill 1096.

Rommel also states that after the capture of the three companies at Jevscek, but before returning to the fighting on 1096, he took the surrender of 'an Italian regiment of 37 officers and 1,600 men . . . with full equipment and armament' in a hollow north of Jevscek.[22] Rommel gives no further details of this remarkable episode, except to say that he had difficulty in finding enough men to supervise the prisoners. He does not state which enemy units were involved or where they had come from, presumably because his attention was fully occupied in reaching Hill 1096. However, some details may be inferred from the Italian Official History.

The ridge from Kuk to Matajur was garrisoned by the IVth Bersaglieri and the Salerno Brigades of the Italian 62nd Division, which had only begun to arrive in the early hours of 24 October (Section 2.6). During the morning the IVth Bersaglieri were deployed on either side of Livek, with the 14th Regiment on the left and the 20th on the right. After the enemy advances on 24 October, Cadorna issued an order at 23.00 setting out new lines of defence should the 2nd Army be forced to withdraw still further (Section 3.2). On receipt of this order, the 62nd Division issued various instructions. The Salerno Brigade was to hold its positions on Matajur 'at all cost'. The units around Livek were to 'defend tenaciously to gain time', and 'some battalions' on the rest of the front were 'to draft a deployment (*abbozzare un schieramento*) on the line Matajur – Cepletischis – Monte San Martino' (Maps 7 and 5).[23]

There seems little doubt that the 2,000 men of the Bersaglieri Brigade captured on 25 October were the greater part of the 20th Regiment which had been forced back from Kuk and Livek by the 12th German Division and the Alpine Corps (Section 3.3), and was marching down to occupy new positions on the next defence line. The IOH does not mention any encounter with the WMB, but the next reference to the Regiment occurs only some days later when it is described as *resti* (remnants).[24]

The IOH makes no mention either of the 14th Regiment to the left of the 20th, after its arrival at Livek until several days later when it too is described as *resti*.[25] Hence, it was probably part of this Regiment which Rommel encountered between Jevscek and Hill 1096, as it was retiring to join the 20th Regiment on the new defence line. Marching

107

down the road these units found themselves in the middle of a fire-fight, assumed that they were completely cut-off, and surrendered.

(b) Hill 1192 and Mrzli vrh

The Wurttembergers were now urged on along the broad ridge leading first to Glava (1192m) and then to Mrzli vrh (1358m). During the fight for 1096 the detachment had spread over the hillside and was now 'badly mixed'. All the officers of the 2nd Company had become casualties, the Company was now commanded by Technical-Sergeant Hügel, and some men had still to arrive at 1096. However, rather than pausing to regroup, Rommel sent the still incomplete 2nd Company along the ridge towards 1192. At the same time he sent back runners with orders to the rest of the detachment to hurry up the Matajur road to join the 2nd Company.

Rommel does not give much detail of the advance to Hill 1192, but the enemy appears to have been holding the quite broad ridge with a series of outposts to protect the main positions on Mrzli. The 2nd Company under Sergeant Hügel worked its way steadily forward, employing the usual WMB tactics of attacking from the flank and rear, and 1192 was captured by 08.30.

The next objective, Mrzli, was now in sight, about a mile further along the ridge, but Rommel was forced to pause. Enemy troops could be seen deployed in strength on the south-east slopes of Mrzli, and heavy machine-gun fire was striking the summit of 1192. Moreover, during the fighting for 1192, the 2nd Company had become so spread out over the slopes of the hill, that Rommel and Sergeant Hügel arrived on the summit leading only a platoon. In addition, sounds of fighting from the right and rear suggested that the other companies, and other units of the Alpine Corps, were still engaged with enemy forces probably trying to retreat to the Savogna road.

Rommel realized that he would need at least two rifle and a machine-gun company to advance further, and went back down the road to contact the liaison officer of the rear companies. He found no liaison officer, but was nearly shot himself, so he returned to Hill 1192 and sent out a 'strong assault detachment'[26] to contact the other units with orders to close up on 1192. Eventually, by 10.00, a force equivalent to two rifle and one machine-gun company was assembled on 1192, and Rommel was ready for the next move forward.

The attack began by Rommel sending a light signal asking for artillery support, which was quickly followed by the 'surprising result' of German shells falling on the south-east slope of Mrzli.[27] Then, under covering fire from the machine-gun company, the two rifle companies advanced along the Matajur road, perhaps 30 metres or so below the edge of the ridge on its south-west side. Near the col between 1192 and Mrzli the two companies, led by Rommel, came into close combat with enemy positions near the road, which were attacked from front, flank and rear. A few dozen prisoners were taken while the remainder retreated towards the east slope of Mrzli.

Rommel continued along the ridge road and brought up his machine-gun company. By now it was clear that something very unusual was happening on the broad col about 20 metres below the twin summits of Mrzli, now about 1,000 yards away. Hundreds of Italian soldiers could be seen standing about, seemingly 'irresolute and inactive', apparently just watching the German advance.[28] Bearing in mind his experiences during the previous two days, Rommel extended his column behind him in considerable depth, and walked in front waving a white handkerchief. Nothing happened at first, and Rommel wondered if the mass of troops would beat a retreat or descend in force on his small detachment.

About 700 yards from the col, the road on the south-east face of Mrzli ran into a dense wood. Rommel was uneasy. He could no longer see the enemy, and was aware that a very much larger force might well descend through the wood and fall on the detachment from above. The shortest way through the wood was by going straight up the slope rather than following the zig-zag road. Therefore, leaving the detachment with their heavy loads to proceed along the road Rommel, with only Lieutenant Streicher, Dr Lenz, and a few soldiers climbed straight up through the wood on a broad front with a hundred yards between each man. Emerging from the wood they saw a huge mass of men, on the far side of the Matajur road, shouting and gesticulating.

All the Italians had weapons in their hands, and there seemed to be a group of officers in front. Rommel realized that he had to maintain the initiative, and walked steadily forward waving his handkerchief, and calling for the men to lay down their arms and surrender. He was now a hundred yards from the wood and felt he could neither return nor stand still. He kept walking. Then suddenly there was a movement in the mass of troops. Most threw their weapons away, and hundreds hurried towards him, sweeping any resisting officers aside. Almost immediately he was surrounded and carried shoulder high amid cries of 'Viva Germania' (Long live Germany).[29] An Italian officer who hesitated to surrender was shot down by his own troops. Thus Rommel had now captured a further 43 officers and 1,500 men, almost the entire 89th Regiment of the Salerno Brigade.[30] (Rommel refers to the 89th and 90th Regiments only as the 1st and 2nd Regiments of the Brigade.)

By now the main Rommel detachment was emerging from the

wood, and was ordered to march straight on along the Matajur road, except for an officer and three men detailed to marshal the prisoners. The 43 officers were separated from the men and guarded by Sergeant Goppinger. Eventually when they realized how small the Rommel detachment had been, they became 'pugnacious' and an attempt was made to re-establish control over their men, but without effect, for 'Sergeant Goppinger carried out his duties rigorously and conscientiously'.[31]

(c) Matajur

As Rommel continued on towards Matajur, some of the prisoners told him that the 90th Regiment on Matajur was a famous one, which would certainly fire on him, and that he would need to be careful. Indeed, as soon as the road swung round towards the west slope of Mrzli, the detachment came under well-directed fire from Glava (1450m) and Point 1424, enfilading the road and forcing the detachment to take cover in dense bushes below the road. The detachment was now on the east side of the valley formed by the ridge running up from Mrzli to Glava, and the ridge running up from Kraguonca to Point 1424 and then to the summit of Glava (Map 7). (Rommel's sketch of this region shows two heights labelled 1467 and 1424, but the first clearly refers to Glava (1450m) on the IGM and Slovene maps, and the second to a small unmarked knoll clearly shown on both maps south of the summit of Glava.)

The road to Matajur high up on the side of the valley was exposed to enemy fire, but Rommel saw that by descending about 200 metres down into the valley, and using thick clumps of bushes as cover, he could arrive unseen at the bend in the road to the south of 1424, and then come up behind the enemy positions. A few machine guns were set up on Mrzli to engage the enemy positions on Glava, and the main detachment made its way undetected to the road south of 1424. Then, as Rommel was preparing for the attack on this point, he received a message from Major Sproesser, who on arriving at Hill 1096 had found so many prisoners that he assumed that all resistance was over, and had sent Rommel an order to withdraw. The order was very clear, and had to be obeyed. On the other hand, Rommel was quite sure that Sproesser was unaware of the present situation, so he decided on a compromise. All the units of the detachment were ordered back to Hill 1096 except the leading hundred riflemen and six heavy machine-gun crews already with Rommel on the road south of 1424. These would go on to attack 'in spite of our ridiculously small numbers'.[32]

A hundred riflemen and six heavy machine guns might well seem

110

'ridiculously small' to attack a regiment, but Rommel's decision was based on more than just the ambition to be first on Matajur. The ridge from Mrzli vrh to Matajur is broad and undulating, and about a mile long. It was similar ground to that traversed already, and Rommel no doubt expected that it would be defended from positions among the hollows and hillocks, and would be vulnerable to his infiltration tactics.

Standing on the road south of 1424, Rommel sited his machine guns with fields of fire towards the rear of the enemy positions on 1424 and Glava (facing east). The Italians were surprised by fire from this direction, and by the heavy fragmentation of the rocks produced by the shots. Soon some Italians began to retire to the north side of 1424. Then Rommel's riflemen moved forward both along the road and up the west slope of 1424, and the enemy vacated his positions there.

As Rommel continued to advance along the road south of Glava, with his machine guns moving up behind in echelon, an enemy battalion tried to move away from Glava, but were halted by the machine guns close to the head of the column. The topography as described by Rommel is not entirely clear, but it appears that as the Wurttembergers moved along the road with some waving of handker-chiefs, the firing on both sides ceased, and it became very quiet. Suddenly coming round a sharp bend in the road they saw, about three hundred yards away, the greater part of the 90th Regiment of the Salerno Brigade gathered together laying down its arms. 'The Commander of the Regiment sat by the side of the road, surrounded by his officers and weeping with fury and shame at the refusal of obedi-ence by the soldiers of his once proud Regiment.'[33] One can only surmise that the Regiment which had only recently arrived, with no prepared positions, had been mesmerized by the steady and visible progress of the enemy from Livek to Matajur.

Before the Italians could realize how small a number of the enemy had disgraced their regiment, Rommel had separated the 35 officers, and sent some 1,200 men down the road to Livek at the double. Then he hurried on towards the summit of Matajur, about a mile away and 200 metres higher, still held by the rest of the Regiment. Rommel's first move was to order an attack from below Glava directly to the summit, covered by his machine guns, but this approach was quickly aban-doned in the face of very heavy enemy fire.

Rommel turned back towards Glava, and moved over on to the north-facing slopes below the ridge, apparently unobserved by the enemy. His group was now able to move along the slope out of sight, seeing as they went small squads of Italians with and without weapons moving down to where the other regiment had surrendered.

Six hundred yards short of the summit of Matajur they came up behind the rear of an Italian company facing north, which was engaged with scout squads of the 12(g) Division who had come up from Caporetto. Completely surprised by the Wurttembergers with weapons at the ready the Italians surrendered immediately.

The weather was now gloriously fine with brilliant sunshine and freshly fallen snow sparkling on the ground. Standing on the summit of Matajur, the highest peak for miles around, the Wurttembergers looked at the wide panorama around them, with Cividale at their foot to the south-west, the Adriatic beyond, and Udine also in the distance. Rommel ordered a 'well deserved rest', of one hour during which he dictated his daily combat report for Major Sproesser. Then, very wearily, they descended some 900 metres of rough slopes (taking the captured Italian officers with them), and by the early afternoon had arrived at the pleasant village of Masseris still at an altitude of 760 metres, where they spent the night. Leaving before dawn they continued down the road to join the rest of the WMB on the outskirts of Cividale.

5.5 Summary

From first light on 25 October to midday on 26 October Rommel and his detachment captured the greater part of five different Italian regiments on five different occasions. Never more than a battalion in strength, and on Matajur less than a company, the Rommel detachment had taken, in round terms, the surrender of the order of 9,000 officers and men, at a loss to themselves during the three days 24 to 26 October of 6 dead and 30 wounded.[34] The IOH does not usually quote losses suffered in particular actions, but all the five regiments claimed by Rommel (the 213rd on Hill 1192, the 20th Bersaglieri at Polava, the 14th Bersaglieri at Jevscek, the 89th on Mrzli, and the 90th on Matajur) either disappear completely from the IOH after 25 October or are mentioned only as *resti* (remnants).

Rommel's progress was a remarkable achievement, but many circumstances had contributed to his success. During the war all the opposing armies had been driven to much rethinking and retraining. The German Army had been in the forefront of developing techniques of attack and defence, and the Allies had found it difficult to catch up. Even after two years of war the British on the Somme in 1916, and the Italians at Caporetto in 1917, were woefully behind German methods. Moreover the XIVth Austro-German Army had attacked a region so mountainous that since 1915 it had been been a quiet sector, and seen no action. The defence systems had laid out on the line of greatest advance in 1915, and had fundamental weaknesses which only began to receive serious attention at the beginning of October 1917, and then in an atmosphere of increasing consternation and confusion.

The German plan of attack, detailed by General Krafft, deployed some of the best German and Austrian troops against some of the weakest Italian troops in a region offering great possibilities for a breakthrough. The troops of the XIVth Army were presented with opportunities undreamt of on the Western Front, and there are many references by Krafft to other officers and their units who distinguished themselves by their rapid progress and substantial gains. Even in such company Rommel stood out in his determination to attack the enemy, in his skill in tactics and encirclement techniques, and in his ability to foresee enemy intentions and reactions.

On 25 October it was solely due to Rommel's drive and foresight, backed by the support of Major Sproesser, that the Rommel detachment of two rifle and one machine-gun company set off along the Kolovrat, while the main body of the Alpine Corps was held up at Na Gradu and Monte Piatto. By 09.15, after some anxious moments overcome by Rommel's personal leadership, the Wurttembergers had captured the Italian 213th Regiment, and gained possession of half a mile of the Kolovrat and Hill 1192. This, in itself a striking feat, opened up the way forward towards Monte Kuk and Livek as soon as reinforcements arrived.

Following the arrival of Major Sproesser at 10.30, Rommel's detachment was increased to two rifle and three machine-gun companies for an attack to take Monte Kuk. Rommel soon realized that the enemy were not very resolute, and in typical Rommel fashion, decided to enlarge the scope of the attack. Leading his two forward rifle companies and one machine-gun company, he raced along the road on the south side of the Kolovrat, in order to outflank and encircle any enemy positions beyond the summit of Kuk on its west-facing slopes. However, after surprising and putting to flight the unsuspecting Italians at Ravne, Rommel saw that the western slopes of Kuk appeared deserted, but that there was much traffic around Livek and on the Livek-Savogna road.

Rommel reviewed the situation and decided that, irrespective of any action by his detachment, Kuk would soon fall to the remainder of the WMB and the Life Guards, and that the detachment would now be better employed by blocking the Livek-Savogna road in order to cut off any enemy troops retreating from Livek. Racing downhill at full speed and arriving with only one rifle company and one machine-gun company, he next ambushed an entire regiment marching down in good order to take up new defence positions in the rear. Finally during the afternoon he met up with Major Sproesser near Livek, and was

113

given three rifle companies and a signal company for an assault on Matajur the next day.

In recording the events of 25 October the IOH states that the Arno Brigade on the Kolovrat, facing north, was taken from the flank so that 'one by one' its battalions were surprised by attacks from unexpected directions.[35] As described above, the Rommel detachment continued the next day in similar fashion, starting with the capture of the 14th Regiment Bersaglieri, retiring like the 20th Regiment in good order. Then followed the advance to the summits of Mrzli and Matajur, arriving at the latter by midday with only one company, and receiving en route the surrender of two further regiments, which appear to have been mesmerized by the steady and rapid progress of the XIVth Army along the ridge from Livek to Matajur.

To set Rommel's achievements in perspective one must remember that all the units of the XIVth Army had been selected to overwhelm the Italian defences and to move fast; and move fast they did. Krafft repeatedly praises the different units involved, as for example the 12(g) Division for its march up the valley to Livek and Caporetto, and the 22(a) Schützen for its occupation of Monte Stol. The advance of the XIVth Army during the first three days of the offensive was made all along its front by all the front-line divisions, and would have surely been made had Rommel and the WMB not been present.

The Rommel detachment was but a small part of a much greater whole, but there remain at least three very striking aspects of Rommel's performance. First, his extraordinary capacity to assess the possibility of a situation, to devise the most suitable plan of attack, and to carry it out with skill, courage and determination. Second, the attack on the Kolovrat and Matajur was made by two of the best German mountain divisions, the Alpine Corps and the 12(g) Division, and it was Rommel who made the fastest progress, always in the lead of the advance, out-distancing no doubt equally ambitious officers in other units. Third, Rommel's capture of the 20th Regiment Bersaglieri is particularly worthy of note. Most of the prisoners taken by Rommel would probably have been rounded up by other units of the Alpine Corps and the 12(g) Divisions, but this is not the case with the 20th Bersaglieri. It appears quite certain that but for Rommel's speed, judgement and audacity, a whole regiment in good order would have marched down the road towards Savogna, ready to carry on the fight the next day.

Rommel's arrival on Matajur had been a great moment for him. When Krafft and von Below had planned the opening stage of the offensive, it was clear that Na Gradu (1114m) opposite Tolmin, and Matajur (1461m) commanding the road from Caporetto to Cividale, were critical initial objectives which must be taken with all possible speed. Therefore, von Below had obtained authorization to announce that a *Pour le Mérite*, the highest German decoration open to junior officers, would be awarded for the capture of Hill 1114, and another for the capture of Matajur. Not only would this encourage some already very competitive officers, but by enabling the awards to be made immediately in the field, would encourage further great efforts. Hence when Rommel stood on the summit of Matajur on 26 October after capturing its garrison, the Salerno Brigade, he must surely have felt that he had won the coveted *Pour le Mérite*. Therefore Rommel, and the WMB, were much surprised by the German High Command Bulletin for 27 October signed by Ludendorff which stated, inter alia, that the well-fortified summit of Matajur had been taken at 07.00 on 25 October by 2nd Lieutenant Schnieber with four companies of the 63rd Regiment of the 12(g) Division.[36]

Krafft's account of Schnieber's visit to Matajur states no more than that Lieutenant Schnieber with his 4th Company (not four companies) had been sent out on the north side of Matajur, and had brought back a report saying only that he had reached a point 100 metres north of the summit![37]

Presumably, his company had been sent as a strong scout squad to make a reconnaissance of the enemy positions, but why had he stopped 100 metres short of the ridge? To make any sort of a reconnaissance it would have been necessary to go right up to the ridge and the summit, for only then would it have been possible to obtain a clear view over all the possible enemy positions. It is sometimes suggested that Schnieber had reached a subsidiary outlier of Matajur, Monte Colonna, about half a mile north of the summit and about 200 metres lower,[38] but if the weather was clear at that time it is difficult to imagine how one could confuse the two summits. If the weather was cloudy and the visibility poor then his reconnaissance was of very limited value. Even so, the 12(g) Division reported to XIVth Army that Matajur had been reached, and shortly afterwards Schnieber received the coveted *Pour le Mérite*.[39]

Despite various discussions of this episode there is no evidence that Schnieber's walk up Matajur made any significant contribution to the XIVth Army. Indeed on the evidence presented, Schnieber might well have faced a charge of failing in his duty to make a proper reconnaissance. Krafft makes no mention of the 'Mérite', but comments that from a tactical point of view, Schnieber thought that he had done all that was necessary, and had decided not to engage with the Salerno Brigade in the conviction that it would be difficult to do so with any probability of success.[40] This remark is immediately followed by a fulsome tribute to the Rommel detachment for its powers of endurance, its clear sense of duty, its ability and independence.

When von Below promised a *Pour le Mérite* for the capture of Matajur, he had certainly not foreseen such an outcome, but the award was now made. According to Fadini, von Below asked General Baron Lynckner, the Kaiser's Military Secretary, for a further 'Mérite', but his request was firmly refused.[41] However, this episode might well have spurred Rommel on to even greater efforts.

6

The Advance to the Tagliamento

6.1   The Tagliamento and its Bridges

The Tagliamento presents a substantial barrier to an invading army, as was once stressed by Napoleon.[1] For much of its course, from above Tolmezzo to above Latisana (Map 8), the Tagliamento runs in channels in a wide gravelly bed, in places over a mile across and sometimes partially covered with scrub, which forms a most prominent feature of the plain when viewed from the mountains to the north. The width of the bed is greatest at the junction of the Tagliamento with its main tributary, the Fella, about four miles below Tolmezzo, where the beds of the two rivers spread out to produce a triangular-shaped stony waste with sides about two miles in length. In most places the flow of the water is confined to one, two, or several relatively narrow channels, but after heavy rainfall in the mountains the flow may rapidly increase and spill out across the whole bed.

When the river reaches Pinzano it finally emerges from the mountains into the plain, where the wide and stony bed continues until a few miles above Latisana, where the river assumes a more normal form, completely filling its bed, about 100 to 200 yards wide with green fields or woods on either side. Finally in the last five or six miles to the sea, the land on both sides is very low and intersected by drainage channels, which make any military operations very difficult, especially if flooded.

On the whole of its course below Pinzano the bed of the river is bounded by high dykes rising 6m or more above the bed to contain the waters when it floods. The river thus provided a considerable military obstacle. The high dykes gave excellent positions for machine-gun and other posts which could sweep fire across any troops attempting to cross the wide bed of bare sand and pebbles. The water in the main channel or channels is generally deep enough to require serious bridging techniques, particularly as the speed of the river can greatly increase after rainfall and be capable of damaging any temporary structure. Indeed with heavy flows the river becomes a raging torrent totally impassable except at the bridges.

117

The main bridges in 1917 are shown in Map 8. (Note that the named town or village adjacent to each bridge lies on the east bank, except for Trasaghis, Cornino and Pinzano on the west bank.) The principal crossings were those near the towns of Codroipo and Latisana. About three miles west of Codroipo there was a stone road bridge, a railway bridge and a footbridge, all about a mile long. At Latisana there was a stone road bridge and a railway bridge each about 200yds long. Less substantial crossings were available at Madrisio by a floating road bridge on pontoons, and above Codroipo by a wooden trestle bridge near the villages of Dignano (and Bonzicco).[2] Further upstream at Pinzano, where the mountains begin, the Tagliamento flows through a short but narrow gorge before emerging into the plain, and was crossed by a stone road bridge high above the river. Then about three miles further upstream, where the valley floor begins to widen out, the river was crossed by a railway bridge at Cornino. Finally before Tolmezzo there were other road bridges at Trasaghis and Venzone.

6.2   The Austro-German Pursuit (27, 28 October)

(a) 27 October

During 27 October the 1(a), 5(g), 26(g) and 200(g) Divisions, and the Alpine Corps marched over the hills and down the valleys on the south side of Monte Matajur and the Kolovrat towards Cividale (Map 5). The town was occupied during the afternoon and the advance units continued towards the line of the River Torre (Map 8), thus producing a substantial salient jutting out beyond the line of the 3rd Army positions south of Gorizia. Hence, the Austro-German forces on the southern edge of the salient had begun to pose a threat to the lines of communication of the Italian 3rd Army, and to endanger its flank during a withdrawal.

As early as 25 October Cadorna had instructed General Sagramoso to set up a force of six divisions to hold the line of the Torre in order to give time for the 3rd Army to draw back to the line of the 2nd Army. However, all six divisions had subsequently been redirected to meet other and more immediate demands during 25 and 26 October,[3] and on 27 October General Sagramoso was left with no forces at his disposal. Therefore Montuori, in command of the 2nd Army, ordered Sagramoso to 'consult with corps commanders to cover the inconveniences and inefficiences that have arisen'.[4] As the IOH comments, this order to 'cover the inconveniences' was rather remote from Cadorna's original order to set up a line of resistance behind the Torre.[5]

The original plans for the XIVth Army offensive had made no

119

Udine. Fighting in the dark, they crossed the river against opposition from the battered Italian VII Corps on the far bank, took 600 prisoners and 16 machine guns, occupied Beivars, and repelled subsequent counter-attacks. At about the same time the XXIII Battalion crossed the Torre somewhat further to the south and captured 200 Italians and 10 machine guns.[10]

The XVIII Battalion continued towards Udine and reached the outskirts at about 10.00. They found the town almost deserted with broken windows, plundered shops, dead drunk Italian soldiers and dead citizens. There was a critical moment about midday when an Italian force said to consist of several battalions supported by artillery and armoured vehicles attempted to move back into the city. Conscious of their inferiority in numbers, the Germans rushed forward and found that the attack broke up surprisingly quickly, although the situation was not stabilized until the arrival at about 15.00 of the XXIII Battalion and a battalion of the 3rd Jäger Regiment. Krafft states that the XVIII Battalion of the 5th Jäger had been 'on the move for 72 hours, on short rations, soaked by rain, penetrating deep into the enemy line without any support save their own, they speeded the collapse of the Italian line on the Torre and collected an enormous booty'.[11]

The 26(g) Division of the Berrer Corps also reached the Torre, somewhat to the south, in the early hours of the morning after a weary march on disconnected and muddy roads, and found an efficient opposition on the opposite side of the river. An attack across the Torre supported by a battery of Austrian mountain artillery was planned for the afternoon, but the river was in full flood and impassable. However, it was then found that the bridge at nearby San Gottardo (about a mile to the east of Udine) although partly destroyed was still passable, so the Division was able to make its way to Udine, already occupied by the 200(g) Division.[12] This was good progress but the Corps had suffered a serious misfortune. General von Berrer, always forward with his troops, drove too soon into Udine and was shot dead in his car by two carabinieri.[13] Krafft writes a glowing tribute to a man of great energy and ability, while von Below refers to 'a grave loss which would be felt all too soon'.[14]

South of the Berrer Corps, the 5(g) Division of Scotti's Corps marched in heavy rain to Remanzacco four miles east of Udine, where they paused for the night, ready to move to Codroipo next day. The 1(a) Division, which had suffered heavy losses in the first two days, had spent the night not far beyond the Judrio river. At 08.00 orders were received from Corps which Krafft describes as 'a very onerous request', namely to capture with all speed the bridges at Codroipo going by way of Udine. The troops were tired and a start was made only at 16.00.

121

The orders were amended and the Division told to concentrate at Udine and take charge of the city.[15]

North of the Berrer Corps, the Alpine Corps advanced in two columns, somewhat delayed by flooding. The head of one column reached the Torre beyond Salt in the late afternoon, and then with covering fire from the 200(g) Division on their left, managed to seize the bridge before it was blown, and spent the night on the far bank. The other column of the Alpine Corps including the Wurttemberg Mountain Battalion reached the Torre at Primulacco, about two miles north of Salt, at about 15.00 and found the opposite side defended.[16] The WMB, worn down by the previous days and nights, found dry clothes in an Italian laundry depot and went to sleep.

An hour before midnight an order came that the Rommel detachment of the WMB, reinforced by a platoon of mountain artillery, was to take the opposite side during the night or at least by daybreak. Supported by fire from their artillery the WMB worked through the night, using all the vehicles that could be moved, to form a temporary footbridge across all the numerous arms of the flooded river.[17] At daybreak there was still about a hundred yards of swiftly flowing stream unbridged and no more vehicles, but a strong rope stretched across the stream allowed the riflemen to get across without losing their footing. (It was at this crossing that an Italian prisoner carrying a heavy medical kit was swept away by the current, apparently unable to swim, and was rescued by Rommel dashing into the stream on his horse, as 'I felt sorry for the poor devil'.) On the right of the Alpine Corps the 12th Division was also held up by flooding and broken bridges on 28 October, but reached the Torre during the evening.

At the extreme north of the front, after a cold and stormy night, patrols of the CCXVI Brigade of the Edelweiss Division reached Sella Prevala on the main ridge of the Canin group, and took the surrender of 200 exhausted Italians, while the Jäger Division moved down Val Resia and Val Raccolana (Map 6).[18] Further south, the adjacent 22(a) Division took the unmanned fort on Monte La Bernadia north-east of Tarcento and reached the town in the evening, where they were halted at the Torre by a blown bridge covered by machine-gun fire. The 50(a) Division was held up by flooding, but arrived at Nimis and Attimis south-east of Tarcento by the evening (Map 6).[19]

At the end of 28 October the rearguards of the Italian 2nd and 3rd Armies were facing the Austrian and German forces along the line shown in Map 8. Although the 3rd Army had moved forward during the day it was still well to the east of the incipient salient extending beyond Udine.

6.3 The Disordered Retreat

The Italian retreat was much restricted by the congestion on the roads caused by the enormous numbers of troops, vehicles and refugees, all flowing westward. The strength of the 3rd Army on 6 October was about 380,000 men and that of the 2nd Army about 685,000. In addition intermingling with the troops was a great mass of refugees estimated by Cadorna to number 400,000. Many were peasants who had completed their harvest, and were now fleeing with only the few possessions they could carry with them.

Moreover, while the 3rd Army was largely in a state of full efficiency the condition of the 2nd Army was very different, with units in varying degrees of order and disorder. Among the retreating 2nd Army troops was Sandro Pertini, a future President of Italy, then a twenty-year-old lieutenant in a machine-gun unit on the Bainsizza. His unit facing the Austrian IInd Army was not the target of the initial attacks but was soon involved in the general retreat. Pertini describes how his unit prepared to leave their trenches on the Bainsizza, leaving behind what they could not carry with them, and then setting off on the long retreat.

There was much continuous rain and their uniforms became sodden rags. 'Command now depended not on the insignia of rank but on respect and trust.' After leaving the Bainsizza in at least a minimum of order, Pertini's unit found itself mixed with crowds of soldiers separated from their units without order or discipline, the *sbandati*. In the general chaos each acted as he thought best. Some threw away their rifles, some insulted their officers, some took to looting. Carabinieri tried to set up control posts but were soon overwhelmed by the human flood. The more energetic officers sought out their own men to establish some order of march and found that their troops responded positively.[20]

There were at least four English observers present. The bibliography lists books by the historian G.M. Trevelyan in charge of a British Red Cross ambulance unit with the Italian 2nd Army; by the writer Freya Stark, then a nurse in Trevelyan's unit; by Geoffrey Young, a distinguished alpinist also with Trevelyan; and by a future Chancellor of the Exchequer, Hugh Dalton, then a young gunner officer. Trevelyan[21] describes how his ambulance unit was ordered to leave its base at Cormons near Gorizia on the evening of 27 October and work its way into one of the retreating columns. Progress was very slow, moving only a few yards at a time. For half the night the men and horses stopped to snatch a few hours sleep and then at dawn the movement began again in fits and starts. As they advanced the stream of traffic was increased by vast numbers, thousands of farm carts carrying fugitive peasants and piled high with their belongings, miserable debris of the war.

Virtually no attempt was made to organize or control the traffic and Trevelyan comments that

> The entire absence of traffic control, either general or detailed, must, I think, have doubled the number of cannons lorries and carts that fell into the enemy's hands. Everyone did what was right in his own eyes, but being Italians they were a good natured crowd, and although most of them were starving and all discipline had disappeared there was neither violence nor fear of it.

Passing through Udine at midday (28 October) he found that no one was even pretending to keep order on the streets, anyone who wished was looting. As they left Udine on the road to Codroipo they heard the sound of shooting as the Italians strove to hold up the Germans on the east side of the town. Eventually the road became completely blocked by vehicles, many deserted. Trevelyan's party skirted the block by turning off the road to drive across open fields, and having the luck to find their way to by-roads which by a twenty-mile detour took them back close to the bridge at Codroipo. They crossed the mile-long wooden bridge in the dark, the river below swollen to a torrent.

(The following day Trevelyan was joined by two other sections of his unit who had started some hours earlier. The journey of one of these sections is told by Geoffrey Young in his book *The Grace of Forgetting*. At the time he was still in the state of convalescence from a leg amputation after being wounded while driving an ambulance on the Bainsizza. Because of the mass of traffic the section was finally forced to abandon its cars and the final stage of his journey was made during the night across muddy fields partly on a stretcher, partly on his crutches.)

6.4   The Race to the Bridges

(a) Codroipo, Latisana (29 October)

The Austrian armies adjacent to the XIVth Army had so far played little or no part in the campaign. At the start of the offensive the Xth Austrian Army north of the XIVth Army, and the IInd and Ist Austrian Armies to the south, had been ordered to bring pressure against the enemy lines, but except for some attacks by the IInd Army on the Bainsizza no large-scale effort had been made. Hence, the Italian 3rd Army with its seven front-line divisions and two reserve divisions had been left more or less undisturbed, and was still in a state of full efficiency. It was therefore vital for Italy that this efficiency be maintained and that no part of this Army be lost in the retreat. However, on the night of 28 October some units of the Berrer Corps near Udine were appreciably nearer the bridges at Codroipo and Madrisio than some 3rd Army units, and as near to the bridges at Latisana as other 3rd Army units (Map 8). Hence the next two days would decide if the still intact 3rd Army could be cut off.

The capture of the 3rd Army would be a great prize but the Austro-German force had now been in action for a very strenuous week. The congestion on the roads caused by the crowds of troops and prisoners, and by bridges broken by the Italians, hindered the bringing up of supplies, guns and munitions. Nevertheless the XIVth Army continued to press on all through 29 October along the whole length of its front, cheered at times by the capture of very large Italian dumps providing supplies of food and drink.

The Berrer and Scotti Corps were ordered to make for the bridges at Dignano and Codroipo, moving in the zones shown approximately in Map 8.[22] At dawn on 29 October the main body of the 200(g) Division of the Berrer Corps was crossing the Torre at Salt, but for some unknown reason, they only set out towards the Tagliamento at 11.30. However, by the evening the troops had reached a point about 3 miles east of the Tagliamento, and found that the Italians still held the area around Dignano on the east bank, and that the river was in flood and not fordable.[23]

The other division of the Berrer Corps, the 26(g), spent the day in various ways. Three battalions held a parade with singing and a band in Udine, deserted except for thousands of Italian prisoners. The advance guard of the 121 Infantry Regiment reached the Tagliamento south of Turrida (Map 8). Elsewhere a battalion of Grenadiers went to the aid of artillery under attack in the south-east outskirts of Udine, and during the night with units of the adjacent 5(g) Division captured Pradamano about four miles south-east of Udine, taking 1,800 prisoners, 35 machine guns and 18 guns. The grenadiers lost 5 dead, 11 wounded and 1 missing.[24]

South of the Berrer Corps, the very bad weather on 28 October had interrupted radio communications. Hence the 5(g) Division (General von Wedel) received its orders to advance on Codroipo as soon as possible, only by hand in the early hours of 29 October. The Division was then still east of Udine. The 52 Regiment left at 05.00 to find the roads through Udine blocked by vehicles and enormous masses of prisoners, and by the afternoon had only reached Campoformido five miles south-west of Udine.[25] The 8 Grenadier Regiment advanced to the region of Paparotti about three miles south of Udine where they were held up by the Italian rearguards, but after fighting during the night they captured 5,000 Italians.[26] The 12 Grenadier Regiment was ordered to move with two batteries of mountain guns to a line through Campoformido, and although delayed outside Udine by roads encombered with wrecked vehicles they reached Campoformido by 11.00.[27]

As the day went on, General Wedel became increasingly concerned that his left flank was becoming exposed by the slow progress of the 1(a) Division on his left. Therefore at 12.30 he modified his orders, so that only the advance guard of the 12(g) Regiment was charged with seizing the bridges of Codroipo, and the rest of the Regiment and the 52(g) Regiment would go no further than Campoformido (Map 8), and the 8(g) Regiment would remain in positions south of Udine.

Following the new orders, the advance units of the 12(g) Regiment set off from Campoformida towards Codroipo. Arriving at the village of Basagliapenta, half-way between Udine and Codroipo, they repelled a very gallant cavalry charge by three squadrons of Italian cavalry who were soon shot down by machine-gun fire. A fight then developed and the village was finally occupied in the early evening with many prisoners taken. But by nightfall no unit of the XIVth Army had reached Codroipo, and Krafft comments on the loss of precious time during the halt at Campformido.[28]

Meanwhile Scotti's 1(a) Division, south of the Berrer Corps, had been delayed by a partially destroyed bridge over the Natisone south of Cividale. The VII Mountain Brigade eventually crossed and, despite some flooding, reached San Gottardo on the eastern outskirts of Udine. The XXII Brigade, marched to a bridge across the Natisone about three miles south of Cividale, but finding it impassable had to make a deviation via Cividale, and by the evening were encountering some resistance to the north-east of Udine. Thus neither brigade arrived at Udine by the end of the day as had been expected.[29]

On the Italian side, the Duke d'Aosta commanding the 3rd Army had issued precise and detailed orders at 05.00 on 29 October to regulate all the traffic crossing the Tagliamento bridges. The XI Corps and those 2nd Army units south of the salient were to cross at Codroipo, and XXIII Corps and XIII Corps were to cross at Latisana. Senior named officers were to be responsible at Codroipo and at Latisana, with instructions to ensure an orderly and uninterrupted passage of the troops across the bridges, and were fully authorized to take whatever action might be necessary to achieve this end.[30] Shortly after these orders were issued news arrived that the level of the river had fallen somewhat and that the bridge at Madrisio was now available, so XIII Corps was directed to cross there, with XXIII Corps crossing at Latisana as previously.

Carta 21 of the IOH shows the locations of the Italian forces south of the salient and east of the Tagliamento at 24.00 on 29 October. Four of the eight divisions of the 3rd Army were crossing the bridges at Madisio and Latisana, or were about to cross, but the other four divisions were still further from the bridges than some forward units of the XIVth Army. (Carta 21 also shows the location in this zone of nine 2nd Army divisions and of four more described as *resti*.)

The retreat of the remaining 3rd and 2nd Army divisions is described in some detail in the IOH and by General Caviglia[31] who was in command of XXIV Corps. Although some of the 2nd Army divisions had collapsed, a group of other divisions was now being deployed in a coherent plan to cover the approaches to Codroipo, under the direction of General Ferrero, commanding the left wing of the 2nd Army.[32] Units were being drawn up around the east end of the Codroipo bridges, along the south side of the salient, and along a north-south line running from near Pozzuolo (Map 8) down almost to the coast.

The day of 29 October probably saw the peak of the congestion on the roads in the area around Codroipo where the main roads from Udine and Palmanova converge on the town which stands about three miles east of the bridge. Caviglia later wrote that on approaching Codroipo on 29 October, at about five to seven miles from the town, there began a mass of lorries, guns, all kinds of waggons, beasts, supplies, services, civilians, a great part of the impedimenta of the 2nd Army, and some of that of the 3rd Army; all forming a huge cauldron which was ready to fuse and disintegrate any coherent and efficient unit that fell into its clutches.[33]

During the retreat there was certainly great confusion and failure of morale, but any mass movement on such a scale at short notice, and harassed by the enemy, is not likely to be totally efficient. It should also be added that much of the disorder on the retreat arose not from failures of the troops but from inefficient or non-existent traffic control, and the breakdown of the supply services. General Caviglia states bluntly that during the retreat the supply services did not function, so the troops were both lacking supplies and food.[34]

Trevelyan gives a sympathetic picture of those days as seen through the eyes of 'Giuseppe' plucked from his family and his little farm in the Appenines in 1915. His officers have disappeared and it seems to him that the war must be over. Someone suggests throwing away their rifles. Well, says Giuseppe, the rifles are very heavy and we have not eaten for two days. 'Andiamo a casa' (We go home). Nevertheless many units continued to operate steadily with their officers main-taining some grip on the situation.[35] Caviglia states that his troops of XXIV Corps marched away from Italian territory, already deserted, 'sad but in perfect order, all at their posts'. The last troops blowing the bridges and burning the remaining stores.[36]

(b) The Upper Tagliamento (29 October)

North of the Berrer Corps, the Stein and Krauss Corps had orders to make for the bridges at Pinzano, Cornino, Trasaghis and Venzone (Map 8). The advance of the Stein Corps was delayed by the bad weather which completely disrupted radio communications. It was only at 02.10 on 29 October that General Stein learnt that the road bridge over the Torre at Salt had been captured the previous day, and was now available. At 04.45 the radio station at Cividale put out a summary of the Army Orders issued at 19.00 on 27 (sic) October saying that the XIVth Army was to seize the Tagliamento bridges and cut off the enemy's retreat, and it was only at 10.45 that Stein received a message from Krauss giving official confirmation. The message laid down the boundary lines of the Corps for an advance to capture the bridges at Trasaghis and Cornino, and stated that it was then the intention to cross the river and to continue the advance.[37]

At 12.30 Stein informed the 12(g) Division and the Alpine Corps that their next objective was to cross the Tagliamento. During the day the 12(g) Division moved towards the bridge at Pinzano and the leading troops arrived at the outskirts of the small town of San Daniele, about three miles east of the bridge, after another very wet march.[38] The main body of the Alpine Corps left Salt at 08.00, and by 09.00 the leading units were about three miles north of Udine. There they received orders for a surprise attack on the bridge at Dignano, using parties of volunteers to be brought up in lorries. However, no lorries were available, so the columns marched on to spend the night at Fagagna, half-way between Udine and Pinzano.[39]

In the Krauss Corps at the north end of the front (Map 9), General Wieden's group made good progress in Valle di Resia. Monte Staulizze, on the north side of the valley overlooking Val Fella, was taken after an attack begun the previous evening, and all resistance in the village of Resiutta was overcome by 18.00. Meanwhile the 8th Jäger Regiment marched over the ridge on the north side of Val Resia, descended into Val Fella, and had crossed the river to arrive at Roveredo about two miles east of Resiutta by 12.00. Later the same day units of the Xth Austrian Army, on the right of the XIVth, descended Val Raccolana (Map 9) and captured the defenders of the half-destroyed fortifications at Chiusaforte about three miles above Resiutta.[40]

South of Val Resia the column which had been sent over Forcella Musi (Section 6.2a) arrived at the outskirts of Venzone on the Tagliamento where they were joined by units of the 22(a) Division. The latter,

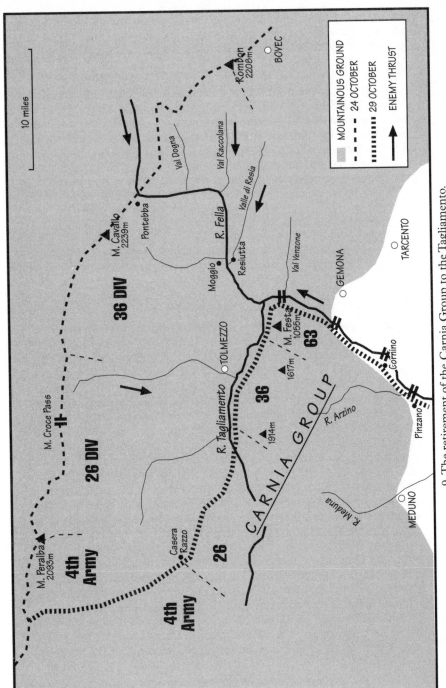

9. The retirement of the Carnia Group to the Tagliamento.

after starting the day by crossing the Torre on a temporary footbridge, had taken Gemona and nearby defence works on the Tagliamento at Ospedaletto and Osoppo, and then gone upstream towards Venzone.[41]

The line reached by the Stein and Krauss Groups at the end of 29 October is shown in Map 8, and details of the Italian units in Carta 21 of the IOH. The Italian front line was held by the 13th, 16th and 2nd (Cavalry) Divisions, with the 34th Division to the rear. The other units (either from IV and VII Corps or those reserve divisions which had been brought up) had now reached the far bank of the Tagliamento, where Di Georgio's Special Corps (20th and 23rd Divisions) had taken up positions behind the bridges at Pinzano, Cornino and Trasaghis, the latter being blown early on the 29th.

On the most northerly section of the front the 26th and 36th Divisions of the Carnia Group had been joined by the 63rd Division sent from the 3rd Army on 26 October to plug a gap between the Carnia Group and IV Corps. All three divisions had now retired before the advancing Xth army, more or less intact, to a line behind or near the upper Tagliamento (Map 9).

(c) Codroipo, Madrisio, Latisana (30 October)

We now come to the final attempts of the XIVth Army to forestall the Italians crossing the bridges over the lower Tagliamento. The first German units to reach the river were the V and VI Battalions of the 4th Jäger Regiment of the 200(g) Division, which arrived in the region of Dignano on the evening of 29 October (Section 6.4a). The next morning at 05.30 the two battalions, with some brief artillery support, attacked and captured the village of Bonzicco, about a mile south of the east end of the bridge. Then, crossing the mile-long trestle bridge in the morning mist, they came to the far end and found that the last forty yards or so were missing (destroyed by flooding on the night of 28 October). The river in the unbridged channel was running fast, four metres deep, and covered by Italian machine guns on the far bank.[42] For the moment, at least, there was little prospect of crossing the river at any point between Codroipo and Pinzano. Hence the actions north and south of Dignano then proceeded independently of each other.

For the first few days of the campaign the progress of the XIVth Army recalled that of a precise and well-oiled machine, but by 30 October its performance south of Dignano began to shows signs of faltering. The troops had now been on the move for a very hard week, and one senses that Krafft was impatient of delays due both to transport difficulties and to the attractions of the food and wine found at Udine and elsewhere.[43] Moreover, both Krafft and von Below had a high opinion of General Berrer, and regarded his death on the outskirts of Udine as a serious loss, particularly at this crucial time when speed was essential to capture the bridges. It was also unfortunate that on 29 October Krafft and von Below, unaware of Berrer's death, were moving their HQ from Kranj, now at least fifty miles behind the front, to Cividale. Leaving Kranj at 08.00, their car was delayed on roads crowded with endless columns of prisoners, and they did not learn that Berrer was dead until they reached Cividale at about 17.00.

Meanwhile, the command of the Berrer Corps had been assigned to General von Hofacker, previously commanding the 26(g) Division. The XIVth Army had continued to advance towards the bridges at Pinzano, Dignano and Codroipo, and by the evening of 29 October had reached the line shown in Map 8. The orders to the Berrer Corps had been to capture the bridges at Dignano and Codroipo but Hofacker, no doubt full of enthusiasm in his new command, saw an additional possibility. A drive to the south-west by his 26(g) Division and the adjacent 5(g) Division in the Scotti Corps should be able to capture the bridges at Latisana and Madrisio before the 3rd Army reached the river. It so happened that a Major Osius, on the staff of the 5(g) Division, met Hofacker at Udine at 13.00 on 29 October to discuss the liaison of his Division with the adjacent Berrer Corps, and Hofacker took the opportunity to propose that the 200(g) Division should deal with both the Codroipo and Dignano bridges while the 26(g) and 5(g) Divisions would drive south to Latisana. Major Osius agreed with this suggestion, subject to the approval of his HQ.[44]

The new plan had of course to be confirmed with the Army Command, but during 29 October Krafft and Von Below had been on the move from Kranj, and only arrived at Cividale at about 17.00.[45] After hearing the latest situation reports Krafft went on to Udine, and at about 20.00 talked with Hofacker, and then returned to confer with von Below. It is clear from Krafft's book and from von Below's diary that speed and surprise were always the essence of their plans, and now their overriding consideration was to capture at least one bridge intact, either at Pinzano, Dignano or Codroipo, so that the XIVth Army could immediately continue its pursuit across the Tagliamento. Therefore orders were given that both divisions of the Hofacker Corps, 26(g) and 200(g), were to concentrate on the capture of the bridges at Codroipo; while the Scotti Corps, 5(g) and 1(a) Divisions plus the 117(g) Division hitherto in the rear of the Stein Corps, were to make for Latisana and Madrisio.[46] This was obviously a sounder arrangement, even though Hofacker might not capture so many bridges.

The subsequent German advance on Codroipo and its three bridges is described by Krafft and von Below. They state that at 09.00 on 30 October, in pouring rain, a Jäger battalion of the 200(g) Division was approaching the bridge from the north, and a battalion of the 121

131

Infantry Regiment from the north-east. The Italians had placed a considerable rearguard around the large number of their troops in the bridgehead still waiting to cross, but the Germans managed to infiltrate and fight their way to near the east end of the bridges, where their presence produced confusion in the columns of retreating troops.

The bridges were much obstructed by abandoned and ruined vehicles, and enemy fire was coming from the far end, but at about midday an advance guard of the Jäger battalion attempted to force their way along the railway bridge. However, as they approached the far end the Italians exploded mines to destroy the last fifty yards across a deep channel, and the Germans were hurled into the water.[47] It appears that all three bridges were blown at the same time and were then impassable. (The IOH, unlike other accounts, states briefly that the railway bridge was less damaged and that a much reduced number of troops continued crossing over it.[48])

The 200(g) Division then turned its attention to mopping up the great number of Italians cut off near the bridge, and these operations continued for the rest of the day. Krafft refers to an encounter of the 200(g) Division with an entire Italian division which, surprised by the presence of the Germans fought hard until the death of its commander. Meanwhile the 26(g) Division had marched to the outskirts of Codroipo, about 3 miles east of the river, and by 19.30 had fought their way in, gained complete control of the town, and taken 27,000 prisoners, 85 guns, 250 motor vehicles, 1,200 carts, a thousand horses, 2 aeroplanes and a mass of other stores.[49] However, despite this great haul of prisoners and equipment the Germans had failed to secure any of the three bridges at Codroipo. The river was four metres deep in places, and the 26 and 200 Divisions remained on the east bank.

(Several accounts, including the IOH, take the view that the bridges were blown prematurely.[50] However, a footnote in the IOH refers to a discussion by the Commission of Enquiry which concluded that most of the prisoners taken at the bridges would in any event have been captured before they could cross. Moreover it would have been disastrous to have blown the bridges too late, and according to von Below's account the charges were only exploded when German troops had reached the west end of the more northerly road bridge.[51])

Further south the three divisions of the Scotti Corps, the 5(g), 1(a) and 117(g), were making for Latisana and Madrisio, starting from the neighbourhood of Campoformido and Udine (Map 8). These divisions soon encountered units of the Italian 2nd Army deployed as rearguards, including the 10th and 49th Divisions of XXIV Corps, the 30th Division recently transferred to XXIV Corps, and cavalry units. Their determined resistance, including the valiant action of the Italian cavalry in the region of Pozzuolo, held back Scotti's divisions who as a result were still some way from the bridges at nightfall.[52] Meanwhile the Italians had been crossing the river all day at Latisana and Madrisio. By 06.00 the following day (31 October) the 10th, 30th and 49th Divisions, the last of the Italian rearguard, had crossed at Madrisio. General Caviglia commanding XXIV Corps had crossed at Latisana at 02.00 (31 October) and reported that by then the bridge was deserted.[53]

(The events of the day have also been described by Caviglia in his book *Caporetto*, which suggests that Caviglia had a much greater grasp and control of events in his corps than some other corps commanders. In a typical aside he recounts how on the night of 29 October he and three of his staff officers in their car were passed by infantry of the 10th Division marching in the pouring rain, and dripping with water. Some soldier observed, 'There go the *attendenti* [batmen]!' Caviglia stopped the car and got out, 'The *attendenti* have a gun in their hand like you. There is work to be done for everyone.' The soldiers recognized Caviglia and the officers marched by saluting. Shortly afterwards Caviglia congratulated the Division on its performance during the march from the Bainsizza to the Tagliamento.[54])

For the XIVth Army it had been a disappointing day. No bridge had been captured intact and the main body of the Italians including the whole of the 3rd Army had been able to cross the river and to take up positions on the far side of the Tagliamento. The river was in flood and bridging equipment was required. The advance had come to a halt.

(d) Pinzano and Cornino (30 October – 1 November)

On 30 October the 200(g) Division, having found the Tagliamento impassable at Dignano the previous day (Section 6.4c), turned south towards Codroipo. Units of the Alpine Corps in Stein's Corps (including the Wurttemberg Mountain Battalion) coming up to Dignano were ordered to turn north towards the bridge at Pinzano. However their patrols reported that the roads towards Pinzano were choked with a hopeless tangle of horse-drawn columns, refugees and their vehicles, and pack animals. None were able to move. Starving horses and pack animals were eating blankets, canvas and leather harnesses. Therefore the Wurttembergers remained near the bridge and tried to get across the flooded river, but all attempts failed.[55]

On the evening of 29 October, the other leading division of Stein's Corps, the 12(g), had arrived on the outskirts of the small town of San Daniele, on a low hill about three miles south-east of the bridge at Pinzano, and about four miles south of the railway bridge at Cornino. The next morning the Division advanced on San Daniele. Krafft states that the Italian rearguards put up a fierce resistance, with ten field batteries and many machine guns, while the main body of the Italians continued to retreat over the bridges. However, by 16.00 two of the German battalions had captured the town by skilful flanking attacks. A great quantity of booty was also taken, much equipment and many waggons from four or five divisions, fifty guns, 10,000 prisoners and the baggage of an entire cavalry division. Meanwhile, a Bosnian battalion of the 55(a) Division in the Krauss Corps had been advancing on the bridge at Cornino from the north.[56]

By the end of 30 October most of the Italian troops around the two bridges had either crossed to the west bank of the Tagliamento or been captured, apart from a rearguard consisting primarily of the Bologna Brigade of the Di Giorgio Corps, sited on the hill of Monte Ragogna immediately to the east of the bridge leading to Pinzano. Cadorna was now much concerned lest any enemy troops should cross the Tagliamento before the 2nd and 3rd Armies had at least some time to prepare defence positions. The Bologna Brigade was therefore ordered to maintain its positions, and deny the enemy the road leading across the lower slopes of Monte Ragogna to the bridge.

The next day, 31 October, the XIVth Army was still held up by the rearguards protecting the bridges at Pinzano and Cornino. The 12(g) Division was joined by the 50(a) Division of Stein's Corps for the drive towards Pinzano, and the 55(a) Division attempted to cross the bridge at Cornino. Their attacks were repulsed during the day, and continued through the night. Finally, at 04.30 on 1 November, the Italians gave orders for the bridge at Cornino to be destroyed, but the destruction was only partial, and the east end remained almost intact. (Hence by the next afternoon, 2 November, the 55(a) Division reached the little island of Clapat in the middle of the river, where they were halted by fire from the west bank.[57])

The attacks on the Bologna Brigade on Monte Ragogna by the 12(g) and 50(a) Divisions after continuing during the night were followed by a further assault the next day (1 November), prefaced by three hours of violent artillery bombardment. These attacks were at first contained but then the enemy penetrated into the village of San Pietro close to the Pinzano bridge, where fighting continued among the streets and houses, and eventually enemy patrols reached the end of the Pinzano bridge. General Sanna, charged with the destruction of the bridge at the appropriate moment, was already concerned that enemy shelling of the bridge might cut the electrical leads to the demolition charges already in place. Therefore on the arrival of the first enemy patrols he gave orders for destruction, and at 11.25 the large arch of the bridge was blown into the air.[58]

When the bridge was broken the Bologna Brigade was still fighting strongly on Monte Ragogna. The Austrian Official History refers to their 'heroic defence', and General Krafft to 'their courageous defence', but cut off from supplies and reinforcements there was little more they could do but surrender, and 3,000 officers and men were taken prisoner. Then followed a rather unusual incident. Their surrender was taken formally at a parade with military honours attended by Generals Krafft, Stein and von Below, and the latter made a short address acknowledging the honour and valour which the Brigade had shown.[59]

(The loss of one of the best brigades in the Italian Army was one of the episodes considered by the Commission of Enquiry. Comments had been made that the country would have been better served by withdrawing the brigade with the rest of the troops, but the Commission took the view that in any event most of the Brigade would probably have been captured. Silvestri condemns Cadorna in strong terms for ordering the troops to hold their ground at all costs,[60] but does not acknowledge the need of the Italian Armies for a pause behind the Tagliamento in order to reorganize and take up positions against the next onslaught of the XIVth Army.

6.5   The Defences of Carnia

The defence of the Italian frontier in the Carnic Alps (Maps 1 and 9) was the responsibility of the Carnia Group (XII Corps), an independent command between the Italian 4th and 2nd Armies, commanded by General Tassoni. On 24 October the frontier, and the front line of the war, ran along the main ridge of the Carnic Alps from Monte Peralba to Passo Monte Croce Carnico and Monte Cavallo, and then across Val Fella at Pontebba to follow the line of summits at the head of Val Dogna, up to but not including Monte Rombon above Bovec (Map 9). This very mountainous sector of the front was held on one side by the Austrian Xth Army, and on the other by the Italian 26th and 36th Divisions forming the Carnia Group (XII Corps).

At the start of the battle, the Austrian Xth Army had orders to exert pressure on the Carnia Group from the line of the frontier, but at first did no more than some limited shelling and the sending out of some patrols. It was only on 28 October, after the Italian 26th and 36th Divisions had begun to withdraw, as part of the general retirement to the Tagliamento, that Xth Army units moved forward towards the retreating Italians. Hence, the only threat to the Carnia Group during the first days of the offensive had come from the XIVth Army, as the Edelweiss and Jäger Divisions marched west and north-west from Zaga, through the mountains and down Val Venzone, Valle di Resia and Val Raccolana, thus posing a threat to the rear of the 26th and 36th Divisions.

135

As early as the beginning of September, Cadorna had foreseen the possibility that the 50th Division of the Italian IV Corps might be forced to retreat down Val Uccea, and had asked General Tassoni to draw up contingency plans to cover such a withdrawal, and to ensure that a firm front was maintained between the Carnia Group and the 2nd Army.[61] However, it was only on the night of 25 October that he ordered the 63rd Division (General Rocca) from the 3rd Army reserve, plus six alpini battalions and five bicycle battalions of Bersaglieri, to reinforce the right of the Carnia Group.[62]

Thus, by the time the Austrian Xth Army moved forward on 28 October, the new support had joined the Carnia Group as the 26th and 36th Divisions were withdrawing to new positions on either side of the Tagliamento, harassed by only weak enemy pressure.[63] By 29 October the Italian 26th, 36th and 63rd Divisions had taken up new positions (Map 9): the 36th and 63rd on the right bank, and the 26th mainly on the left bank, on a line drawn back from the river to join the 4th Army at the high and lonely farmhouses at Casera Razzo.[64] (Carta 20 of the IOH shows the whole of the 26th Division on the left bank, but Schizzo 11 shows a lesser part on the right bank, and General Tassoni's order N.214 of 2 November refers to parts on both banks.[65])

During the retreat the Italians had carried out demolitions on the bridges and track of the railway line in Val Fella, and at the station of Carnia near the junction of the Fella and Tagliamento rivers, all of which Krafft and von Below had hoped to capture intact. By 31 October the bridges at Trasaghis and Venzone (Map 8) had been destroyed, and the 26th, 36th and 63rd Divisions were ready to oppose both the XIVth Army coming down the valleys west of the upper Isonzo, and the Xth Army coming down from the north. In particular the 63rd Division held the strongly fortified positions on Monte Festa which overlooked the junction of the Tagliamento and Fella rivers, and dominated half a mile of the main road on the left bank of the Tagliamento above Venzone.[66]

6.6   Friction between Allies

It had been envisaged that while the main weight of the Austro-German offensive would be provided by the XIVth Army, the Austrian IInd and Xth Armies would give support by bringing pressure on the Italians on either side of the XIVth Army. As mentioned above, on 24 October two divisions of the Austrian IInd Army made some initial advances against the three divisions of XXVII Corps on the left bank of the Isonzo, but by the evening were back on their start line.[67] The same evening the Headquarters of the XIVth Army was informed that the IInd Army intended to resume these attacks the next day, but had not sufficient supplies of ammunition for the artillery.[68] To the north of the XIVth Army, the Austrian Xth Army did little more than produce some sporadic artillery fire.[69] However, news of the successes of the XIVth Army soon reached the Emperor Karl, and at 10.00 the next day (25 October) he arrived at XIVth Army Headquarters, anxious that the Austrian IInd Army should play a larger part.[70]

The assassination of the Archduke Ferdinand, the heir to the throne of Austria, at Sarajevo on 28 June 1914, meant that his nephew Karl was now the successor to the Emperor Franz Joseph, nearly eighty-four years old. Karl was then aged twenty-seven, and had followed a relatively conventional career as an army officer until November 1912, when he was posted as major to a regiment in Vienna. There, he was engaged on staff work and other studies to prepare him for the still far-off day when he would succeed his uncle the Archduke Ferdinand as Commander-in-Chief of the Austro-Hungarian Armies.

Unlike the position in Italy, the Emperor was not only the titular head of the Army, but was the actual Commander-in-Chief. However, when war broke out in 1914, Franz Joseph was well over eighty, so the effective commander was the Chief of Staff, General Conrad von Hötzendorff. Nevertheless, the old Emperor began to involve Karl to an increasing extent in political and military affairs. In 1916 he was given the command of a corps during the Strafexpedition against Italy, and when Karl became Emperor on the death of Franz Joseph in November 1916, he was able to assume the role of Commander-in-Chief. Thus, when Karl arrived at XIVth Army HQ, he came as the Commander-in-Chief of all the Austrian forces, and he desired a larger role for Austria in the now successful operation. However, as the roads around the Tolmin bridgehead were already seriously overcrowded, it was agreed that the IInd Army would only cross the river after the XIVth Army had gained sufficient space on the right bank. Karl then returned to his HQ, but this was not the end of the matter.

At one stage during the planning of the battle, the Austrian Command had suggested that the front of the XIVth Army should be extended to the south to include the line Plava – Cividale (Map 8). However, by 26 October something rather different was envisaged. It became known at XIVth Army HQ that Karl had already ordered that the right-hand boundary of the IInd Army's sector should extend to the line Na Gradu – Cividale (Map 5), which lay well inside the XIVth Army's sector.[71] General von Below immediately protested to the Army Group Commander, the Archduke Eugene, saying that the order would seriously compress the front of the Scotti and Berrer Corps at a time when the IInd Army units were still far behind, and would compromise the chances of reaping the full gains of the present success. Eugene agreed that such a change was neither opportune nor practical at that moment, and the order was not passed on.[72]

The next day, 27 October, Krafft learnt that the Austrian IInd Army had already sent six divisions across the Isonzo between Rocinj and Plava, that three more were to follow, and that this army was to advance against Monte Korada (Maps 8 and 5).[73] Any such additional and unplanned traffic would threaten the supplies of the XIVth Army, and particularly its ammunition supply. Therefore, between 08.00 and 09.00 Krafft telephoned General von Waldstatten, the first assistant to General Arz, the Austrian Chief of Staff, to ask him to intervene, and to suggest that these Austrian divisions be sent immediately to the Conrad Group to carry out an attack in the Trentino. Waldstätten said he would consider the matter, and subsequently ordered Boroevic to suspend, at least temporarily, any sideways movement of his troops.[74]

Later on 27 October, the XIVth Army orders issued at 22.00 fixed the southern boundary of its sector as the line Udine – Codroipo (inclusive) (see Map 8).[75] But during the late evening of 28 October Eugene defined the northern boundary of the IInd Army sector by a line from Udine lying further to the north, so that the sector now included the bridges at Codroipo.[76] However, since the IInd Army was far behind the XIVth Army, von Below was sure that the XIVth would arrive at Codroipo well before the IInd, and decided not to pass on Eugene's order.

For much of 29 October Krafft and von Below were occupied in moving their HQ from Kranj to Cividale. On finally arriving at Cividale they issued orders to Scotti and Hofacker to make for the bridges at Latisana and Codroipo respectively (Section 6.4c).[77] However, during the day Scotti's 5(g) Division had been held up by Italian resistance in the area of Basagliapenta, and his 1(a) Division was delayed by flooding between Cividale and Udine. On the other hand, the IInd Army had encountered less Italian resistance and was now moving more rapidly in their sector which, as laid down by Eugene, extended to the north of the Codroipo bridges. There was now a clear lack of unity between the allies: von Below was anxious to capture the bridges and cross to the far bank with all speed; while Eugene appears to have received orders to obtain the maximum role for the Austrian Armies.[78]

The next day, 30 October, the 5(g) Division of the XIVth Army, moving south-west towards Latisana, encountered the 28 Division of II Corps of the Austrian IInd Army, which was moving north-west towards Codroipo. General Wedel, commanding the 5(g) Division, was told by the Commander of the 28(a) Division that he had orders to make for Codroipo, and if need be, would march there across the German columns.[79] This news was passed to the Command of the XIVth Army. During the night, the German High Command

138

telegraphed von Below saying that 'The arrival of part of the XIVth Army at Latisana could be decisive for the complete destruction of the Italians.'[80] Next morning General Pfeffer of the reserve 4(a) Division of the XIVth Army was at Cividale, and was told by the Chief of Staff of the Austrian II Corps that the Corps had three times received precise orders to move to the west even if the German troops turned to the south. Whereupon, General von Below being absent at General Berrer's funeral, General Krafft ordered the Austrian II Corps to halt immediately, an order unreservedly approved by von Below on his return. However, by midnight or shortly after, the Italians had completed their crossing of the Tagliamento and blown all the bridges, so both the IInd and the XIVth Armies were brought to an enforced halt.

Krafft and von Below were also concerned at the slow progress of the Austrians at the other end of the front, where the Austrian Xth Army faced the Italian Carnia Group. As described in the previous section, the Xth Army only began to move against the Carnia Group when the Italian 26th and 36th divisions began to retire on 28 October, and then not very vigorously.[81] Nevertheless, on 26 October the Austrian High Command at Baden proposed that the two divisions on the right of the Krauss Group, the Jäger(g) and the Edelweiss(a) Division, should pass to the Xth Army. This was rejected by von Below who saw no point in the scheme which, he said, would only weaken the right wing of the XIVth Army, and disturb the rapport between the two commands.[82]

A further disagreement arose on 29 October, after General von Wieden's column of the German Jäger Division and four battalions of the Austrian Edelweiss Division arrived in Val Fella after a five-day march from the Isonzo described by Krafft as 'truly brilliant'.[83] The road and railway in Val Fella were of great importance as they linked Villach in Austria with Gemona and Udine on the east side of the Tagliamento, and would provide a much better line of supply for the XIVth Army which was still supplied from the railhead at Tolmin. The Italians had carried out some demolitions on the road and railway bridges, but their work appeared to have been hurried, and not too difficult to repair. A more serious and immediate obstacle was the fact that the road down to Gemona, and the area around Carnia railway station, were dominated by the guns on Monte Festa, high above and overlooking the great stoney area at the junction of the Fella and Tagliamento rivers (Map 9).

On 28 October General Krauss ordered General von Wieden to capture the defence works at Chiusaforte in Val Fella, the bridges at the railway station for Carnia, the defence works on Monte Festa, and to clear the road to Gemona.[84] During 29 October Val Fella was

139

completely cleared of the enemy, and von Wieden's orders for the next day stated that the Jäger Division with four mountain batteries was to march to Tolmezzo, and there cross the river to take the fortress on Monte Festa.[85] At 11.00 on 30 October von Wieden arrived at Resiutta and found the Division, after five very hard and successful days, resting in the neighbourhood. He also learnt of damaged bridges across the Fella near the railway station, that half a mile of the road to Gemona was under shell-fire, and that the Tagliamento was in flood. He therefore decided that the Division must wait for nightfall before making a move.

During the day von Wieden received news that a battalion of the LIX Brigade of the 94 Division of the Austrian Xth Army had arrived in Tolmezzo with orders to precede the Jäger Division, and cut off any Italian units retreating down the road from Passo Monte Croce Carnico (Map 9). It was also reported that the XIX Brigade of the Division had reached Moggio from the north, and was proceeding towards Tolmezzo. Therefore von Wieden consulted Krauss as to how he should respond to these changed circumstances, in particular, was he still to move against Monte Festa? Krauss ruled that his group should now proceed to Gemona, away from the Xth Army sector, and this move was made the next day (31 October).[86]

On 1 November the road to Gemona was still blocked by the Italian guns on Monte Festa, and von Below saw no sign that the Xth Army would be able to respond quickly to this situation. In his view, most of its troops were not 'very vigorous in combat', and Krauss should have sent the von Wieden group back towards Tolmezzo to carry out 'that which had been neglected'. As this ground was now clearly in the Xth Army sector, von Below now believed that the Edelweiss and 22nd Divisions, two of the best Austrian units, should be transferred to the Xth Army, to aim for Tolmezzo and Belluno.[87] However, following an objection from Krauss, only the Edelweiss Division was transferred, on 3 November.[88] In fact, Monte Festa was not taken until 7 November, and then by General von Wieden's Jäger Division.[89]

6.7   The Italian Armies on the Tagliamento

By the end of October the Italian Armies from Carnia to the sea were aligned on the right bank of the Tagliamento (Map 10) where they hoped for an appreciable pause while the XIVth Army brought up the supplies and equipment which would be needed for any attempt to cross the river.

The north wing of the front (Map 10) was still held by the 26th and 36th Divisions of the Carnia Group, now taken into the 2nd Army, and augmented by the 63rd Division transferred from the 3rd Army

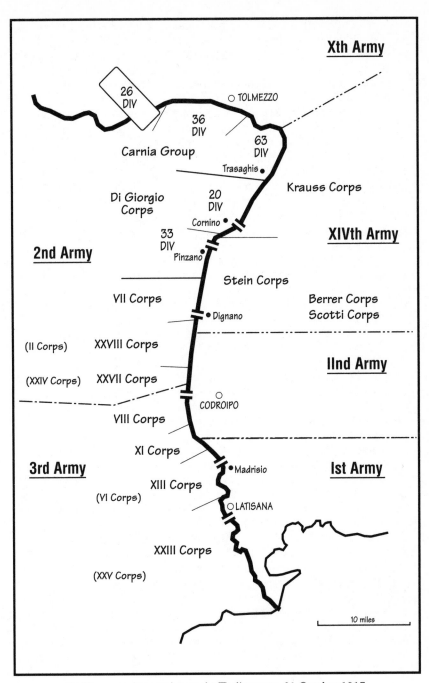

10. The opposing armies on the Tagliamento, 31 October 1917.

reserve. The south wing of the front was still held by the 3rd Army with its initial three front-line corps, plus VIII Corps formerly in line with the 2nd Army. Between these two wings much had changed. South of the Carnia Group the line was held by the 20th and 33rd Divisions from the 3rd Army reserve, now forming a corps under General Di Giorgio.

The relatively short stretch of front between the Di Giorgio Corps and the 3rd Army was held by three corps of the much changed 2nd Army: VII, XXVII and XXVIII, of which XXVIII Corps had been brought from the 2nd Army reserve. Hence, the only corps which had been in the front line of the 2nd Army on 24 October, and which were still somewhere in the front line, were VII Corps, XXVII Corps and VIII Corps. But the map hardly gives a complete picture because very many moves had been made transferring divisions between corps, brigades between divisions, and battalions between brigades, as in the examples noted in Chapter 3.

With the exception of II Corps and VIII Corps, all the front-line corps of the 2nd Army were now much changed, as is made clear by comparing the details of their constituent divisions on 24 October and 31 October as given in the IOH.[90] For example, VII Corps was initially constituted by the 3rd and 62nd Divisions, but a week later is described as the remnants of the 3rd Division and of one of the brigades of the 62nd Division. The situation map for 12 November[91] shows Badoglio's XXVII Corps still present as a fighting unit, but this is somewhat misleading. On 24 October the Corps consisted essentially of eight regiments deployed in four divisions, the 19th, 65th, 22nd and 64th. But by 31 October it had been reconstituted with the 13th and 67th Divisions, with six brigades in all, of which only one (Belluno) was present on 24 October.

Besides holding its stretch of line along the Tagliamento, the 2nd Army now faced the daunting task of reorganizing its shattered units. The effective strength of the 2nd Army on 1 October 1917, as given by the official statistics, was 685,000 (officers and men),[92] but by the end of October was greatly reduced. The IOH quotes the Austro-German communiqué of 1 November which claimed 180,000 prisoners and 1,500 guns,[93] virtually all of which would have been taken from the 2nd Army. In addition the IOH estimates that about 300,000 *sbandati* (stragglers) were now pouring back from the front.[94]

G.M. Trevelyan described the change in atmosphere on crossing the bridge at Codroipo: 'once we reached the far shore of the Tagliamento we set foot on a more hopeful and active world, where officers and carabinieri were sorting out the men as they arrived over the bridge, and orders were being given and obeyed'.[95] Today Trevelyan's account appears perhaps unduly low key. A more chilling picture of the crossing of the Tagliamento at Codroipo was given by Ernest Hemingway in his famous novel *A Farewell to Arms*. His hero Frederic, an American Red Cross worker, wearing an army-style officer's uniform and with an American accent, was arrested at the bridge by carabinieri. He found himself in the company of an Italian lieutenant colonel and an Italian major, who like himself had arrived at the bridge without any troops. It soon appeared that all such officers were being picked out, arrested, taken away, and summarily shot, but the resourceful Frederic managed to make a dash to freedom. (Hemingway himself served with the American Red Cross on the Piave front in 1918, but was not in Italy at the time of Caporetto. Even so, his novel was researched with such care[96] that it remains one of the best general accounts of the retreat.)

There was certainly need for action. Hundreds of thousands of troops were retreating in various degrees of order and disorder, among them many thousands of deserters who had taken the opportunity to make for home. Firm measures were needed and Cadorna was well known for his belief in an unrelenting discipline. All through the war he had regarded executions as an excellent method of maintaining morale and had tried hard (and unsuccessfully) to obtain the government's permission to discipline units by the Roman practice of decimation (Section 2.2). Hence it was not surprising that his order N.4988 on 26 October to the Headquarters of the 2nd and 3rd Armies makes it clear that all commanders were personally responsible for enforcing, where necessary, the most severe measures, and would have the full backing of the Comando Supremo.[97] Aosta's order N.10013 on 27 October stated that appropriately sited artillery and machine guns would fire on runaways.[98]

There are no exact figures for how many were summarily shot during the period of Caporetto. During the whole war some 729 soldiers who appeared before military tribunals were sentenced and executed for offences against military discipline. These tribunals followed formal procedures and kept full records, as described by Forcella and Monticone (who give details of two cases of desertion across the Tagliamento at the Pinzano bridgehead).[99] During November and December 1917 the official record gives the number condemned by tribunals as 100,[100] but the number of summary executions which went unrecorded was certainly much greater. According to Mack Smith 'Cadorna unfairly blamed the defeat on his men's cowardice and thousands were executed.'[101] According to President Pertini, who was a junior officer in the 2nd Army at the time of the retreat, the reorganization was sometimes accompanied by shootings en masse and drastic decimations.[102] Further discussions are given by Melograni,[103] and by De Simone who quotes a figure of 5,000

143

executions during the period of Caporetto.[104] (According to the latter the remains of the Unknown Soldier interred in the Victor Emmanuel Monument in Rome was selected by a war widow from one of eight remains brought from the eight main sectors of the front. But the eight sectors did not include the 2nd Army sector at Caporetto, to ensure, so it is said, that the Unknown Soldier had not been summarily executed.[105])

By 6 November *The Times* was able to report a despatch dated 5 November saying that the Italian Army was sorting itself out, and that the roads from the Tagliamento were now in a much more orderly state. Men of the same branch of the services had been collected together and were being directed to places of assembly for re-equipment.[106] The next day *The Times* also quoted a 'stern proclamation by Cadorna' dated 5 November which was posted in all towns behind the new line saying that all soldiers separated from their units were to report within five days. If not they would be considered as deserters liable to the death penalty, and all those assisting absent soldiers were liable to three to fifteen years in prison.[107]

From the Tagliamento to the Piave

7.1 The Move to the Piave

The Austrian High Command had initially envisaged the offensive across the Isonzo as a quite limited operation, but after discussion with Krafft and von Below at the conference on 15 September, Eugene issued an order stating that the aim was to drive the enemy back across the frontier 'and if possible to reach the Tagliamento'.[1] But General Boroevic had been very doubtful that his troops would ever get so far (Section 1.4).

The successes of the XIVth Army on and after 24 October produced an immediate change of mood. The XIVth Army had asked for more bridging equipment to be sent from Rumania.[2] The Austrian High Command had agreed with the German High Command that the Austrian Army Group of the Tyrol should now mount an offensive in the Trentino, and on 27 October allocated two extra Austrian divisions to form part of a five division offensive on the Asiago plateau to commence on 10 November.[3] Even so, the Austrians still appeared reluctant to commit themselves to crossing the Tagliamento. According to Krafft, Eugene prepared an order on 28 October setting out the demarcation lines between the XIVth and the Austrian IInd Armies for a crossing of the river, but then held it in abeyance.[4] The next day the German High Command informed the Austrian High Command that as soon as the Tagliamento was reached, it intended to withdraw the German divisions. On receiving this news, Eugene said that he intended to continue the campaign across the Tagliamento; the German High Command agreed to let its troops remain until further notice; and at 22.00 on 30 October Eugene issued orders for the offensive to continue across the river.[5]

Cadorna hoped that the line of the Tagliamento could be held for at least some days, so that the 2nd Army could reorganize and stabilize its units, but Krafft and von Below were determined to advance as rapidly as possible so as to obtain the maximum result from their already considerable successes. From 03.00 on 2 November the 55(a) Division of the Krauss Corps fought to force a way across the bridge at

Cornino, which had not been completely destroyed. The Italians fought back but were unable to prevent a Bosnian brigade of the 55(a) Division reaching the far bank by nightfall.[6] Meanwhile the 12(g) Division of the Stein Corps had been striving all day to ford the river at Pontaiba between Cornino and Pinzano. Finally, spurred on by the news that the 55(a) Division was now across, they reached the far bank at 22.00, and began work on a temporary bridge.[7]

During the next day, 3 November, the 55th and the 12th Divisions continued to cross the Tagliamento. The Italians in the Di Giorgio Group fought back, but once the bridgeheads had been established, Cadorna had little choice other than move back to the Piave. Hence, at 10.35 on 4 November he ordered the 2nd and 3rd Armies to retreat to the line of the Piave and Monte Grappa (Maps 1 and 11)[8] as outlined in preparatory directives on 31 October and 1 November.[9]

While the 55th and 12th Divisions had been crossing the Tagliamento, Eugene was holding discussions with von Below and Krafft, and heard their recommendations on how best to exploit the new breakthrough. The next day, 4 November, Eugene issued orders to the Army Group of the South-West, greatly extending the scope of the Austro-German offensive. All the Armies of his group were now to take part in a great effort, not just to reach the Piave, but to drive the Italians back, at least to the line of the River Brenta![10] Krafft and von Below give only a short summary of these orders, but Eugene's intentions appear clear. Boroevic's Group of the IInd and Ist Armies was to cross the Piave from a sector extending from Nervesa to the sea, and then make across the Venetian plain to the Brenta, while at the same time sending a force with all speed to capture Venice. The XIVth Army would advance to the Piave in a sector north of Nervesa, lying partly in the plain and partly in the mountains. Its principal task would be to advance along the line Belluno – Feltre – Fonzaso – Bassano, and thus cut through the lines of communications of the Italian 4th Army, still high up in the mountains near the frontier (Maps 1 and 11). The Xth Army in Carnia would advance down the Piave to Belluno, and then proceed via Feltre to Val Brenta, where it would co-operate with Conrad's Group in an attack on the Asiago plateau.

We now turn to the retirement of the Italian Armies, beginning with the retreat of the 2nd and 3rd Armies across the Venetian plain to the Piave. This almost flat expanse was traversed by an extensive system of roads, and the only obstacles to movement were the relatively small rivers flowing to the sea between the Tagliamento and the Piave. According to Cadorna's orders, the 2nd Army was to retire in stages with rearguards on the intermediate rivers, the Cellina, the Livenza and the Monticano.[11] The 3rd Army, with less distance to cover, was to move in two stages, first to the Livenza and then to the Piave.[12] The

146

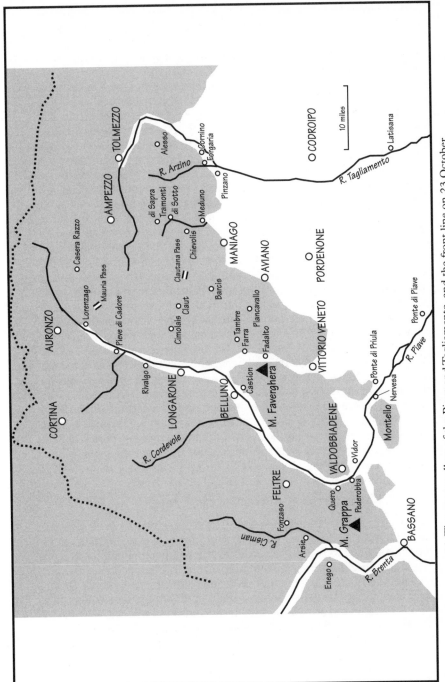

11. The upper valleys of the Piave and Tagliamento, and the front line on 23 October.

rearguards were to be provided by the 2nd and 3rd Armies, with three divisions of cavalry all under the command of General Sagramoso,[13] the whole operation being the responsibility of the Duke of Aosta.[14] Material and non-combatants were to be sent back immediately and the main bodies were to begin to retire on the night of 4 November.

Although the Austrians and Germans were across the Tagliamento at Pinzano and Cornino on 4 November, most of their units had still to bridge the river, so the Italian 3rd Army and those units of the 2nd Army already on the plain were able to withdraw to the Piave with little interference from the enemy. (According to von Below, Boroevic ordered the Ist and IInd Austrian Armies to take no action until the heavy artillery arrived, but then Eugene intervened to order an advance at any cost.[15]) The most difficult situation for the Italians was at the foot of the mountains where Krauss's 55(a) Division had crossed the bridge at Cornino the previous night, and where fighting was in progress on the right bank. However, this did not much affect the general retreat, and by the end of 5 November most of the Italians had made good progress across the plain, and reached the line of the Livenza about 18 miles back from the Tagliamento. Meanwhile the enemy were beginning to cross the Tagliamento in strength.

The retreat across the plain continued the next day, 6 November, with little interference by the Austrian Ist and IInd Isonzo Armies, though some rearguards on the Livenza came under pressure from two columns of the Stein Group. On 7 November the main bodies of the 2nd and 3rd Armies reached and began to cross the Piave. At the same time the rearguards came under pressure from a build-up of enemy forces, and withdrew to the line of the Monticano. By the end of the next day the bulk of the Italian troops had crossed the Piave with the rearguards holding the Monticano. Then on 9 November most of the rearguards crossed the Piave, and all the bridges were blown at midday. Thus virtually all the troops retreating across the plain arrived safely behind the Piave.[16]

7.2   The Retirement of the Carnia Group

The Carnia Group and the 4th Army, over 300,000 men in all, faced a difficult retreat. We first consider the move of the Carnia Group, comprising the 26th, 36th, and 63rd Divisions, then holding the line on the upper Tagliamento shown in Map 9.

The main line of supply and communication for the Carnia Group had been along the valley of the Tagliamento, but by 3 November this route was blocked by the enemy presence around Pinzano. Hence, to reach the plain and the new Army line on the Piave, the 36th and 63rd Divisions would have to traverse some 25 miles or so of high and steep mountains lying to the south of the upper Tagliamento. The only practical routes through these mountains followed the roads leading to the head of the Meduna and Arzino valleys, and then down the valleys to the plain (Map 11). The 26th Division, higher up the Tagliamento, also had the possibility of following the road from Tolmezzo which led through Ampezzo over the Mauria Pass, to Lorenzago in the valley of the upper Piave.

On 2 November General Tassoni, the Commander of the Carnia Group, issued order N.214 outlining the arrangements for a retreat if that were necessary.[17] The 36th Division would retire directly by the Arzino valley. The 63rd Division located lower down the Tagliamento would first move to Alesso (Map 11), and then take a mountain track to the Arzino valley, where it would await the passage of the 36th Division and then follow on behind. The eleven battalions of the 26th Division on the left bank of the Tagliamento would leave by the Mauria Pass. The other four battalions of the Division, on the right bank of the Tagliamento, would form a column commanded by Colonel Danise, and retire down the Meduna valley as far as Chievolis, and then follow minor roads and tracks from Chievolis through the mountains to the valley of the Piave.[18]

The order for the retreat was issued at 11.20 on 3 November by the Commander of the left wing of the 2nd Army, General Etna. It included an instruction to attack the right flank of any enemy troops at the foot of the Arzino valley moving towards Meduno. At 11.45 General Tassoni sent out the Operational Order n.4 to the 26th, 36th, and 63rd Divisions. The latter was sent by radio telegraph and stated that if the 36th and 63rd Divisions found the mouth of the Arzino valley blocked by the enemy, they were to make their way by minor roads and tracks through the mountains to the Meduna valley, and there join the units of the 26th Division.[19]

Already the Group appears to have been somewhat disorganized, for Tassoni's order n.4 began by saying that the 26th Division was to use all methods at its disposal to communicate the order to the other two Divisions, implying that contact had already been lost between Tassoni and the 36th and 63rd Divisions, Hence, it is not surprising that the Italian accounts of the retreat of the 36th and 63rd Divisions are in places somewhat incomplete. However, the general picture is evident from the accounts given by Krafft and the IOH.

The next day, 4 November, General Tassoni issued further orders, saying that the 36th and 63rd Divisions were to march down the Arzino and Meduna valleys, and fall on the flank and rear of any enemy units pursuing the Di Giorgio Group as it withdrew across the northern edge of the plain.[20] These moves were to be coordinated by General Rocca (63rd Division) who would assume command of all the 36th and 63rd

149

Division units in the Arzino valley, while General Alliana of the Benevento Brigade (36th Division) would be in command of the units moving down the Meduna valley.

The above plans for the withdrawal assumed that the Italians would hold the initiative, but this was not the case. The XIVth and Xth Armies were aiming to block off the exits from the whole mountain area delineated roughly by the square Ampezzo – Tolmezzo – Forgaria – Meduno. By 4 November the 55(a) Division of the Krauss Group was across the Tagliamento at Cornino, and marching westwards along the road at the foot of the mountains. During 5 November the 55(a) Division reached Cavasso two miles beyond Meduno, and was followed by the Jäger(g) Division with orders to block off the exits of the Arzino and Meduna valleys. Meanwhile, to the north, the 94th Division of the Austrian Xth Army and the Edelweiss Division (now in the Xth Army) were crossing the river at Tolmezzo, and preparing to descend the Arzino and Meduna valleys (respectively).

The column led by General Rocca in the Arzino valley encountered the German Jäger Division coming up from the plain on 6 November. The Italians repulsed the first attack, but found themselves hemmed in; some attempted to escape over the mountains to the west but most were captured.[21] Krafft states that 4,000 Italians were taken prisoner in the Arzino valley by the Jäger Division and another 1,000 by the Edelweiss Division.[22] General Alliana's units of the 36th Division descending the Meduna valley were caught in the region of Tramonti (Map 11) between the 94th Division of the Austrian Xth Army coming from behind them and units of the Edelweiss Division that had come across the mountains from the Arzino valley.[23] Fighting continued until the morning of 7 November, but the Italians were trapped and some 5,000 men and 24 guns captured.[24]

Colonel Danise's column of the four battalions of the 26th Division on the right bank of the Tagliamento went from Ampezzo to the Meduna valley, with orders to establish a rearguard across the valley at Redona just south of Chievolis, to protect their retirement over the Clautana Pass against any attacks from the south.[25] (The road system hereabouts has since changed considerably because of a hydro-electric scheme creating Lake Selva and Lake Tramonti.) But on 6 November 1,200 of Danise's troops were captured south of Tramonti by units of the 22(a) Division which, having crossed the Tagliamento had been directed first to Meduno, and then up the Meduna valley.[26] Adding these losses to those at Tramonti we obtain a minimum loss of 11,000 captured, while von Below gives the total losses as 19,000 to 21,000.[27]

We now return to the eleven battalions on the left of the 26th Division which were to retire over the Mauria Pass. In fact, since 30 October four battalions of I Corps on the right of the 4th Army had been sited around the pass to prevent any incursion by the Austrian Xth Army into the Piave valley, the Corps' supply route, and way of retreat. Therefore, on 3 November the eleven battalions were transferred to I Corps, and three of them ordered to remain at the pass to support the units already in place.[28] This augmented force now spread over the high ground on either side of the pass to cover both the pass and other minor roads. They were attacked on 7 November by the 94(a) Division,[29] and after a day of hard fighting the Austrians gained control of the pass, and the Italians retreated towards the village of Lorenzago in the Piave valley.[30]

The fate of the troops in the Carnia Group remains somewhat obscure. Most of the 36th and the 63rd Division were trapped in the mountains, the Commission of Enquiry refers to 'the loss of the 36th and 63rd Divisions',[31] and the divisions do not appear again in subsequent pages of the IOH. Most of the 26th Division retired over the Mauria Pass and the rest by the Clautana Pass, and the only account we have of any major losses by capture is that of the 1,200 prisoners taken near Chievolis from the group making towards the Clautana Pass. Yet this Division, also, is not mentioned again in the IOH.

The total strength of the Carnia Group on 6 October, apparently including fortress troops, is given by Italian official statistics as 2,838 officers and 86,773 men, a total of 89,611.[32] In addition the Group had been augmented on 26 October by the 63rd Division. Hence, its total strength was of the order of 100,000. Yet Krafft mentions a total only of 14,000 prisoners, and von Below a total of 19–21,000. On the other hand, the IOH gives the number of Italians captured up to the establishment of the new line on the Piave as about 300,000,[33] and quotes an Austrian bulletin on 1 November which claimed the capture of 180,000 prisoners.[34] These two figures imply that about 120,000 prisoners were taken in the first nine or ten days of November. Possibly some of this number came from the Carnia Group. Be that as it may, the loss of the Carnia Group was another heavy blow to the Italian Army.

7.3   The Tardiness of General Di Robilant

We now turn to the retreat of the 4th Army from the frontier in the mountains to the new line running from the valley of the River Brenta, over the high ground of Monte Grappa to the Piave, and then along the right bank of the river as far as Vidor (Map 11). This Army of some 230,000 men,[35] commanded by General Di Robilant since September 1915,[36] had spent some thirty months of the war guarding the frontier on and around the high mountains of the Dolomite peaks.

During this time the 4th Army had established well-built defences

151

and barracks, in the harsh environment of the high mountains, so that positions could be maintained all through the year, with some units even on the ridges and summits of the Marmolada, the Tofane, and Monte Cristallo. Since 1916, preparations had also been made for a line of ultimate resistance, the so-called Yellow Line, which was sited up to 20 miles behind the front line, and at its north-east end ran through the area known as Fortezza Cadore Mae.[37] This 'Fortezza' consisted of a group of forts in the region of Pieve di Cadore, often high up, and commanding the road along the Piave to Cortina and much of the surrounding ground. In fact, most of the guns in the Fortezza had long been removed and sent to other fronts, but the very existence of the Fortezza, together with the Yellow Line, appears to have produced a feeling of security.

At the start of the battle, the 4th Army guarding the mountain frontier (Map 1) was constituted with three corps: XVIII (51st, 15th, 56th Divisions), IX (17th, 18th Divisions), and I (1st Division).[38] The I Corps was anomalous in that it had only one division, but this was an unusually large unit divided into four separate sectors, three holding the front line, and the fourth garrisoning the rear defence areas. For most of these troops the retreat from the frontier to Monte Grappa and the Piave would involve longer marches than for the 2nd and 3rd Armies. Moreover, the main routes of withdrawal were largely defined by the valleys of the Rivers Brenta, Cismon, Cordevole, and Piave. Hence there was a very real possibility that a rapid advance by either the XIVth or the Austrian Xth Army might trap units before or when they reached the lower ends of the valleys, a danger particularly serious for I Corps which was closest to the enemy and had furthest to move.

Already on 26 October, as the full extent of the disaster at Caporetto was becoming clear, Cadorna had seen the inevitability of a retreat to the Tagliamento, and the strong possibility that this would be followed by a further retirement across the Piave. Therefore at 16.20 Cadorna sent order N.4998 to Di Robilant warning that the 2nd and 3rd Armies might be forced to retire to the Tagliamento, and in that case the 4th Army would retire to the defences of the Yellow Line. At the same time he ordered that the less obsolete and less mobile guns of large and medium calibre retire to the right bank of the Piave between Pederobba and Montebelluno; and then for further guidance added that 'this partial and prudent retirement of the artillery must not in the slightest way affect the conduct and resistance of the troops of the defence'.[39]

At 05.45 the next day, 27 October, Cadorna informed Di Robilant that he had decided on the retreat of the 2nd and 3rd Armies to the Tagliamento, and that the left wing of the Carnia Group would draw back to Casera Razzo (Section 6.5). Therefore the 4th Army was to start 'this day' on the first stage of the retirement to the Yellow Line; and also to complete various defence works on Monte Grappa. Cadorna also stated that the Army was to move 'calmly, steadily, slowly'.[40]

For most of the war the 4th Army had held largely static positions, and had not been involved in any major battles. Its experience so far had been gained in actions on a relative small scale, often in rather impressive places high up in the mountains, where it had shown considerable expertise. (When the XIVth Army launched its offensive, the 4th Army was engaged in an action to dislodge the Austrians from the summit of the Marmolada (3343m), the highest peak in the Dolomites.[41]) Hence the 4th Army, in well-constructed and relatively comfortable positions, had little or no experience of movements on the required scale. In fact the IOH states that the Army now found itself in 'a situation of undoubted gravity for which the Command of the 4th Army was totally unprepared; and did not easily come to terms with the situation either conceptually or psychologically'.[42]

In response to Cadorna's order of 27 October, Di Robilant issued order N.11298 on the same day, setting out 'arrangements for the retreat', including preparations for the movement of guns, material and animals not needed by the troops.[43] There were to be no changes in the positions of the front-line troops until further orders. Two days later, on 29 October, Di Robilant issued order N.11389 on the same subject which stated that 'It is the intention of the Comando Supremo to pause on the Tagliamento and then retire to the Piave. On this latter hypothesis [sic] the Army will occupy the front Grappa – Ponte Priula.'[44] The order continued that the 'idea' was to get all the heavy and medium guns back to the zone between Bassano and Monte-belluno on the right bank of the Piave, and that the artillery and engineers were to 'prepare' what each would be required to do during the move.

On 30 October Di Robilant, in message N.11387 informed the Comando Supremo that some realignment had been made on the right of his front to maintain a junction with the Carnia Group at Casera Razzo (Section 6.5), and that no other changes had been made in the 4th Army front line, except that some units were being sent to reinforce the right of I Corps.[45] On the same day, Di Robilant also sent his chief of staff, General Businelli, to suggest to Cadorna that the 4th Army should activate a scheme, proposed in 1916, to create an isolated redoubt in the region of Cadore Mae, and that the 4th Army be sent an additional Army Corps for this purpose![46] This suggestion, both un-realistic and untimely, was not adopted.

On 31 October Cadorna informed Di Robilant of the worsening

situation and told him that it was absolutely essential to speed up his retirement and give complete priority to the movement of troops and guns.[47] Di Robilant replied by saying that he had heard from General Montuori that the situation had improved.[48] (Why Montuori might have made such a remark is hard to imagine.) Therefore Di Robilant went on to ask if it was really necessary to accelerate the withdrawal as much as possible because this would imply abandoning all the guns (which were now supposed to be en route to the Piave). Cadorna replied at 21.00 saying that the situation was always grave, and it was therefore necessary to speed up the withdrawal, not to maximize speed, but to save the artillery, especially the heavy guns.[49]

At 23.15 the next day, 1 November, the Headquarters of the 4th Army notified Cadorna that it was continuing to garrison the Yellow Line, which was now sufficient to protect the retirement of the other troops, and that it had arranged for the speedy withdrawal of the guns.[50] However, on 2 November Di Robilant further reported that the Yellow Line could not be held firmly because arrangements to maintain troops there were not yet in place. Also, if the troops were moved from their present positions (still on the front line) it would not be possible to guarantee any resistance on an intermediate line because all the medium guns had been sent to the Piave. He then suggested various possible ways in which the retirement might be speeded up, such as moving a battalion a day by train.[51] Yet again, Cadorna had to reaffirm his explicit orders for a speedy withdrawal behind the Yellow Line, and at 23.30 Di Robilant ordered the move to begin the next day.[52] Thus the front-line troops only began the long move to their new positions on 3 November, seven days after Cadorna had ordered the first stage of the retreat.[53]

7.4   Plans and Concerns of the XIVth Army

Krafft and von Below were very aware that the scale of their successes would depend on how quickly they could exploit their initial crossing while the enemy were still disorganized. According to Eugene's orders of 4 November the aims were now, inter alia, to cut off the 4th Army and the Carnia Group from the rest of the Italian forces, and to link up with Conrad's forces on the Asiago plateau. His order also laid down that the task of the XIVth Army was to reach Belluno with all speed, and thus cut the lines of communication of the Italian 4th Army.

There now followed some disagreement between von Below and Eugene regarding the details of the order, and between von Below and Krauss regarding the execution of the order. Both Krafft and von Below believed that the quickest route to Belluno would be to follow the roads and tracks which led through the mountains, from near Meduno to the valley of the Piave at or below Longarone, and then down the river to Belluno. However, according to Eugene's orders, the XIVth Army's sector appeared to extend only to the left bank of the Piave, the right bank being in the sector of the Xth Army coming down from the mountains to the north. This part of the order did not make sense to either Krafft or von Below. They were confident that they would arrive at Longarone on the Piave before the Xth Army; and the main road, the railway and the village itself all lay on the right bank of the river beyond the XIVth Army sector. However, on 5 November the Emperor Karl paid a visit to XIVth Army HQ, accompanied by General Arz, his Chief of Staff, and von Below was able to obtain their permission to attack Longarone on the right bank as soon as possible.[54]

Although Krafft and von Below had insisted to Eugene that they would reach Longarone before the Xth Army, one might comment that the performance of the XIVth Army after crossing the Tagliamento had not shown quite all the precision so brilliantly deployed on the Isonzo. Although the 36th and 63rd Divisions of the Carnia Group had been captured by the combined action of the 94(a) Division of the Xth Army, the Edelweiss(a) Division temporarily in the Xth Army, and the Jäger(g) Division of the Krauss Corps, some time had been lost. On 3 November the 22(a) Division, sent towards Tolmezzo to support the Xth Army, was first held up by broken bridges near Carnia station, and then recalled by Krauss, as Eugene regarded this support as unnecessary. Therefore the Division ended the day by marching back to Gemona which it had left five days earlier(Section 6.4b).[55] One of the Jäger regiments, after crossing at Cornino on 4 November, took a road too much towards the north. Also on the same day, the CCXVII Brigade of the Edelweiss Division missed their way, and marched up the wrong side-valley on the north side of the Tagliamento.[56]

The disgreement between von Below and Krauss arose over the choice of routes to Belluno. The sector of the Krauss Corps was defined to the north by the summits north of the line Cimolais – Claut – Chievolis (Map 11), and to the south approximately by the road running at the foot of the mountains from Meduno to Aviano and Vittorio Veneto. The task of the XIVth Army, as laid down by Eugene, was to advance to Belluno and beyond, and thus cut off the Italian 4th Army. It was therefore unfortunate that while Krafft and von Below favoured a direct route through the mountains, Krauss had little enthusiasm for any route through the mountains.

To follow the events of 5 and 6 November we first recall that on 3 November the Edelweiss Division had been transferred to the Xth Army (Section 6.6) and the Krauss Corps then comprised four divisions, the 55(a), Jäger(g), 22(a) and 50(a), the latter recently transferred from the Stein Corps. The Jäger and the 22 Division had been involved in the actions against the Carnia Group. The Austrian 55th Division had crossed the Tagliamento at Cornino on 4 November, and followed the road at the foot of the mountains to the neighbourhood of Meduno, where it passed the night. The 50th Division had crossed the Tagliamento at Pontaiba, and was following on behind the 55th. Thus by the night of 4 November the 55(a) Division, near Meduno, was in the lead position for the drive to the Piave and Belluno.[57]

Between the Meduna and Piave valleys lay twenty miles of rough mountains rising up to 2300 metres, crossed by only a limited number of roads and tracks. Yet the shortest route from Meduno to the Piave was certainly through the mountains via Chievolis and Cimolais to Longarone. Moreover Krafft and von Below judged, correctly, that the minor roads to Chievolis and between Claut and Longarone were passable for carriages, and that the track over the Clautana Pass (1342m) between Chievolis and Claut was at least adequate for their mountain troops. However, Krauss was reluctant to move into the mountains, and preferred to take the good roads which led round the foot of the mountains to Vittorio Veneto and then to Belluno, even though this route was at least twenty miles longer, and near Faldalto (between Vittorio Veneto and Belluno) was confined in a steep and narrow valley which would provide the Italians with very good defensive positions.

Krafft and von Below were probably expecting that on 5 November the 55(a) Division would continue from Meduno to Chievolis and Longarone. However, Krauss had no such intention, and directed the Division to take the route via Vittorio Veneto.[58] Likewise he also ordered the 50(a) Division, which had been following behind, to take a route through the plain, by roads a few miles away from the edge of the mountains. Thus on 5 November two divisions were moving towards the Piave by the long route via Vittorio Veneto on the edge of the Krauss sector, and there was no sign of any move towards Longarone in the rest of the sector, ten to thirty miles wide.

Krafft and von Below were now much concerned because not one of Krauss's four divisions appeared to be moving fast enough to cut off any Italian forces retreating down the Piave. In his diary for 6 November von Below wrote that the Krauss Corps was the only one to have done less than its assigned task, saying that Krauss should have advanced swiftly through the mountains, with the greater part of his corps, to cut off the Italians retreating in front of the Xth Army. Instead, wrote von Below, he had directed all his forces on to the plain, where his most advanced divisions found themselves in front of Stein's Corps. 'Thus we lost a whole day.'[59]

On 6 November von Below suggested to Krauss the advantage of sending the 22(a) Division, which had now reached Meduno, by the shortest route to the Piave. Orders were then given for the Division to make a two-pronged attack through the mountains west of the Meduna valley, to cut off the Italians escape route down the Piave. The XLIII Brigade was to make for Longarone via Chievolis and the rough track over the Clautana Pass (1432m) to Cimolais, and then down the road to Longarone. The IIC Brigade was to make for Belluno from Barcis, by way of Piancavallo (1259m), then by a mountain track over a 1700m pass to Farra (Map 11).[60]

To support this thrust through the mountains further changes were made on 7 November. The Edelweiss Division (now with the Austrian Xth Army) together with the LIX Brigade of the 94(a) Division were to form the main part of a new corps, located at the junction of the Xth and XIVth Armies, with its objective Longarone.[61] However, although the CCXVII Brigade of the Edelweiss Division had arrived at Chievolis, the other brigade was very tired and needed a brief rest, so the Division was ordered to follow behind the 22nd Division. Further south the 50(a) Division and the Alpine Corps(g) were grouped into a new corps under Scotti on the edge of the plain, leaving Krauss with the 22(a), 55(a) and Jäger(g) Divisions.

General von Below was also concerned that although the Archduke Eugene, the Army Group Commander, had agreed to the XIVth Army attack on Longarone, he had reserved the right to assign any of von Below's units operating on the right bank to the Xth Army.[62] This reservation was quite unsatisfactory to von Below, not only because it involved a fundamental change in the conduct of the operations, but also because of the rather moderate performance shown so far by the Xth Army. In particular, von Below saw the need for a single command in the region of Feltre at the foot of the Grappa massif to avoid problems arising from any crossing and intermingling of the two armies. He was sufficiently concerned that on 7 November he asked Major Jansa, Eugene's liaison offficer, to speak confidentially to the Archduke.[63] Apparently this had a satisfactory effect, for on 10 November the South-West Command ordered that the offensive against Monte Grappa was to be led by General Krauss; that the Xth Army remain temporarily halted in the rear; and that the Edelweiss Division rejoin the XIVth Army.[64] Thus the XIVth Army sector would now extend as far as Conrad's Group on the Asiago plateau.

For the troops on the left wing of the XIVth Army, facing the Piave between Pederobba and Nervesa, there was only one way to advance: across the river. Although the XIVth Army had quickly breached the Italian defences on the Tagliamento, Krafft and von Below knew that the crossing of the Piave would be a more difficult enterprise. The Italians were now defending a much shorter front, while the river itself offered good defensive positions. On 7 November news was received that work on defence fortifications along the Piave had been in progress since 25 October, and aerial reconnaissances showed the presence of considerable numbers of troops.[65]

A further factor now influenced the situation. As early as the night of 26 October the Italian Government had asked for assistance from its French and British allies, and by 31 October two French divisions had begun to arrive in Italy.[66] Then during November there was a buildup to a total of six French and five British divisions, in all over 200,000 men.[67] The first news of this development mentioned by Krafft is a report on 7 November that French and British troops had been seen in Treviso (Map 11), and that the Command of the South-West front believed that about ten Allied divisions were already in Italy.[68] On 10 November a source 'thought to be reliable' reported that General Foch had taken command of all operations in Italy, and that a Franco-British Army of 360,000 troops under General Mangin was on its way.[69] (General Foch had certainly not taken command of all operations in Italy, though he was there from 30 October to 23 November helping to advise the Comando Supremo.[70])

It was now clear to Krafft and von Below that the Austro-German forces must move rapidly to extend and consolidate their gains before the full deployment of the Allied troops. Yet, before the XIVth Army could attempt a full-scale crossing of the Piave, more bridging equipment would be required as almost all its supply had been used at the previous rivers. Guns and ammunition would have to be accumulated in sufficient quantities to force the crossing and for the subsequent fighting on the far side, yet the supply of ammunition to the front was disappointingly slow. On 10 November Krafft commented on the need for caution, for a full-scale offensive across the Piave would only be possible after lengthy preparations. Hence it was thought that the best course would be for the XIVth Army to attack across Grappa, while at the same time Conrad's Group launched an attack at Asiago.[71] In fact the last stage of the offensive, known in Italy as *La battaglia di arresto*, was fought largely in these two regions, although some attempts were made to cross the Piave.

7.5 The Retirement of the Italian 4th Army (3–12 November)

The three divisions on the left of the 4th Army, the 51st, 15th and 56th, were to take up positions on the Grappa massif. The other units of the Army, the 17th and 18th Divisions and I Corps, were to hold the line of the Piave between Pederobba and Nervesa (Map 12).[72] Before describing the move of these units we first give some picture of the characteristic terrain within the Grappa massif.

The principal summits (Map 13) stand on the south side of the

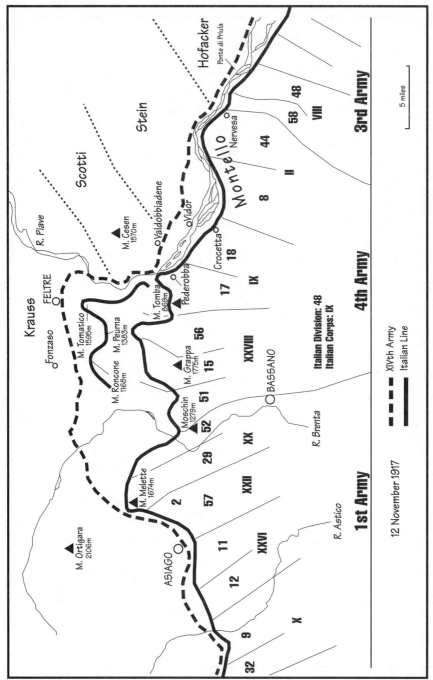

12. The new line on the Piave and Monte Grappa. (After IOH (IV, 3, Carta), 25)

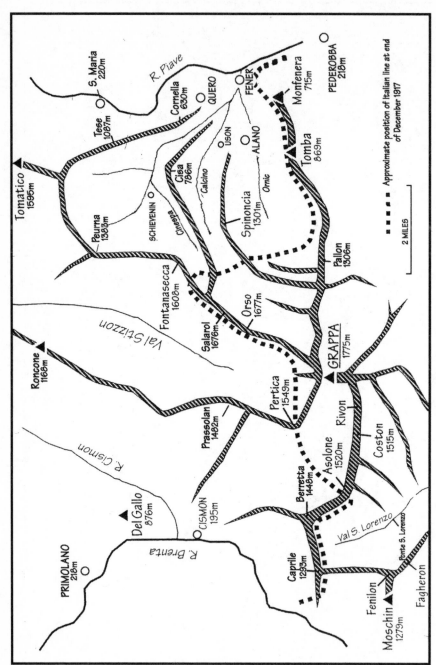

13. The ridges of the Grappa massif.

massif, only 2 or 3 miles from the edge of the Venetian plain, which runs along a line from Bassano to Pederobba, a distance of about 12 miles. The heights of these summits range from about 1500 to 1775 metres. Lower down the hills are well wooded, but the higher slopes are open and grassy, forming a lonely area giving summer pasture for sheep, goats and cows, which in 1917 was traversed by only a few tracks and paths. Long ridges run down from the line of the summits in a northerly direction; their tops are generally broad and grassy, though occasionally interrupted by steep cliffs. On its west side the massif is divided from the Asiago Plateau by the gorge-like valley of the River Brenta. On its east side, the valley of the River Piave (hereabouts largely confined in a single channel) separates it from the mountain group of Monte Cesen (Map 12).

The view from Monte Grappa on a fine clear day is extensive and splendid, stretching away into the distance as far as Venice, the Adriatic and the Appenines. From the summit the ground drops steeply to the plain which lies all before one, scarred by the great stony bed of the Piave; turning one's back on the plain the view is totally different. Long ridges run out northwards from the summit ridge, and slowly decrease in height to end about seven miles away at Monte Roncone (1168m) and Monte Tomatico (1594m), overlooking the road from Fonzaso to Feltre. To the north-west the mountain is bounded by the dark cleft of the Brenta valley, while to the north stands a backdrop of innumerable Dolomite peaks.

Monte Grappa and its outliers formed a natural strategic bastion linking the Piave and the Asiago fronts, the high ridges providing sites for gun positions which could dominate the surrounding ground. At first this ground was remote from the front line, but after the Austrian offensive in the Trentino in 1916, the so-called Strafexpedition, it was realized that the massif might form an important part of the defences of Val Brenta, and Cadorna ordered the construction of a good military road from Bassano to the summit up the southern slopes of the mountain. This was now complete and the principal route of access. In addition the summit could be reached by a cart track from Covolo south of the main summit and two cable ways had been installed, one from near Covolo to near the summit, and one from Val Brenta to Monte Raniero (1248m) south-east of Col Moschin (Map 13).[73] Following the Strafexpedition, defence positions had been prepared high up, but most faced north-west rather than north-east, so further defence works had been ordered by Cadorna on 27 October.[74]

All the divisions faced a long march to their new positions, and on 5 November Cadorna, worried by their slow progress, set up a group of four battalions and three batteries of field guns under his secretary General Bencivenga, with orders to occupy the line of the summits on

Grappa with all speed. They were to go directly into the massif from the north, by taking the mountain tracks leading from Seren near Fonzaso into the remote Val Stizzon (Map 13).[75] The group set off the same day and occupied the line of the summits Col Caprile – Asolone – Pertica – Prassolan – Col d'Orso – Tomba by 7 November. Subsequently by 12 November the three divisions assigned to Grappa had arrived at their new positions (encountering little or no interference from the Austrian Xth Army) and had set up forward defence positions on Monte Tomatico (1595m), Monte Peurna (1383m) and Monte Roncone (1168m), at the end of the two main ridges leading up to the summit.[76]

The other units of the 4th Army faced longer marches to their positions on the fifteen mile stretch of the Piave below Pederobba (where the river emerges into the plain) and Nervesa: I Corps down the Piave, and the 18th Division of IX Corps first down Val Cordevole and then down the valley of the Piave. One of the key points on the new front was the bridge at Vidor (Map 12), which offered the enemy the best prospect of crossing the river to attack the flank of the troops on Grappa. (The present bridge near Quero (Map 11) was built much later.) Therefore, as soon as the retirement commenced on 3 November, two battalions of I Corps were sent down the Piave valley by train to Pederobba, as the advance guard for the 18th Division of IX Corps which was to cover both the bridge at Vidor and the end of the valley running down from Valdobbiadena (Map 12).[77] By 6 November the 18th Division was largely in position, but I Corps had still to arrive in strength on the Piave, so II Corps of the 2nd Army then temporarily at Nervesa was put at the disposal of the 4th Army and took over the front line between Vidor and Nervesa.

Meanwhile, on 5 November the main body of I Corps still had a long march through the mountains down the valley of the Piave, where its left flank lay open to attack by enemy forces approaching from the east, in the first case by way of the Mauria Pass. However, the Italian rearguards on the pass held their ground, and Carta 19 of the IOH shows that by 7 November the troops had filed past Lorenzago and the road from the Mauria Pass, and on 8 November were continuing down the Piave protected by rearguards about two miles north of Pieve di Cadore. Yet the 94 Division of the Austrian Xth Army was close behind, and occupied Pieve di Cadore on the morning of 8 November,[78] as the Italians set up rearguards near Rivalgo (Map 11).

Both brigades of the 22(a) Division were now moving towards the Piave from the east in separate columns. As we describe in the next chapter, the XLIII Brigade led by the Wurttemburg Mountain Battalion reached the Piave opposite Longarone at about midday on 9 November when the Italians were still marching down the valley.

Then, by a masterly action, the Italian retreat was halted. Some of the Italian troops took to mountain tracks to the west, but the greater part was trapped between the Xth and XIVth Armies. The bulk of these forces, of the order of a division, surrendered the next morning, while the main body of the XLIII Brigade continued down the Piave to enter Belluno at 22.00.

The IIC Brigade of the 22(a) Division had taken a track through the mountains further to the south, and spent a very cold night on 8 November bivouacking in the snow at 1650 metres above Piancavallo (Map 11). The next day they descended to Tambre above the road from Vittorio Veneto to Belluno, and on 10 November captured the bridge at Farra on the valley floor together with 600 prisoners. Other nearby Italians were forced to retreat down the valley towards Vittorio Veneto and were captured by the 55(a) Division coming up from Fadalto. Also on 10 November, the Edelweiss Division arrived at Longarone via the Clautana Pass, and the 55(a) Division crossed Monte Faverghera (1611m), north of Fadalto, and descended to Castion near the Piave opposite Belluno (Map 11).

The Carnia Group had been unfortunate in that the first crossing of the Tagliamento, by the XIVth Army at Pinzano, had cut off its main way of retreat. The losses of I Corps in the 4th Army are not so easily excused. Most could have been avoided if the Army had retreated a day sooner. (According to Faldella, Cadorna was sufficiently moved on 3 November to say that if the 4th Army was not saved he would have Di Robilant shot.[79]) As already mentioned, the IOH states that the Headquarters of the 4th Army was totally unprepared both conceptually and psychologically to handle the situation in which it found itself. However, despite Di Robilant's procrastinations, most of the Army, XVIII and IX Corps, moved effectively to their new positions, with their guns deployed along the summit ridges.

Rommel at Longarone

8.1 The New Assignment (26 October – 6 November)

After the capture of Matajur, the Rommel detachment descended about 900 metres along narrow paths to the small village of Masseris (760m), where the tired troops were billeted among the few farms for at least part of a good night's rest. Next day (27 October) they were up before dawn to continue their descent and join the rest of the WMB in the neighbourhood of Cividale.

The Alpine Corps had now reached the edge of the mountains, and for the next six days took part in the general pursuit of the Italians across the plain towards the Tagliamento. The day of 28 October was cloudy and extremely wet, and on reaching the River Torre at Primulacco, about seven miles north of Udine, the WMB found that the river was swollen to a width of 600 yards, and was under fire from a determined Italian rearguard on the far bank. The Rommel detachment discovered dry clothes in an Italian laundry depot, and went to sleep, hopefully for the night. However, at 23.00 they were woken up by an order from Major Sproesser saying that the river must be crossed during the night, or at least before dawn. By daybreak (29 October) a passage had been constructed across most of the width, using all the available carts and lorries as bridges over the several branches of the main channel. The Italians had now withdrawn, and the detachment was able to cross by negotiating the last unbridged hundred yards aided by a strong safety rope stretched across the fast-flowing river. The next evening (30 October) the WMB reached the Tagliamento, and this also was very swollen, and presented a more considerable barrier.

During the next two days other units of the XIVth Army were arriving at the Tagliamento and were also unable to cross. However, as described in Section 7.1, by the night of 2 November the 55(a) Division and the 12(g) Division had secured bridgeheads on the far bank at Cornino and Pontaiba, and on 3 November the XIVth Army began to cross in strength.[1] Both Krafft and von Below were very conscious that further successes would depend on the speed of the advance, and had been concerned at the sometimes slower rate of progress achieved by the Krauss Corps, and particularly by the adjoining Austrian Xth Army.

Major Sproesser states that he met General Krafft at XIVth Army HQ in Udine on 3 November, but gives no account of their conversation, other than that Krafft greeted him by saying 'I congratulate the Mountain Battalion on its prodigious success.'[2] After this conversation Sproesser talked with Krafft's Director of Operations, Major Willisen, who told him that the WMB was to be transferred from the Alpine Corps either to the German Jäger Division or to the Austrian 22nd Division in the Krauss Corps, in order to act as the advance guard in a thrust through the mountains to reach the Piave at Longarone. Moreover, he was told: 'to allow no power on earth to stop you before you arrive at Longarone',[3] a verbal order confirmed by an entry in von Below's diary which reads that the WMB 'were to be put in front to lead the way'.[4]

The next day, 4 November, the WMB left the Alpine Corps to join the Jäger Division, and marched to within about four miles of Cornino. The following day the WMB crossed the river as dawn was breaking, and received orders from General Krauss attaching the Battalion to the Jäger Division 'to lead the way on the march to Longarone by Chievolis, Forcella Clautana, Claut and Cimolais' (Map 11).[5] The WMB then marched on to spend the night at Travesio, about five miles short of Meduno. Meanwhile the Jäger Division was still engaged in operations against the Italian 36th and 63rd Divisions in the Arzino valley, ten miles to the east of the Meduna valley (Section 7.2).

The WMB left Travesio before dawn on 6 November, and marched first to Meduno, and then up the Meduna valley towards Chievolis at the entrance to the Silisia valley. At Redona just south of Chievolis they encountered the rearguard of the Danise column (Section 7.2), and after a brief fight captured 85 prisoners. The remainder of the rearguard took flight and were pursued by a WMB squad on bicycles, acquired near the Tagliamento, and another 230 prisoners were captured near Chievolis.[6] Meanwhile, the main body of the WMB continued westwards up the Silesia valley and by the evening had reached Pecolat at the foot of the Clautana Pass.

Also on 6 November, the Austrian 22 Division (General Müller) arrived at Meduno, and it was then decided that it should substitute for the still distant Jäger Division and lead the thrust to the Piave (Section 7.4). Therefore the WMB, already on its way to Chievolis, was transferred from the Jäger to the 22(a) Division, and allocated to the XLIII Brigade (General Merten). The Brigade set off on the road to Chievolis, en route to Longarone. However, before arriving at Chievolis, General Merten received news of an enemy force further north beyond Tramonti, so most of the Brigade marched past Chievolis and after a brief encounter towards evening captured an 'Italian general and 1200 men',[7] presumably all part of the Danise column. The Brigade then resumed its march to arrive back at Chievolis during the night, by which time the advance scouts of the WMB were making a reconnaissance up the Clautana Pass.

8.2   The Clautana Pass (7,8 November)

The WMB were now in the mountainous area lying between the rivers Meduna and Piave (Maps 11 and 14), which is divided by the river Cellina and its tributary the Cimoliana into two lines of summits, each running approximately north – south, one passing between Chievolis and Claut, and the other between Claut and Longarone. Thus the route from Chievolis to Longarone falls naturally into two stages, over the Clautana Pass to the villages of Claut and Cimolais, and then over the San Osvaldo Pass to Longarone. The lower slopes of the mountains are well wooded but the main summits, which rise to between 1500 to 2300m, often present steep and broken rock faces, particularly on east-facing slopes (Plate 23).

On 6 November the WMB marched 15 miles or so from Travesio, four miles east of Meduno, to the huts of Pecolat and Tronconere at the foot of the Clautana Pass. The Battalion was then about two miles from the top of the pass, but 900 metres lower down. In addition, Major Sproesser had been informed that the Ist Battalion of the 26 Schützen of XLIII Brigade, and the 377 Mountain Howitzer detachment, would come under his command for the operation, and were on their way.

During the evening Major Sproesser, conscious of his orders to move with all speed, considered his plans for the next day. It is not clear how good a picture Sproesser had of the ground to be covered. The day had been sunny,[8] but it is doubtful if Sproesser would have had any view of the pass as he came along the road to Pecolat. (Today the final stretch of the road lies above the south side of the man-made lake of Selva, but in 1917 there was no lake and the road kept mainly on the north side of the stream,[9] and the view would have been more limited.) Nor would his maps have been of the quality of the 25,000 maps available today. Even so, it was no doubt clear that the top of the pass, at 1432m, was the lowest crossing of a ridge which on either side rose steadily to heights of over 2000m.

During the evening, two advance scout squads from the 4th Company made 'excellent'[10] reports that the summit of the pass was occupied by about two Italian companies with several machine guns and three mountain guns. Moreover, the track to the pass soon turned into a side valley which eventually opened out into a high combe, with its base at an altitude of about 800m, encircled by a length of the main

166

ridge between the summits 1715m and Monte Gialina (1634m) on either side of the pass. The track kept high up on the right-hand side of the combe (as viewed looking up), and an enemy deployed near and under the pass would have a commanding view of any troops moving towards them, so it appeared impractical to attempt any direct advance up the track. In addition the pass was guarded on either side by steep cliffs on the main ridge.

It was clear 'that the pass could only be captured by some encircling manoeuvre, and that the expert in encirclement was Rommel'.[11] Sproesser now issued his orders for the next day. Rommel with the 1st and 2nd Companies and the 1st Machine-Gun Company would carry out an encirclement by crossing the ridge to the south of the pass and attacking the enemy from the rear. To the north of the pass, part of the 6th Company would climb the steep slopes of Monte Gialina and attack from that side. The 4th Company with the 3rd Machine-Gun Company would make a frontal attack. Captain Gössler with the 5th and 6th Companies would follow behind the forward troops. The attack would be supported by the Austrian mountain battery sited above Pecolat. The Ist Battalion of the 26 Regiment would remain at Pecolat.[12]

(Both Sproesser's and Rommel's accounts contain some minor contradictions. Sproesser states that the Rommel detachment consisted of the 1st and 2nd Companies and the 1st MG Company, whereas Rommel states that he had four companies, the 1st, 2nd, 3rd and 1st MG,[13] but gives no information at all on the part played by the 2nd Company. Sproesser's text makes no mention of the 3rd Rifle Company, whereas his accompanying map shows it to the left of the 4th Company in a position below and facing the pass. Even so, the general run of events can be sufficiently well described without going into uncertain details.)

Sproesser states that during the day of 8 November 'there was no success with the 4th and 6th Companies attempt to take possession of the pass with a frontal attack'.[14] The Rommel detachment also had a difficult time. It was soon harrassed by machine-gun and artillery fire, and was forced to move in bounds from rock cover to rock cover. Eventually it reached dead ground in the fold of a lateral side valley, and was able to move up and obtain a good view of the main ridge south of the pass, high above them and protected by a line of cliffs, covered in snow and ice.

Rommel gives little detail of how his detachment spent the day, but it seems likely that they paused for some time while reconnaissance squads sought and failed to find a route through or around the cliffs. Therefore he decided that the attack would have to be made frontally, and the detachment traversed across the mountain side towards the pass. The men were carrying very heavy loads, including the machine guns, over very rough ground, and when they arrived near the pass they were 'völlig erschöpft' (utterly exhausted).[15]

As night came on the detachment took up positions on some snow-covered knolls a few hundred yards from the pass. While the men rested, Rommel began to plan a surprise attack on the enemy positions. Accompanied by Lieutenant Streicher and some scout squads he went out into the night to reconnoitre the ground immediately below the pass. (Rommel's account describes the night as dark, but leaves us wondering how dark was dark.) The noise of Wurttemberger boots breaking through the frozen snow alerted the enemy, who responded with fire thus revealing some of their positions. In all several hours of hard effort were spent reconnoitring positions for his machine guns and for the start positions for the 1st and 3rd Rifle Companies.

The attack was launched at midnight with the machine guns concentrating their fire for two minutes on the enemy positions immediately about the pass. Then, as this fire shifted to the enemy positions on either side of the pass, the two rifle companies should have taken the pass by surprise and storm, but there was no immediate response. Rommel had indicated that he would lead the assault, but he had misjudged the time, and was still some distance from the companies at the moment the fire lifted from the pass. He rushed up to them and found to his dismay that they were still waiting to move. The attack was then made, but the effect of accurate timing had been lost. The Italians responded stoutly and, after some close fighting with hand grenades, Rommel broke off the attack.

It was now about midnight and the Rommel detachment was still close to the pass, and with the coming of daylight would be in a hopelessly exposed position. They were also sorely in need of food and rest, and there was no possibility of either in their present position, so Rommel had little choice but to order a return to Pecolat. The detachment made its way down in the dark, leaving the Gössler detachment to keep watch on the pass. About half-way down Rommel made his report at Major Sproesser's command post among the rocks. The detachment arrived at Pecolat before dawn and the cooks provided plenty of hot coffee.

The outcome of any night action is always somewhat uncertain, but for Rommel the night was a great disappointment. He writes that this was the first time he had failed since the beginning of the war, and he was very angry. The WMB had been selected to spearhead the march on Longarone, and their first action on the march had failed, probably as the result of his ambiguous orders to his two rifle companies. Yet the attack was by no means a complete failure. Two hours later, as the sun began to rise, news was received from Major Sproesser that a patrol from the 5th Company had found that the Italian rearguard had now gone from the pass (having received orders to withdraw and block the roads leading out of the Cimolais basin).[16]

Very soon Major Sproesser issued orders for the march to be continued to Claut and Cimolais, with the Gössler Detachment as advance guard, followed by the staff, the bicycle company and the Rommel Detachment, plus the Ist Battalion of the Austrian Schützen and the 377 Howitzer Detachment, which had now arrived to join his command.[17] A detachment under Captain Gössler was soon on their way up the pass, followed by the Rommel Detachment. The latter, despite their heavy loads and having to face the 900m climb for a second time, were apparently invigorated by the news that the enemy had given up such good positions, and they caught up with the Gössler Detachment before reaching Claut at the foot of the pass.

Arriving at Claut at about 14.00, the column paused for a short rest and a welcome from the local population. Major Sproesser then issued orders for the pursuit to continue as would have been expected. However, in a subsequent account he states that these orders disobeyed XLIII Brigade orders which had laid down that the WMB should spend the night at Claut, yield their position as advance guard to the Ist Battalion Schützen, and then follow on with the main body of the Brigade.[18] When and how these orders were received by Sproesser is not clear, but the WMB was now setting the pace of the advance. Hence Sproesser, bearing in mind his meeting with Major Willisen, took it upon himself to ignore the order, and instructed his column to continue its march towards Cimolais.

Captain Gössler with the 5th Company and the 3rd MG Company was sent ahead to secure the road junction two miles further on, where a road led off to Barcis. Here they encountered, and attacked, some of the enemy who thereupon withdrew towards Cimolais at the foot of the San Osvaldo Pass leading to Longarone. The main body of the WBM marched on to Cimolais with the Rommel detachment as the advance guard, preceded by Lieutenant Schöffel and a few cyclists and mounted staff acting as a scout group in front. Behind them followed the Ist Battalion, 26 Schützen.

Arriving at Cimolais as it was becoming dark, the WMB again received a friendly reception, as at Claut. They found food and billets, and then a few hours sleep to recover from their thirty-two hours of marching and fighting since first leaving Pecolat. Meanwhile Lieutenant Schöffel's mounted scout group, which had gone forward along the road to Longarone, reported that the enemy was taking up positions on both sides of the road no more than half a mile west of Cimolais.

The Headquarters of XLIII Brigade now repeated its earlier order that the WMB was to halt and hand over the lead to the Ist Battalion Schützen. Major Sproesser replied that as the WMB was in close battle contact with the enemy, it was impossible to obey this order.[19] General Merten, commanding XLIII Brigade, was clearly anxious that his Austrian Schützen should play a prominent part in the operation, but his orders were falling behind the flow of events, for this last order included an instruction that the WMB act as a flank guard to the Schützen in the Silisia and Cellina valleys.[20] But these were the valleys on either side of the Clautana pass, through which the WMB had already marched on its way from Pecolat to Cimolais several hours previously!

8.3   Cimolais to Longarone (9 November)

The mountain range lying between Cimolais and the Piave, rising to over 2000 metres, is traversed by only one road, that from Cimolais to Erto and Longarone by the San Osvaldo Pass (Map 14). The summit of the pass is quite close to Cimolais, about two and a half miles away and only about 150 metres higher. However, immediately after leaving the village the road enters a narrow defile (Plate 24) where steep and often rocky slopes rise up to Monte Lodina (2020m) to the north, and to Monte Cornetto (1792m) to the south, and here the Italian rearguard had prepared to make a stand.

Major Sproesser, eager to reach Longarone, was determined that the San Osvaldo Pass should be crossed without the delay occasioned by the enemy defence of the Clautana Pass. About midnight, after studying his own maps, and some captured Italian maps, he issued the orders for the next day (9 November). All nine companies of the Battalion were to be involved, but only one company was to advance up the road, while the other companies developed three separate encircling movements along various tracks through the mountains. A detachment of two rifle and one machine-gun company would follow a track round Monte Lodina, probably across Forcella Lodina (1860m), and then descend to the road beyond the enemy positions. On the opposite south side of the road, a similar sized detachment would move along tracks encircling Monte Cornetto and rising almost to the summit of Monte Gallinut (1755m). Further south still, a rifle company and a machine-gun company under Captain Gössler would go west from Il Porto over Forcella Ferron (993m) and Forcella Liron (1398m) and then, keeping to the south side of the Vajont gorge, would follow tracks down to Dogna on the Piave.

Rommel was allotted the command of the northern-most group charged with encircling Monte Lodina, and for once he was

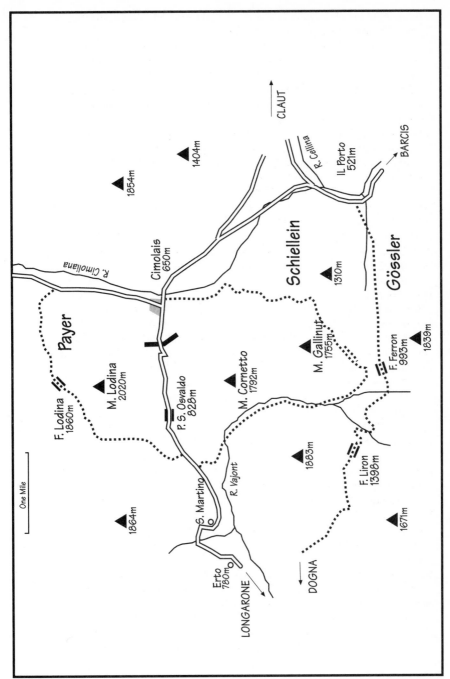

14. The attack on the San Osvaldo Pass. (After Sproesser (1933), Map 45).

disconcerted to receive his orders. His detachment had endured a very hard two days during the crossing of the Clautana Pass, and it now faced another day with heavy loads, starting in the dark along unknown tracks, with an ascent and descent of some 1200 metres. Moreover he had not seen the ground, and no doubt wished to avoid a repeat of the attempts to encircle the Clautana Pass. On being informed of the plan Rommel protested to Sproesser saying that his men were too tired to make the arduous climb involved in the encirclement. He therefore proposed that his detachment should take a much shorter route and attack the positions frontally from Cimolais. Sproesser reluctantly agreed, and amended his orders. Only the 2nd Company under 2nd Lieutenant Payer would take the route round Monte Lodina, while Rommel with the 1st and 3rd Rifle and 1st MG Company would take the much shorter route straight up the road. On the south side of the road, the 4th and 6th Rifle and 2nd MG Company under 2nd Lieutenant Schiellein would encircle Monte Cornetto and Monte Gallinut, while the 5th Rifle and 3rd MG Companies under Captain Gössler would take the tracks towards Dogna.

2nd Lieutenant Payer found a local inhabitant to act as a guide on the track round Monte Lodina, and set off on the northern encirclement about three hours before daybreak. Meanwhile 2nd Lieutenant Schöffel had been reconnoitring the enemy positions around the road west of Cimolais, and by 05.00 had reported back to Rommel that there was no sign of the enemy. Therefore Rommel decided to reconnoitre himself, together with his company commanders, as soon as it became light.[21] At about 05.00 a visitor arrived at Major Sproesser's HQ, Colonel Pasetti, the Commander of the Austrian 26 Regiment, who brought a verbal message from XLIII Brigade, saying that the WMB must halt in Cimolais and wait for the Brigade to come up. In reply Sproesser gave the Colonel a message to the Brigade Commander, General Merten, saying that the WMB had already begun battle during the night in the direction San Osvaldo and Longarone, and it was not possible to stop them.[22]

Meanwhile Rommel and his company commanders had ridden out to view the enemy positions, with a squad of cyclists as an advance guard. All was quiet as they left the village, but they soon came under rifle and machine-gun fire, and hurriedly took refuge in the roadside 'chapel of La Crosette' 150 yards west of Cimolais.[23] (This could hardly be the chapel at La Crosetta on the modern 25,000 map, which is at least a mile further up the road. Rommel's La Crosette was probably an unnamed chapel just beyond the village.[24])

The relief felt at finding this cover was soon diminished by the strength of the fire from quite close range, which began to splinter the slates on the roof. There was no future here, particularly if the enemy brought up any artillery. To avoid this trap, Rommel detailed the party to return individually, each man running out in a different direction to the nearest cover, and then moving off again from another part of the cover. Hence, despite heavy fire, all succeeded in reaching Cimolais uninjured. But Rommel comments that if the Italians had waited for them to advance another 100 yards they would all have been killed.

The reconnaissance had been watched by Sergeant Dobelmann and an observation squad from the tower of Cimolais church, assisted by an Italian x40 telescope captured on the Tagliamento. Dobelmann had observed the flashes from the rifles and machine guns, and was able to give Rommel an assessment of the enemy positions. The view from the church tower, shown in the sketch[25] on page 174 (prepared for a lecture in 1918 given by Rommel to senior officers),[26] was not encouraging. The Italians were holding a line running across the road about 500 yards from the outskirts of the village. To the left of the road this line ran along the top of a low but steep band of rock precluding any direct attack. Then further to the left, at about 150 yards from the road, the line continued higher up the hillside with riflemen in positions protected by piles of rocks and stones, where they could give covering fire over the lower positions. To the right of the road the ground was less favourable to the enemy, but here the line was protected by wired barricades. Moreover, any frontal attack here would come under enfilade fire from the positions to the left of the road.

Rommel had assured Major Sproesser that the attack would succeed, and he now realized that his task was more difficult than he had imagined. His book gives some insight into the thoughtful way in which he resolved the situation. It was clear that the best chance of success lay in an attack to the right of the road, supported by the heavy machine guns. But Rommel could see nowhere to site these guns in positions which would give some cover against fire from the Italians on the left of the road.

Three hours or so were spent in reconnaissance and preparations, which included the laying of telephone lines from the command post to the three companies and to a detachment of six light machine guns sited to the right of the road on the slopes about eight hundred yards north of Cimolais. The attack began at 09.00, with the six light machine guns of the 1st Rifle Company opening fire on the Italian positions to the left of the road, concentrating at first on those higher up in the more open situations on the hillside. At a range of fourteen hundred yards the fire was not particularly accurate, but was sufficiently scattered that some of the Italian riflemen could be seen in the telescope moving down to seek refuge in the better-prepared positions nearer the road. Soon an entire platoon appeared to be on the move, with some

173

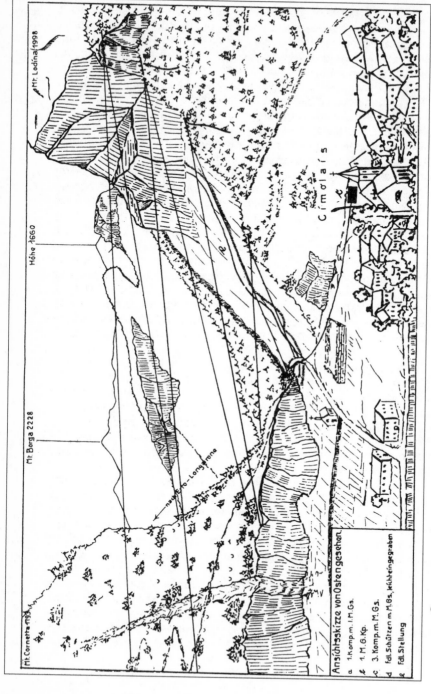

Contemporary sketch showing view towards Passo San Osvaldo from Cimolais. The straight lines indicate the lines of fire of the German machine guns. (*Haupstaatarchiv Stuttgart*)

troops making off to the rear, and Rommel decided that it was now safe to move his machine-gun company into positions lower down and much closer to the enemy line.

As the heavy guns added their fire to that of the light guns, the Italians on the southern slope rushed to find some protection, and crowded into a narrow trench near the road, while those trying to escape to the rear were shot down. Now that the south side of the enemy line was completely pinned down, the 3rd Rifle Company began to work its way forward, widely extended, and covered by the fire of the light and heavy machine guns. With this support the company broke through wire defences and took the enemy positions astride the road, but the enemy forces higher up on the slopes to the north of the road still held out. Rommel sent back a message reporting his progress and ordering up cyclists, mounted runners and horses in order to exploit the success as rapidly as possible. He then went up the road towards the captured enemy positions, whereupon 2 officers and 200 men still in position on the slopes to the north of the road laid down their arms and surrendered.[27]

Rommel ordered an immediate pursuit, but there was a few minutes delay as the 1st Company did not immediately realize that the 3rd Company had occupied the enemy positions, and continued to fire on them. Nevertheless, Rommel, Lieutenant Streicher, and the leading units of the 3rd Company were soon on the road moving as fast as they could go. From the top of the pass the road ran gently downhill for about three miles to the villages of San Martino and Erto (Map 14), only three miles in a direct line from the Piave. But below Erto the Vajont river has cut a steep and narrow gorge which drops down very abruptly to the Piave at Longarone. The road negotiated this ravine by a rather spectacular system of bridges and tunnels which could all too easily be demolished, or blocked by well-placed machine guns. Therefore speed was essential to prevent the Italians from taking up positions there, or carrying out demolitions.

(Today the modern road, built during the construction of the huge Vajont dam (Plate 28), keeps to the north side of the gorge. The valley behind the dam has been largely empty of water since the catastrophe of 9 October 1963,[28] when a quarter-mile length of the mountain side, high above the water, sheared off and fell into the lake, thus displacing its own volume of water over the dam. This tremendous mass of water rushed down the gorge with increasing velocity, and hurled itself across the Piave against the small town of Longarone, killing 2,000 of the 4,000 inhabitants.)

At San Martino Rommel was joined by the staff, and horses and cyclists ordered up from the rear. The head of the column now moved with increased speed. Coming up to Erto the column caught up with

175

small parties of Italians also making down the road. A light machine gun was set up ready to fire, but this was not necessary. Rommel says that he shouted to them to surrender and disarm, and they were sent marching back towards Cimolais.

After Erto the road began to descend, and the cyclists drew away from Rommel and the other mounted staff. They soon overtook more Italians before disappearing round a bend in the road; shots were heard; and an Italian motor car was seen making down the road. As the horsemen raced through 'a pitch-black tunnel',[29] they were checked by the shock of a large explosion ahead of them. Emerging from the tunnel they saw that a sizeable bridge across a side stream had been destroyed, but it was still possible to climb down into the stream, over the ruins of the bridge, and up the other side.

While the sound of shots continued, Rommel's group rushed on, to arrive at the north end of a high bridge, 130 feet long, which spanned the main gorge 150 metres above the river (Plate 26). The WMB cyclists were already there, and told Rommel that they had been firing on an Italian truck which had just disappeared into a tunnel on the far side, presumably carrying the demolition squad which had blown up the previous bridge as Sergeant Fischer was attempting to pull off a smoking fuse. Ahead, at each end of the bridge, demolition charges were clearly visible in holes in the centre of the carriageway. Was the enemy about to explode the charges?

Rommel ordered Sergeant Bruckner, 'an especially brave and daring soldier',[30] to run across the bridge with an axe and chop through the cables which could be seen leading to the bridge. Rommel and the cyclists then raced across the bridge, pulling out the fuses as they went. Sergeant Bruckner with a few cyclists was sent ahead to ensure that no further demolitions were made on the road, and as no signs of firing were heard it seemed that all was well. Emerging from the lowest tunnel into the brilliant sunshine Rommel came upon a sight 'offered to only a few soldiers in the World War'.[31] The Piave lay about 150 metres below, flowing in a narrow valley confined by steep mountains rising up to 1500m on either side. The road and railway ran parallel to the far side of the river, and along the road marched thousands of Italian soldiers retreating in good order unaware of the enemy presence.

Meanwhile Major Sproesser and Captain Kremling, commanding the Ist Battalion 26 Schützen, had arrived at Erto where Sproesser received yet another order from XLIII Brigade: 'The WMB stops, makes camp and spends the night at the mill at Erto; the 26 Schützen Regiment undertakes the lead.' But these orders were now well outdated, and he replied that 'The advanced units are fighting at Longarone. I need support with infantry on the pass road, and please send me the 377 Howitzer Detachment.'[32]

8.4 The Capture of the Ten Thousand

When he emerged from the last tunnel, Rommel was on the upper slopes of Hill 882 (Map 15) on fairly steep ground covered by scrub and trees, dropping to the valley floor about 150m below. The large village of Longarone lay on the far side of the valley, about half a mile distant from the foot of the Vajont gorge. The main channel of the Piave is hereabouts of the order of a hundred yards wide, set in a wide stony bed up to 400 yards wide, so any attempt to cut off the retreating columns would involve fording the river and crossing some very open ground.

Rommel was now in the lead position of a considerable force, the WMB and the Austrian XLIII Brigade, but these had yet to arrive. The time was still only an hour before noon, and Rommel knew that the rest of the WMB, which had been sent on three different encircling movements, had much further to travel, and could not arrive before midnight at the earliest. However, the main body of his detachment (the 1st and 3rd Companies and 1st MG Company) was spread out along the road not far behind, and was closely followed by the Ist Battalion Schützen. So he decided to press on. The events of the next twenty-four hours are described by Sproesser and Rommel in their battle reports written at the time,[33] and in two more detailed accounts in their books published in 1933 and 1937 respectively.[34] All are in substantial agreement though sometimes containing different points of detail.

When Rommel first saw Longarone, columns of marching infantry and artillery were moving down the valley unaware of the threat to their flank. He immediately ordered the few riflemen and cyclists accompanying him to take up fire positions, under cover and away from the road, about a hundred yards to the south amidst trees and scrub. Their best target appeared to be a stretch of road, about half a mile away, where the Italian columns were confined on the far side by a steep rocky outcrop, and on the other by the Piave. Rapid fire caused a column to halt, and then break into two halves, that south of the defile hastened its march, while that to the north of the defile turned back to Longarone.

Italian machine-gun fire began to fall on the road and the Vajont gorge without troubling the well-sited Wurttembergers. The rest of the Rommel detachment were not far behind, and the firing party was joined by a platoon with two light machine guns. Shortly after, a company or perhaps a platoon of Italian troops, probably part of the rearguard over the pass, was seen descending a rock face above and behind the Wurttembergers. However, faced by both rifle and light machine-gun fire while still negotiating the rock face, they soon accepted Rommel's call to surrender.[35]

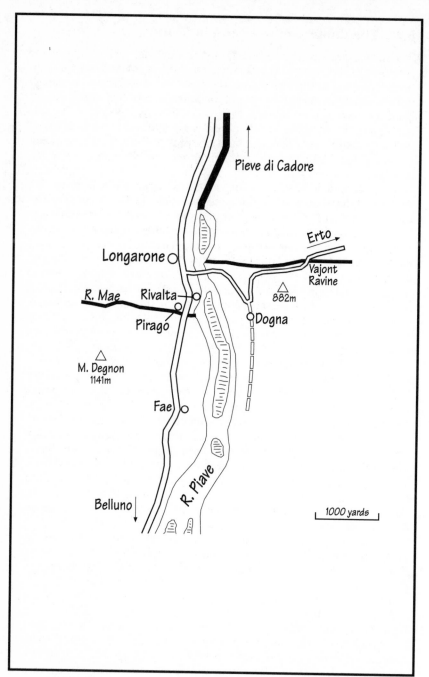

Pieve di Cadore

Erto

Longarone

Vajont
Ravine

R. Mae Rivalta

882m

Pirago

Dogna

M. Degnon
1141m

Fae

R. Piave

Belluno

1000 yards

15. The Piave at Longarone in 1917. (After IOH (IV,3, Carta), 25)

At 11.15 the bridge across the Piave on the road from the gorge to the village was blown up, and rifle and machine-gun fire began to fall around the road leading from Hill 882 down to the river near Dogna (Map 15). During the next half hour most of the 3rd Company caught up with Rommel and were ordered to take up similar firing positions.

By 11.45 Rommel's 1st Rifle Company, which had been following the 3rd, arrived on Hill 882 and was given the task of crossing the river from Dogna.[36] But by now, the exit from the gorge and the road down to Dogna were under heavy Italian fire from machine guns and artillery. Moreover, the fierce fire from the far bank appeared to preclude any attack in company strength across the bare bed of the Piave, so Rommel decided to send out carefully selected squads from the 1st Company with orders to cross the river, block the main road, and send back a sufficient number of prisoners to act as a screen for the passage of all the Wurttembergers.

At first all these squads appear to have been held up by the heavy enemy fire except for an eighteen-man squad led by Acting Officer Huber and Sergeant Hohnecker. This group, spread out widely, descended to Dogna, and made their way across the river bed in the direction of Fae, south of the main enemy fire. Then after fording and swimming the Piave, these troops reached the far bank, and went on to achieve a considerable success, as we describe below.

Shortly after midday, Major Sproesser arrived on Hill 882 with his staff and the Signals Company of the WMB, and with the staff of the Ist Battalion Schützen (which had now come under his command), and set up his command post at a point he refers to as height 830.[37] Covered by the fire of a section of the 1st Machine-Gun Company of the 26 Schützen, the whole of the Rommel detachment was now able to descend cautiously to Dogna, arriving there by 14.00, but attempts to move across the river bed were frustrated by the intense enemy fire.

Meanwhile Huber's party, now on the west bank of the Piave, was making good progress. Huber's own account, quoted by Sproesser,[38] describes how the whole party, soaking wet after swimming the river, contrived to arrive unseen below a low stone wall bordering the edge of the main road. Then, at the appropriate moment, with the head of an approaching Italian column only a few yards away, they suddenly confronted the columnn with guns firing, and produced such confusion that the group halted and allowed themselves to be taken prisoner. Moreover, Huber's squad not only captured these prisoners, but kept secret how very small their own numbers were, and continued to capture subsequent groups still moving south down the road.

By 16.00 two groups of the 1st Company of the WMB, one under Huber and the other under 2nd Lieutenant Schöffel, had succeeded in completely blocking the main road, and by 18.00 the Wurttembergers had captured 50 officers and 780 men, the officers being separated from the men and guarded by two troopers on the top floor of Fae Castle. Finally, as darkness fell, the intensity of the Italian fire declined, so Rommel ordered his 3rd Company and half of his 1st MG Company, and the 3rd Company and the 1st MG Company of the 26 Schützen to follow him across the river in the direction of Fae, while at the same time Huber's prisoners were sent back to the east bank.[39]

On arriving at Fae, Rommel learnt of the successes obtained by Huber's squad, and was also informed that the scout squads had cut all the telephone lines from Longarone to Belluno. However, a hostile battery on Hill 1141 above and to the west of Fae must have observed what was happening, so it seemed probable that some force would be on its way to relieve the trapped Italians. Therefore Rommel's first decision was to deploy the 3rd Company of the Ist Battalion Schützen and half of the 1st MG Company WMB to block the road from Belluno in the neighbourhood of Fae, with outposts about half a mile further south.[40]

Having set up his rearguard, Rommel's next reaction was that he should advance to Longarone, but the enemy was there in great numbers, and Rommel's resources were rather limited. Apart from the rearguard at Fae, he had at his disposal on the west bank only the 1st and 3rd Companies and half the 1st MG Company of the WMB and the 1st MG Company of the 26 Schützen.[41] Meanwhile, on the far side of the Piave, the 1st and 2nd Companies of the Ist Battalion, 26 Schützen, were due to arrive at Major Sproesser's HQ on the east bank, together with the 377 Mountain Howitzer Detachment. (The other companies of the WMB, four rifle and two MG, were also on their way, but were not expected to reach Major Sproesser before midnight at the earliest.)

Many commanders would have thought it prudent to maintain blocking positions against enemy attacks during the night, from both the north and the south, and await the arrival of reinforcements, but Rommel thought otherwise. The enemy might attempt to break out during the night, and he decided to forestall any such move by an attack with his two WMB companies and the 1st Machine-Gun Company of the Schützen.[42]

At 21.00 when it was quite dark Rommel ordered the machine guns at Dogna to cease all firing across the river and led his detachment in extended line along the road towards the village of Longarone. He himself was with the leading squad, and they crossed the bridge over the Mae stream at Pirago almost unchallenged. Then only a hundred yards or so short of the first houses in Longarone they encountered a road block and Rommel gave orders for heavy machine guns to be set up to cover an attack. Almost immediately the detachment came under fire, both from their own machine guns in Dogna who had not received the orders to cease fire, and from the road block where several machine guns opened fire at 80 yards range. Rommel's machine guns were not yet assembled, and the squad lay for minutes in a very poor position. The barricade of the road block was too far away to throw grenades, and the Company Commander of the MG Company, 26 Schützen, lay severely wounded in a ditch.

The attack had failed completely, and could only be aborted. But the detachment was now widely extended, spread out along the road; the night was 'pitch black';[43] and Rommel himself was pinned down at the head of the column in a position 'where death stands right next to one'.[44] Somehow, he sent back a verbal order for the detachment to retire to the bridge at Pirago. The troops further from the road block managed to disengage, but Rommel's forward squad had to wait for any breaks in the firing and then dash back a few yards at a time. Eventually Rommel reached a bend in the road and was then able to hurry back to Pirago, overtaking some of his troops as he went. But on arriving at Pirago he found no one there.[45] Apparently his order had not been received. Nor did he know where his men were, though he suspected that some had yet to get back as far as Pirago.

After a time the enemy ceased firing and Rommel heard the sound of many Italians, shouting and yelling, approaching down the road from Longarone, and was uncertain whether they were going to attack or surrender. The night was still very dark, so he fired flares and saw a close-packed mass of Italians waving handkerchiefs with the head of the group only a hundred yards away. They did not fire and Rommel was uncertain of their intentions, but it was clear that the four or five riflemen with Rommel would not be able to stop that mass of men. So Rommel ran back towards Fae hoping to catch up with the other members of his detachment and organize a more effective resistance.[46]

A few minutes later Rommel had gathered about fifty men to bar the road about 600 yards south of Pirago, between a cliff on one side and a house on the other. Lieutenant Streicher occupied the house with half the men and the rest lined up across the road. When the mob was about 50 yards away Rommel shouted 'Halt' and demanded surrender. There came an answering roar of obscure significance but no one fired. Rommel repeated the call with the same result, and then when only 10 yards away the Italians opened fire. The WMB fired a salvo but had no machine guns available and were overwhelmed, 'killed, wounded, routed', before they were able to reload.[47] Many were captured, including 2nd Lieutenant Schöffel, but some of the garrison in the house escaped in the dark across the Piave as the Italians continued down the road to the south. 2nd Lieutenant Streicher avoided capture and tried to swim the Piave, but was swept down stream and washed ashore unconscious.[48]

Rommel managed to escape at the last moment by jumping over the wall by the side of the road. Then tearing across ploughed land, small brooks, hedges and fences, he made desperate speed to warn the 3rd Company Schützen and the WMB MG platoon at Fae, to turn around and face the impending danger. 'The thought of losing the final remnants of my troops gave me enormous strength.'[49] Rommel arrived at Fae before the Italians, and set up a new front with the 3rd Company Schützen holding a line of 700 yards across the road, from a sawmill on the Piave to the cliffs at the foot of Hill 1141.

Almost as soon as the Schützen were in position the Italians came down the road, and Rommel opened fire when they were about 200 yards away. They slowed down, their machine guns began to rattle, and masses of infantry yelling 'Avanti, Avanti' appeared to be attacking on either side of the road, but rapid fire from the Schützen and WMB troops caused them to stop and take cover. This was a very critical time for Rommel and his now very much reduced 1st and 3rd Companies. He states that his only officers were the CO of the 3rd Company Schützen and Acting Officer Huber. 'All the others appeared to have fallen into the hands of the enemy.'[50] Moreover, the fifty Italian officers still on an upper floor of Fae Castle were guarded by only two soldiers. As Rommel had no telephone communication with Sproesser, his orderly Private Unger offered to swim the river to summon reinforcements from the east bank.

The fighting continued for two or three hours, as the Italians made several attempts to break through the enemy line. Rommel sent out squads to start fires in houses and barns to light up the scene and avoid encirclement. New fires were started as old ones began to go out. Much ammunition was required for this type of fighting in the dark, and supplies would have been short but for the abundant supplies of weapons and ammunition which had been found in Fae Castle. Fortunately Rommel's skilful dispositions prevented the Italians from realizing how few his numbers were. Then about midnight the enemy fire slackened, and the Italians began to draw back from their positions. Rommel sent out patrols to maintain contact. One lost its able leader from close-range fire, but another returned at 01.00 with 600 prisoners who had surrendered, and it now seemed that most of the enemy had withdrawn to Longarone.

Reinforcements were now on their way. At 23.00 Captain Kremling, commanding the Ist Battalion 26 Schützen, received orders from Major Sproesser to cross the Piave with his 2nd Company and move against Belluno, while the Rommel detachment undertook the capture of Longarone.[51] On arriving at Fae, Kremling ordered his 2nd Company to join the 3rd Company of Schützen to strengthen the defence against attack from the south. Between 23.00 and 24.00, 2nd Lieutenant Payer arrived on Height 830 with the 2nd Company WMB after its traverse round Monte Lodina, and was ordered to follow Kremling's Battalion over the Piave, to join Rommel's attack on Longarone. Payer also brought the good news that the IInd and IIIrd Battalions of the 26 Schützen were now on their way to place themselves at Major Sproesser's disposal.

Meanwhile, those WMB troopers scattered by the fight at Pirago had been returning to the 1st and 3rd Companies; and the half of the 1st MG Company still on the east bank crossed over with an abundant supply of ammunition. In addition, the 1st Company Schützen arrived at Height 830, and was then sent across the river to join the 3rd Company blocking the main road to the south. About midnight 2nd Lieutenant Schiellein arrived with the 4th and 6th Rifle Companies and the MG Company which had taken the long route from Cimolais round Monte Cornetto, and they were held in reserve on the east side of the river.[52] The fifty captured Italian officers were transferred to the east bank making their way through the ice-cold Piave encouraged by their escort.

At 03.00, after fierce artillery preparation, Italian attempts to storm Rommel's positions led to hand-to-hand fighting, but Rommel was able to direct his forces to the most threatened positions, and maintain his front despite artillery fire from quite close range. The Italians suffered considerable losses, and after a quarter of an hour or so broke off the engagement, and withdrew towards Longarone. The WMB, wet and shivering, drank Chianti with the Schützen, and waited for the morning (10 November).

Also during the night, the ammunition for the Austrian 377 Mountain Howitzer Company of eight howitzers arrived at Height 830, and Sproesser inspected their fields of fire, and saw that they were well entrenched in positions dominating Longarone.[53] Between 04.00 and 05.00 the commanders of the IInd and IIIrd Battalions of the 26 Schützen arrived at Sproesser's command post, and II Battalion crossed the Piave at daybreak, while III Battalion remained at Dogna.[54] At 05.00 Sproesser ordered the IInd Battalion to strengthen the defences to the south, and ordered the Rommel detachment to advance towards Longarone, and take the road and railway bridge across the Mae stream before they were blown up by the Italians. In fact the bridges were destroyed as the Wurttembergers approached, but the stream was passed with no great difficulty.

The Italians at Longarone were now trapped, with units of the Austrian 94 Division coming up behind them, and their line of retreat blocked by the WMB and the 26 Schützen. Meanwhile, Sproesser had sent an Italian prisoner back to Longarone with a message in Italian saying that the village was surrounded by an Austro-German Division, and that all resistance was useless. Hence, as the Rommel detachment (now the 1st, 2nd and 3rd Companies and the 1st MG company) advanced beyond the bridges, they were met by Lieutenant Schöffel, captured during the night, with a message from the Italian Commander in Longarone. His troops were in no condition to continue fighting and he placed them at the disposal of Major Sproesser.[55] The Rommel detachment now advanced without opposition, and on entering Longarone were greeted by their comrades who had been captured during the night's fighting.

The village was crowded with thousands of Italians cut off from their line of retreat. (Some of these troops tried to escape by traversing the mountains to the west, but most were eventually captured.) The 4th Army had paid dearly for its delay in starting its withdrawal. About 10,000 men, 200 machine guns, 18 mountain guns, 600 pack animals and 250 loaded vehicles were captured at Longarone. Yet the losses in Rommel's detachment from Cimolais onwards were no more than 6 dead, 2 severely wounded, 19 slightly wounded and 1 missing.[56]

(A further casualty was Captain Gössler, the senior company commander in the WMB and an expert mountaineer, who died leading the detachment of the 6th Rifle Company and the 3rd Machine-Gun Company directly towards Dogna over the high pass of Forcella Liron (1398m, Map 14). High up near the pass the ground was icy, no one had crampons, and Gössler slipped to his death while prospecting a route over a steep grass slope. The route was obviously impractical. The detachment, profoundly shaken by the death of the much-respected Gössler, made their way to the Vajont road, and arrived at Longarone about midday on 10 November, bringing with them the body of their dead leader.[57])

8.5   The Victory at Longarone

The Austro-German success at Longarone was announced in the Austrian Bulletin of 10 November which claimed a total of 10,000 prisoners. This is obviously an approximate round number, but one which has been generally accepted (Krafft, Sproesser, Faldella, Rommel, Falls, Pieri) and never seriously challenged. In fact the Report of the Italian Commission of Enquiry in 1919 prints the Austrian Bulletin of the Day without comment,[58] and subsequently refers to 'about 10,000 captured near Longarone'.[59] Moreover, besides the capture of a large part of the Italian 1st Division, the road was now open for the XIVth Army to march down the Piave to Belluno and the Brenta.

Although the Austrian Bulletin appears to be correct in its claim for 10,000 prisoners, the same cannot be said of its account of how this number came to be captured. The taking of Longarone was the finale of an extensive joint operation which began with Krafft and von Below's decision that speed was essential for success, followed by their choice of the WMB to spearhead the attack of the 22(a) Division Schützen. The WMB lead by Sproesser and Rommel then proceeded to set the pace of the whole operation to reach Longarone. Finally, in the fighting of 9/10 November they were joined by battalions of the Austrian 26 Regiment Schützen. In addition the Austrian 94 Division had been following the retreating Italian 1st Division down the Piave valley bringing some pressure to bear. Yet, despite this extensive effort, the Austrian Bulletin credited the success to only the 94(a) Division,[60] which had been following the Italians and was able to take prisoners at Longarone only because the road out had already been blocked. (The Austrian Official History, written later, describes the part played by the Austrian 22 Division, but without any reference to the WMB.[61])

The capture of Longarone was a remarkable achievement for Rommel, all the more so coming only two weeks after the capture of 9,000 prisoners on the Kolovrat and Matajur. Of course, there is no suggestion that Rommel himself, alone, captured these thousands of prisoners. He was always part of the WMB, supported by his troops and by his superiors, and the WMB was itself part of a large operation involving many battalions. Even without Rommel, or even without the WMB, the Kolovrat and Matajur and their defenders would surely have been captured either by the Alpine Corps or the 12(g) Division within a few hours.

Likewise the capture of Longarone was part of a much larger operation, initiated by Krafft and von Below involving the whole of the WMB, particularly Major Sproesser and Acting Officer Huber, as well as the 22(a) Division Schützen. Yet the decisive factor was the determination and speed shown by the WMB. Its advance guard reached the foot of the Clautana Pass on the evening of 7 November, after a march of some 15 miles from Travesio, and a skirmish en route which took some 300 prisoners. Early the next morning the WMB set off to climb to the pass 900 metres above. Rommel's detachment weighed down with heavy loads, including the machine guns, spent the day high up on the mountain ridge, vainly seeking a route to encircle the Italian rearguard on and around the summit of the pass. As already described, they finally delivered an attack at midnight, were resolutely rebutted, and obliged to descend to Pecolat. The next morning the detachment again climbed the 900 metres to the now undefended pass, marched on to Claut and Cimolais, and by the evening had sent out scouts towards the San Osvaldo Pass. Then, on leaving Cimolais early next morning, they set out on what was to be thirty hours of unrelenting effort ending in the capture of Longarone. It is hard to believe that this speed would have been achieved without Rommel.

Major Sproesser also played an essential role in the capture of Longarone, just as his determination and seniority had authorized Rommel to lead his detachment along the Kolovrat to Matajur. As already described, Sproesser during the march to Longarone received at least four orders from his Brigade Commander, General von Merten, to halt his column and allow the Austrian 26 Schützen to take the lead. Each time he replied that his forward troops were in combat with the enemy, and it was not possible to withdraw them. Sproesser had doubtless been encouraged to take such a firm line by Major Willisen, Krafft's Chief of Operations, who had told him in conversation that nothing must prevent him from arriving at Longarone with all speed (Section 8.1). He certainly appears to have had the support of his Divisional Commander, General Müller, whose order of 8 November issued at 20.15 at Claut to XLIII Brigade stressed the importance of arriving at Longarone the next day,[62] while an order from 22(a) Division to the Edelweiss Division sought to expedite the supply of 270,000 rounds of ammunition for the WMB.[63] (We also note that when General Müller issued orders at Claut, he appears to have been much further forward than the Brigade Commander at Tronconere near Pecolat.[64])

Despite such encouragement, Sproesser was aware that military discipline could make any disregard of orders rather dangerous, especially if not accompanied by success. On crossing the bridge at Vajont he must have realized, perhaps for the first time, how critically his success had depended on the Italians failing to explode the charges already laid in the bridge. For if the bridge had been broken there was just no way the WMB could have arrived at Longarone in time to halt the Italian columns.[65] He later wrote of his disquiet on the night of 9 November after the arrival of a rumour from the far side of the Piave that Rommel and his whole detachment had been overrun by the enemy. 'Once again he [Sproesser] was submerged by the spectre of having to justify himself in not following Brigade orders.'[66] Although this false news was soon corrected, Sproesser was shortly after visited by the General Staff Officer of XLIII Brigade who 'talked about the court-martialling of officers who disobey their leaders, and who have then to surrender their swords'.[67]

Following the capture of Longarone the part played by the WMB was widely and speedily acknowledged. A message from General Krafft on 11 November read: 'The Battalion has achieved a brilliant performance of the first order, which as an old mountaineer I well appreciate.' This was followed by warm congratulations to the 22nd

Division from both Corps and the Edelweiss Division, and to Major Sproesser and the WMB from the Wurttemberg Ministry of War, and from King Wilhelm of Wurttemberg.[68]

The following month, on 13 December, the orders of the day for the Jäger Division announced that Rommel and Sproesser had each been awarded a '*Pour le Mérite*', and the next day the Commander of the Wurttemberg Mountain Battalion received a message of congratulation from the Kaiser. The award was announced to the WMB in Sproesser's orders for 13 December, which stated that:

> His Majesty the Kaiser thus wishes to give the highest recognition to the Wurttemberg Mountain Battalion for its support, achievement and success on the Isonzo, the Tagliamento and Piave. Comrades, the Imperial Kaiser's thanks apply to yourselves, the officers, under-officers and men, whose incomparable energy attained all that was humanly possible. It is an honour to belong to the Battalion. The highest honour is to be its Commander.[69]

The award of two *Pour le Mérite* in one battalion was most unusual, but Sproesser had played an essential role in the campaign. In particular his stand against Major Bothmer of the Bavarian Life Guards at Passo Zagradan, and against General Merten of the Austrian XLIII Brigade on the road to Longarone had been indispensable. Hence, the remark made to Sproesser by Captain Kremling commanding the Austrian Ist Battalion 26 Schützen at Longarone: 'I do not know which to admire most, Herr Major, your courage before the enemy or your courage against your superiors.' [70]

(It was unfortunate, but hardly surprising, that Major Sproesser continued to look back to the exploits of the WMB with a mixture of pride and umbrage. No doubt some contribution to his dissatisfaction arose from the traditional rivalry between the Kingdoms of Wurttemberg and Bavaria, and not least between the WMB and the Bavarian Life Guards which had served together in the Alpine Corps in Rumania in January 1917. Both units had been engaged in a successful operation to take Rumanian positions on and around the summit of Magura Odobesti (1001m), with the Life Guards immediately to the right of the WMB. Even so, Rommel's account of the success makes no mention of the Life Guards,[71] even though Sproesser later complained that the Life Guards claimed all the credit.[72]

Eventually Sproesser's irritation erupted in 1926 on the publication of the first volume of Krafft's official monograph *Der Durchbruch am Isonzo* which covered the capture of the Kolovrat and Matajur. It was unfortunate that this admirable account, which in general is careful to make reference to any officer worthy of special note, made no reference to Major Sproesser at all. This omission was soon followed by a very intemperate pamphlet by Sproesser claiming that the WMB had not been given sufficient credit for the capture of Na Gradu (1114m), a claim that is hard to follow. Its capture was an operation by the Alpine Corps in which several units were involved, and in which the Life Guards captured the summit, as is clearly set out by Krafft. Nevertheless the pamphlet declared that Krafft's volume was 'biassed, erroneous and injudicious' and after other remarks in a similar vein, concluded that 'it is expected that Volume II [of Krafft] and all further writings and publications of the Reichsarchiv must include a serious history of the war. We know that the Combatants demand this.'

Volume II of the *Durchbruch am Isonzo*, published later in 1926, contained eight pages of corrections to Volume I, nearly all of a quite minor nature including spelling mistakes. Two paragraphs relating to Sproesser's pamphlet stated that Krafft did not accept Sproesser's views, and that the issues would have to be decided by later historians, and a footnote rebuked Sproesser for his intemperate language. It would seem that Krafft's rejection of Sproesser's claim was not unreasonable, as Rommel's 1937 account provides no support at all.)

The Last Battles of the Offensive

9.1 Italian Reorganization

By about 12 November the Italian armies were established on their new line (Map 12) which ran from Asiago across the Brenta valley, over the massif of Monte Grappa, down to the right bank of the Piave at Pederobba, and then along the right bank of the river to the sea. The map also shows that the line of the Italian 1st Army had been drawn back from its previous positions on the east side of the Asiago plateau so as to maintain contact with the 4th Army on Grappa, and that the Austrians had still to reach this line. The Italian armies had now to prepare for the final stage of the Austro-German offensive, *La battaglia di arresto*.

The total Italian losses from the start of the battle to the retirement behind the Piave are given by the IOH as 10,000 dead, 30,000 wounded, and about 300,000 taken prisoner; together with 3,152 pieces of artillery, 1,732 mortars and 3,000 machine guns.[1] In addition some 300,000 *sbandati* (stragglers) were still to be reorganized into either their own or new units. The bulk of the losses had fallen primarily on the 2nd Army and the Carnia Group; of the 35 or so divisions in the 2nd Army and Carnia Group on 24 October only 3 were to be found in the front line on 12 November, the 8th and 44th Divisions of II Corps, now the right-hand Corps of the 4th Army, and the 48th Division, originally in VIII Corps, which now formed part of a reconstituted VIII Corps on the left of the 3rd Army line.[2]

The outlook for Italy would have been very bleak but for the fact that the length of the front line between Asiago and the sea, previously about 180 miles, was now only about 70 miles. Hence, despite his enormous losses Cadorna still had about enough troops to defend his new and shorter line, but there were virtually no efficient reserves in the rear should the enemy penetrate the new line. However, six French and five British divisions from France had been assigned to Italy, four French had already arrived and the rest were on their way.[3]

The Italians had now to deny the enemy any further progress, and reorganize the vast numbers of disordered 2nd Army troops. When

General Lord Cavan commanding the British forces arrived at Pavia on 5 November he observed many thousands of men marching westwards, on the whole of fine physique, who did not appear to be as demoralized as might have been expected.[4] On the other hand the war correspondent, Warner Allen, arrived at Mantua from Paris on 17 November and commented that Italian stragglers moving back made a poor impression, 'a disorderly rabble of tattered, panic-stricken soldiers'.[5] Lieutenant Colonel Barnett of the British 48th Division wrote of a column of infantry 'straggling along in a rough column; there was no march discipline; the men looked dispirited, apathetic, sullen, and, above all, dog tired. They seem to have hardly any arms and little food. Occasionally a group would fall out and cut up a dead ox by the side of the road, making a hasty meal of raw or half cooked flesh.'[6] Barnett also comments that officers were scarce and appeared no more confident than the men. Other reports refer to senior officers riding in victorias and phaetons and junior officers in pony carts, some playing cards.[7]

Reorganization began apace. By 10 November the remnants of the 2nd Army, 7,000 officers, 250,000 men and 20,000 animals had been reunited in vast camps well behind the front line.[8] Some units were ready to return to the front quite soon. The 66th Division was on Grappa by 22 November, the 7th Division at Asiago by 7 December, and the 50th and 59th on Grappa by 31 December.[9] Other units had become so dispersed that the troops were deployed to separate camps for infantry, artillery, engineers, and drivers, prior to constitution into new units

The disaster at Caporetto marked a turning point in Italy's war with Austria. The debatable aim of acquiring Trieste and the Trentino was now replaced by a much greater and clearer objective. All Friuli-Venezia Giulia, and part of the Veneto had been occupied, and the Austrians were now less than 20 miles from Venice. The enemy was already looking forward to the fruits of victory. At the beginning of November an article in the *Cologne Gazette* foretold retribution against Italy,[10] and an article in the *Vienna Reichpost* called for the dismemberment of Italy.[11] The Foreign Office in London was informed by their Netherlands Embassy of a press report in *Der Tag* of 27 November saying that early vegetables and fruit would be imported into Germany.[12]

The issues were now very stark. Was the invader to be allowed to remain? Was his advance to be halted? On these issues the country was united. The British Ambassador in Rome reported to London that 'deserters trying to make their way back to their homes were badly received, and the women of Calabria drove them with reproaches out of the villages'.[13] The Catholic Church had hitherto been somewhat equivocal in its attitude to the war against Catholic Austria (Section 2.1), but was now reported as continuing 'to do all in their power to rally the people in the face of the enemy' and that Cardinal Maffi had issued 'a noble appeal for union and sacrifice'.[14]

By 24 November the strength of the army in the war zone had grown by the arrival of 170,000 young troops of the class of 1899, by 50,000 troops recovered from illness and wounds, and by 80,000 men returning from leave, in addition to the numbers coming from the reorganization of the 300,000 *sbandati*.[15] The doubts of the previous summer had been largely set aside. For the first time the country was united in its efforts to resist and defeat the enemy. President Pertini, who had served in the 2nd Army during the retreat, was later to remark that the bond between Army and Country had never been so strong and complete as in the months at the end of 1917 and the beginning of 1918.[16]

During this time the great majority of the *sbandati* returned to their units or were regrouped in new units without much difficulty. Yet there remained some underlying air of disquiet. Warner Allen soon after his arrival at Mantua commented that 'the military authorities had been dealing severely with the officers and men responsible for the disaster, and in every town one might see lists of traitors or mutineers condemned to be shot in the back. There was fear in the Italian ranks.'[17] In fact the government and Comando Supremo remained concerned that perhaps several thousand *sbandati* and deserters might make trouble with their pacifist and anti-militarist views, aided perhaps by enemy propaganda (see for example Melograni[18]). However, no serious trouble arose although the authorities continued to keep watchful eyes on the situation.

9.2   The New Italian Commando Supremo

As described elsewhere, the Allied Prime Ministers, Orlando, Painlevé and Lloyd George, met on 5 November at Rapallo to coordinate their military effort, and on 7 November were informed by the King of Italy that it had been decided to relieve General Cadorna of his command and replace him with General Diaz.[19]

The choice of a new Comando Supremo had not been immediately obvious. Until Caporetto, General Capello had strong claims, particularly in view of his successes during the 11th Battle of the Isonzo on the Bainsizza. However, the collapse of his 2nd Army, together with his own collapse into sickness, put him out of consideration. Many regarded the Duke of Aosta as an obvious successor. He had commanded the 3rd Army for two and a half years; it had suffered no disasters; and had retreated in good order. Aosta was respected. His

191

orders were strikingly clear and to the point. But he was a cousin of the King, and the King is said to have vetoed him, perhaps to avoid a close connection between the throne and any future military defeat.[20]

General Alfieri, the Minister of War, appears to have played a large part in the decision to appoint General Diaz as the new Comando Supremo. Colonel Gatti records part of a conversation on 6 November when Alfieri talked with him and mentioned the name of Diaz. Gatti: 'But nobody knows him.' Alfieri: 'He has been a good corps commander . . . has also been fortunate, is intelligent, and adaptable. In these times, when we have to deal with our allies, he could do well.' Gatti: 'For God's sake, as things are, don't make changes.'[21]

Yet Diaz had fought with distinction in Libya, and had subsequently served on the staff of General Cadorna. He had been a successful divisional commander and then a corps commander on the Carso. In June 1917, during discussions prior to the appointment of General Giardino as Minister of War, Diaz had been mentioned as a possible candidate.[22] Hence his appointment as Comando Supremo was not as surprising as Gatti's remarks suggest.

According to General Caviglia, Cadorna had appeared to his contemporaries as 'a figure hewn by destiny in granite'.[23] He was also a Piedmontese aristocrat, Count General Cadorna, and by all accounts with an overbearing personality, with little idea of the life and character of his troops. On the other hand Diaz came from a Neapolitan bourgeois background and was 'more human, in closer touch with his subordinates from the sub-chiefs of the General Staff to the last private'.[24]

Diaz took up his duties on 9 November, and very soon gained some insight into the workings of the Comando Supremo. One of his first actions, presumably after consulting his staff, was to send phonogram N.5468 to the 1st and 4th Armies, suggesting that they should continue to hold a line running from Monte Caldiera near Monte Ortigara (Map 12) eastward to the high ground on the other side of Val Brenta. The Headquarters of the 1st Army replied that this was not possible as a previous order to withdraw had already been carried out.[25]

As early as 27 June 1917 Gatti had confided to his diary that the Comando Supremo hardly existed. 'There is a *Capo*, Cadorna: there is a *Sotto-Capo*, General Porro; there is a secretary, General Bencivenga: and we speak the truth, there is a *Capo*, Cadorna, and a secretary, Bencivenga . . . How is it possible for two people to cope with all the enormous work? If Cadorna had the mind of Napoleon it would not be possible.'[26]

In addition, General Caviglia has described the lack of trust between the Comando Supremo and the troops arising because of 'operational orders which produced grave losses without tangible results'. He also commented that 'almost all the staff officers had never commanded units on the Carso or the Isonzo and had no first hand experience of the war', and when their orders did not produce success they blamed the failings on the troops.[27] However, the government had already taken measures to strengthen the staff of the Comando Supremo. General Porro, the deputy chief of staff, had made an extremely bad impression at the Rapallo Conference,[28] and was subsequently replaced by two deputy chiefs of staff, General Badoglio and General Giardino, a former Minister of War.

The arrival of the new team of Diaz, Badoglio and Giardino soon produced a considerable effect. As already mentioned, Colonel Gatti had been much concerned at the dismissal of Cadorna, so the entry in his diary on 20 November is of particular interest. 'Our chiefs are doing well . . . Things are now much changed. There is something freer in the working of the command. The work done by General Giardino is enormous. Badoglio is reorganizing and visiting the troops. General Diaz takes decisions tranquilly and unperturbed. Calm and confidence has returned.'[29]

Diaz soon turned his attention to various aspects of the problems of command. As in all the warring armies, the enormous expansion of the Italian Army had produced difficulties due to a lack of suitable officers to command the hundreds of thousands called up for service. On 27 June 1917, Gatti had written in his diary that some corps commanders had only been lieutenant colonels at the start of the war, and still had the minds of lieutenant colonels.[30] Inevitably, as in other armies, senior Italian officers from lieutenant colonels to generals including four army commanders had been judged inadequate and removed from their commands.

Cadorna was clearly not a man to shrink from dismissing unsuitable officers, and because of lack of time and understanding, many of those dismissed were judged very harshly and went away bitter against Cadorna. Indeed the number of dismissals was sufficient to create a feeling of 'What I do does not matter much. It's always wrong. We are fired whatever we do.' As one general later told the Commission of Enquiry, 'It was a well known principle. Enemy trenches not taken or trenches lost, dismiss a commander of a brigade or a division.'[31]

Diaz adopted a very different approach. In a memorandum written twelve days after his appointment he said 'severe measures should not be too hastily taken against a man who goes wrong either through inexperience or because an initially sound idea does not meet with success, or for some other reason which well disposed examination may show not to be too culpable'.[32] He also remarked that 'frequently the substituted man is worth no more than the man who has been dismissed', and stressed that he would only support dismissals after other means of correction had failed. Then in January 1918 he established a commission to review previous dismissals. In 206 cases involving brigadiers, major generals and lieutenant generals the commission exonerated 95, and in 669 cases involving all ranks down to lieutenant colonel, 262 were exonerated.[33] (This change of emphasis was certainly timely. Cadorna had long sought to impose a system of iron discipline and had laid the blame for Caporetto on the troops not doing their duty. However, he himself had failed to ensure that his own orders were obeyed by his own Army Commanders, particularly by General Brusati in 1916,[34] and by General Capello and General Di Robilant in 1917.)

The new Comando Supremo gave high priority to the welfare of the troops. During the war difficulties on the farms and in the importation of food had led to a noticeable reduction in the soldiers' rations. However, a decree of 18 December stated that the level of rations was to be restored to rather more than the level at the start of the war, and that stores were to be set up near the front where the troops could buy food, drinks, and other necessities. Then in 1918 the fifteen days of annual winter leave was augmented by an additional leave of ten days.[35]

Diaz was particularly concerned that some commands apparently regarded their best troops as so valuable that they spent the longest times in the front line, and were less likely to be granted leave. He therefore laid down that all troops were to take their turn regularly and equally in the front line, except in quite exceptional circumstances, and that 'the tendency to leave in the line certain units such as batteries, machine gun companies, and technical detachments, on the specious pretext that they are indispensable, must be eliminated'.[36]

As described above, brigades and battalions had been passed feverously from one division to another to meet crises before and during the battle of Caporetto. These moves had generally proved fruitless and Diaz now stressed the importance of the division as the basic tactical unit; that to be successful its components must be trained to work and cooperate with each other; and that reliefs should be organized by withdrawing complete divisions. In a memorandum at the end of December, regarding the changes now required, he wrote that 'To avoid them may appear to be the easier course, but it is nevertheless a dereliction of duty, and defeats our one and only object – the maintenance, at any cost, of the material and morale of the Army in its entirety'.[37]

9.3 The Fighting in November

At the beginning of November the Austrian High Command had decided that the time had come for a final effort on the whole front of Eugene's Armies, and at Asiago by Conrad's Group (Section 7.4). We now outline the form of their attacks and the outcome in each of the three main sectors, beginning with the assaults across the Piave.

(a) Piave

After emerging from the mountains below Pederobba, at the foot of Monte Tomba (Map 12), the Piave enters the Venetian plain, and the waters of the river flow in several channels along a wide bed of stony gravel, which between Pederobba and Vidor is in places over a thousand yards wide. At Vidor the river narrows as it cuts through low foothills on either side, but soon spreads out again on its gravel bed. Two miles below Vidor, the right bank of the river comes hard against the side of a prominent and isolated hill known as the Montello (458m), which forces the Piave to flow in an easterly direction until Nervesa, where it emerges into an almost totally flat plain.

All the way for the 30 miles or so between Pederobba and Ponte di Priula the river meanders in several relatively narrow channels in its shingle bed, which varies in width from 1,000 to as much as 4,000 yards. Rough tracks down to the shingle bed are used by lorries carting away stones and gravel, and much of the bed is covered by low scrub. Seen from the hills on the edge of the plain the Piave, like the Tagliamento, presents a most characteristic sight quite unlike any British river.

The Piave, again like the Tagliamento, has a very large catchment area in a mountainous region subject to heavy storms of rain coming in from the Adriatic, and responds very rapidly to these storms and its waters may then spread right across the whole width of the shingle bed. Therefore, below Pederobba the river is enclosed by massive dykes up to ten metres high to contain the flood waters. In dry seasons these embankments may appear remote from the river, but at any time give very good fire and defensive positions, particularly for machine-gun posts near the crest and in tunnels cut in the outer base. On either side of the river, the ground is traversed by minor streams and canals, often with their own containing dykes, which made any enemy advance very difficult, particularly as matters were so arranged that it was possible to flood certain areas without flooding adjacent areas.

Other features of the plain were not so favourable to the Italians. The land was heavily cultivated with crops of high corn and numerous orchards. The roads were hidden by the bushes and trees at their side,

195

and the fields were divided by high hedges and rows of trees; so it was difficult for the defenders to obtain adequate views and adequate fields of fire. Also, there was always the possibility that an enemy rushing from hedge to hedge might infiltrate defensive positions. Hence, it was necessary for the field artillery to be kept well forward in order to distinguish friend from foe, but it then became liable to capture.

The first attempt to cross the Piave appears to have been made by the Stein Corps on 10 November when the 12(g) Division arrived at the still undamaged bridge at Vidor. However, attempts to cross were foiled by machine-gun fire from the far bank, and the Italians were able to blow the bridge during the night.[38] A further attempt to cross the river the next day, involving all the Corps artillery, was foiled in its preliminary stages by fierce Italian fire.[39] On 14 and 15 November other units of the Division attempted to cross near San Vito west of Valdobbiadena, but failed as their available artillery was insufficient to silence the Italian machine guns. Meanwhile the 13(a) (reserve) Division of the Corps had tried to cross near Mino south of Valdobbiadena, but lacking adequate artillery support was also unsuccessful.[40]

Lower down the Piave (Map 16) the IInd and Ist Austrian Isonzo Armies launched attacks against the 3rd Italian Army. On 13 November the Austrians captured the island of Papadapoli in the middle of the widest part of the Piave, but failed to reach the far bank.[41] Further attempts on 16 November to reach the right bank at and below Saletto also failed, leaving behind 300 prisoners.[42] Further downstream on the same day, a dawn attack near Fagare crossed the river by wading and in barges, and surrounded an Italian garrison of 400 men and two field batteries. However, three hard counter-attacks forced the Austrians to retreat back across the river, leaving behind the captured prisoners and guns.[43]

Below Ponte di Piave, the Piave no longer wanders over a wide stony bed but flows in one channel perhaps one or two hundred yards wide. An Austrian attack at dawn on 12 November gained a foothold across the river near Zenson, which they were able to hold against Italian counter-attacks including a particularly strong one on 20 November beaten back by machine-gun and artillery fire.[44]

Finally, for the last ten miles or so below San Dona di Piave the river passes through the area of its delta, where the very flat ground on either side is intersected by the cuts and channels of drainage and river control systems which form serious obstacles to large-scale troop movements. After the retreat, the Italians below San Dona had taken up positions behind the main channel of the Piave leading directly to the sea near Cortellazzo. Hence, any movement here was unlikely, and the ten miles of front from San Dona to the sea were held by only one

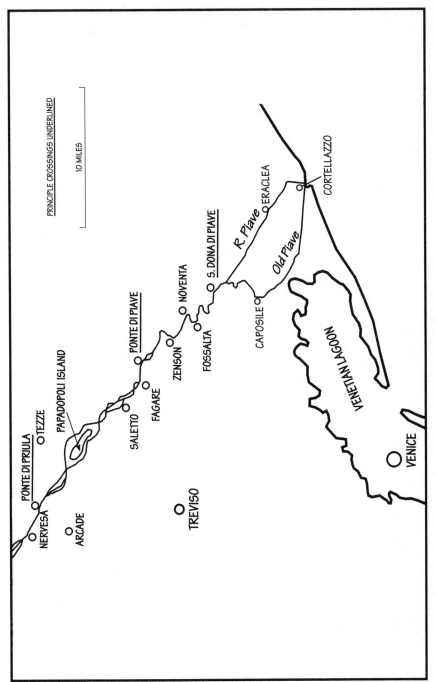

PRINCIPLE CROSSINGS UNDERLINED

10 MILES

PONTE DI PRIULA
OTEZZE
NERVESA
ARCADE
PAPADOPOLI ISLAND
SALETTO
FAGARE
PONTE DI PIAVE
TREVISO
ZENSON
NOVENTA
FOSSALTA
S. DONA DI PIAVE
CAPOSILE
R Piave
Old Piave
ERACLEA
CORTELLAZZO
VENETIAN LAGOON
VENICE

16. The Lower Piave.

division on each side.[45] Yet on 13 November the Austrians launched local attacks at Grisolera (now Eraclea) and reached the course of the old Piave (the Piave Vecchia now draining the Sile river and other streams). Consequently the Italians were forced to take up new positions behind the Piave Vecchia (while retaining bridgeheads near Caposile and Cortellazzo).[46] The Austrians were now at the very edge of the Venetian lagoon, but their way ahead led immediately into the waters, islands and marshes of the lagoon, all organized as the Piazza Marittima di Venezia, a powerful marine fortress with guns of all calibres, on mobile barges and on shore, together with defence lines, trenches and barricades.[47]

(b) Asiago

The small town of Asiago (Maps 1 and 12) stands near the centre of a plateau which extends from east to west for about six miles, and from north to south for about about three miles, at an altitude of about 1000 metres. The plateau is fairly level or gently undulating, and cultivated and interspersed with several small villages. To the north and south the ground rises and is rough and rocky underfoot and given over to forestry.

The plateau is bounded to the west and to the east by the deeply cut valleys of Val d'Astico and Val Brenta, the ground falling steeply to both these valleys. From the northern edge of the plateau wooded hills rise steadily first to altitudes of up to 1500 metres about three miles from the town, and then after a further six miles of mainly wooded terrain to a line of bare summits overlooking Val Sugana, the upper part of Val Brenta. Here the relatively accessible mountain ground extending back towards Asiago ends abruptly above the northern cliffs of Ortigara (2106m) and its neighbours, which plunge steeply down into Val Sugana some 1700 metres below.

South of the town of Asiago, the ground is fairly level for a mile or so, and then rises over rough terrain mainly covered with pine woods to summits at altitudes of up to 1500 metres, standing four or five miles south of the town and about 500 metres above the plateau. To the south of these summits, the ground falls steeply to the plain but in no way as precipitously as the drop from Ortigara to Val Sugana. One must also remember that before the war the whole region was much more isolated than today, many of the present roads being litle more than mule tracks.

The withdrawal of the 4th Army necessitated a considerable withdrawal of the right flank of the 1st Army on the Asiago plateau in order to maintain contact with the 4th Army at the west end of the Grappa massif. At the start of the battle the front line (Map 17) ran roughly north from near the town of Asiago towards Val Sugana over the Ortigara massif where much blood had been shed in the Italian offensive of June 1917. All this ground was abandoned as the Italians retreated, not much troubled by the Austrians, to a line running from near Asiago town across the summit of Monte Melette (1676m) to the south side of Val Gadena. The line then ran down this deeply incised valley to cross the Brenta river near Rivalta and join up with the 4th Army line on Col Moschin in the Monte Grappa massif (Map 17).

The Commander of the Italian XXII Corps believed that these new positions could be held, but General Giraldi Pecori in command of the Italian 1st Army was not so sure, and on 8 November asked the Comando Supremo for reinforcements of men and guns.[48] Diaz's reply the next day stated that four brigades would be sent, and that they would be of young men of the Class of 1899 who should be given good food and lodgings, and their health looked after. No extra guns were available.[49] The following day the Austrians began a series of attacks on the new Italian positions which led to fighting on a considerable scale for the next two months.

On 10 November the Austrians began an offensive all along the Asiago front, with the initial aim of wiping out the Italian salient jutting out to Monte Melette. Four Austrian divisions were engaged. Facing them, reading from left to right were the Italian XXVI and XXII Corps each of two divisions, and part of XX Corps (the 29th Division and part of the 52nd). In the first stage of the battle between 10 and 14 November the Austrians took Gallio and the ruins of Asiago, and the Italians were forced back to a line running through Monte Sisemol and Monte Zomo. Then, after a pause, the Austrians launched a substantial attack on Monte Melette on 22 November which was repulsed with such heavy losses that the offensive was temporarily suspended.[50]

(c) Grappa

On 12 November, the Command of the XIVth Army ordered the Krauss Corps to advance south from the line Feltre – Fonzaso, and occupy the whole of the Grappa massif (Map 12),[51] and on 13 November units of the Corps were moving from Belluno towards the town of Feltre which stands at the north-east corner of the Grappa massif. The 22(a) and 55(a) Divisions arrived during the morning, and found the town already evacuated by the Italians. Krauss, also in Feltre, had little information on the state of the enemy's defences on Grappa, but apparently believed that the line of the main summits, Col Moschin – Asolone – Pertica – Grappa – Pallon – Monte Tomba (Map 13), could soon be occupied by advancing up the long spurs and valleys which run down northwards from the main tops. However,

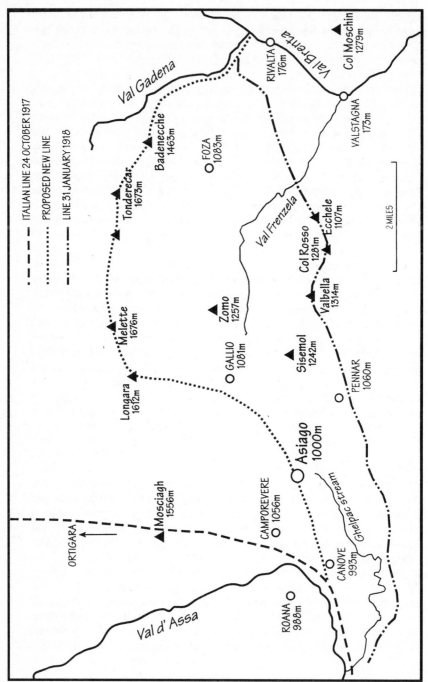

ITALIAN LINE 24 OCTOBER 1917
PROPOSED NEW LINE
LINE 31 JANUARY 1918

Val Gadena

Val Brenta

RIVALTA
176m

Col Moschin
1279m

VALSTAGNA
173m

Badenecche
1463m

FOZA
1083m

Tonderecar
1675m

Val Frenzela

Ecchele
1107m

Col Rosso
1281m

2 MILES

Melette
1676m

Zomo
1257m

Valbella
1314m

GALLIO
1081m

Sisemol
1242m

Longara
1612m

PENNAR
1060m

Asiago
1000m

Mosciagh
1556m

CAMPOREVERE
1056m

Ghelpac stream

ORTIGARA

CANOVE
993m

Val d' Assa

ROANA
988m

17. Asiago.

reconnaissances on 13 November showed that the Italians were working feverishly on the existing fortications on Monte Grappa and the surrounding summits, and had already occupied Monte Tomatico and Monte Roncone at the north end of the massif overlooking the Feltre–Fonzaso road.[52]

Krauss was already concerned both by delays in his supply of food and ammunition, and the fact that his artillery was still some way behind the main body of his divisions. He now appears to have concluded that the occupation of the whole of the Grappa massif would be difficult, and gave orders for the advance to proceed principally by the valleys of the Piave and the Brenta (Maps 11 and 13), which he viewed as easier alternatives. The Corps was therefore divided into two groups. One under General Schwarzenberg, the commander of the 55(a) Division, would consist of the 55(a) Division and the Jäger(g) Division; the other under General von Wieden, the commander of the Edelweiss division, would consist of the Edelweiss Division and the XLIII Brigade of the 22(a) Division.

The main body of the Schwarzenberg group was to force its way down the valley of the Piave to Pederobba, supported by the artillery of the Stein Corps on the left bank of the river. At the same time other units of the group would make for Monte Tomba, Monte Pallon and the summit of Grappa. The main body of the Wieden group was to move down Val Cismon and Val Brenta to take Bassano del Grappa, while a secondary force would go from the village of Cismon to take Monte Asolone. The IIC Brigade of the 22 Division would be held near Feltre as the reserve.[53]

General Wieden and General Müller (22 Division) had serious doubts about the proposed operations. The Brenta and Piave valleys are narrow, steep sided and dominated by the mountains on either side, and both the Edelweiss and the 22 Divisions had outrun their artillery support. Therefore, both Wieden and Müller believed that the principal effort should be a direct assault on Monte Grappa along the ridges sloping up to the summits. General Müller agreed to present these views to General Krauss, but a meeting could not be arranged until the following day.[54] The next morning, 14 November, General Müller sought to persuade General Krauss to amend his orders, but Krauss disagreed, and confirmed that his plan was to continue the operation on 15 November.[55]

Meanwhile, on 14 November, Schwarzenberg's 55 Division led the march down the Piave, and the lead battalion was halted by serious opposition near the village of San Maria where it came under almost continuous fire (Map 13).[56] However, during the day the Austrians captured some of the Italian positions high up on the west bank, on the ridge north of Monte Tese.[57] The Wieden group had orders to move down Val Cismon, but Wieden decided that before doing so it was essential to take Monte Tomatico and Monte Roncone which overlooked his route along the road from Feltre to Cismon. An attack on Roncone by the 3rd Regiment of XLIII Brigade was strongly resisted and the Italians remained in possession despite heavy losses. However, after some very hard fighting, two battalions of the 26th Regiment of the Brigade captured Monte Peurna, but the Italians remained in possession of Roncone and Tomatico.[58]

The following day, 15 November, the XLIII Brigade of 22 Division captured Roncone. The CCXVII Brigade of the Edelweiss Division descended Val Cismon to Val Brenta, and occupied the village of Cismon. But on continuing down the very narrow and enclosed valley of the Brenta it was halted by artillery fire, directed from the village of San Marino, three miles below Cismon, and from higher ground on the east bank of the river.[59] Meanwhile, on the Piave, the 55 Division was still held up near San Maria. During the day, the summit of Monte Cornella, further south and overlooking Quero, was captured but was then lost to an Italian counter-attack.[60]

It was now clear that the Italian forces were fighting with a tenacity, not often shown on the Isonzo. Hence, by 15 November Krauss was becoming increasingly concerned at the slow progress down the Piave, and realized that to secure this route it was necessary to gain control of the Grappa massif immediately to the west of the Piave, particularly Monte Tomba and Monferena. He therefore gave orders for a concentrated effort the next day by General Schwarzenberg to force a way down the Piave as far as Quero, supported by the guns of the Scotti and Stein Corps on the left bank of the river. The Jäger(g) Division would then take over the main thrust of the attack on Monte Tomba.[61]

The morning of 16 November was spent preparing the necessary dispositions of the artillery, and when General Krauss arrived in the afternoon he was surprised to find that the attack he had ordered had not yet started. General Schwarzenberg explained that he was still held up by fire coming down from above and along the road. However, following Krauss's visit, Monte Cornello was taken at midnight by the 2nd Bosnian Regiment (Colonel Mihailic) of the 55 Division,[62] and the village of Quero was occupied somewhat later by the Jäger Division which had come up from Feltre. Meanwhile the Wieden group had a largely unsuccessful day apart from the capture of Prassolan on the ridge from Roncone to Pertica.[63]

On the morning of 17 November Krauss considered the reports on the events of the previous day and decided to launch a new comprehensive attack on 18 November. The main thrust by the Jäger Division and XXVI Brigade of 55 Division would aim to establish positions on a line running from Monte Tomba and Monfenera to the Piave at Fener, two miles above Pederobba, where a footbridge would be built as a link with the Scotti Corps across the river. At the same time, the Wurttemberg Mountain Battalion would attack Spinoncia and Fontanasecca (Map 13), where enemy batteries were firing on Quero and the Alano basin. Also at the same time, the XLIII Brigade in the Wieden group would launch an attack on Monte Pertica. Five and a half battalions of the Scotti Corps on the left bank of the Piave between San Maria and Pederobba would be ready to cross the Piave as soon as the footbridge became available.[64]

Krauss's attack began at 05.30 on 18 November, and fighting continued all day against sustained and effective resistance. By nightfall on 18 November it was clear that the attacks on Monte Tomba, Monfenera, Fontanasecca, Spinoncia and Pertica had all failed with heavy casualties. None of Scotti's units had been able to cross the Piave. Von Below noted in his diary that 'the enemy is defending himself with extreme determination despite the excellent action of our artillery'.[65] The whole offensive was now at a halt, and Krafft makes various suggestions to explain the lack of success: there was no surprise, the enemy knew they were coming; the Austrians had difficulty in bringing forward their artillery, as well as food, water and ammunition; the Italians were deploying their best troops; the Italians were encouraged by the presence of the French and British in Italy, and were now confident that they could hold the line of the Piave and Grappa.[66] Another factor may have been General Foch's advice that both Monte Tomatico and Monte Roncone be defended, for the holding actions here gave a valuable two or three days to the 4th Army troops preparing positions further back in the massif.[67]

(Italian accounts often give detailed descriptions and photographs of well-constructed tunnels and gun positions on Monte Grappa as well as trenches and barracks, but one should note that these developments came only in 1918. The arrangements in place in 1917, though vital, were quite limited. They were essentially the new road from near Bassano to the summit of the massif, a wide mule track and two cable ways, water reservoirs on the dry uplands, a large strong point on the summit, and positions for over sixty batteries of artillery. Moreover, as already mentioned, these works had been designed to counter any further attack similar to the 1916 Strafexpedition coming from the north-west, rather than from the north-east as now.)

Both Krafft and von Below believed that the failure to achieve better progress on Grappa would have been avoided if the force of the attack had not been dissipated by concentrating on the Brenta and Piave valleys, particularly as both these valleys were overlooked by mountains which gave excellent positions for the Italian artillery. Therefore on 18 November von Below ordered a regrouping of the forces on

Grappa as a preliminary to launching a new attack to gain possession of the whole of the massif. The Krauss Corps now comprising the Edelweiss, 55(a), 22(a), and the 94(a) Division transferred from the Xth Army, would concentrate solely on the mountain sector and work with two combat groups. The first under General Wieden comprised CCXVI Brigade (Edelweiss Division), the 3rd Regiment Schützen (22 Division) and XXV Brigade (94 Division), and would operate between the Brenta and Col dell'Orso. The second under General Müller comprising IIC Brigade, the 26 Regiment Schützen and the WMB (now apparently transferred to 22 Division) had the task of occupying Fontanasecca, Spinoncia, Pallon and the ridge to Monte Tomba. The remainder of the front from the summit of Tomba to the Piave was taken over by the Scotti Corps, now comprising the Jäger Division and the Alpine Corps brought up from the reserve.[68]

On 20 and 21 November the Krauss and Scotti Corps were mainly engaged in carrying out the regroupings ordered by von Below, but a joint operation beginning on the night of 20 November by the IIC Brigade of the 22(a) Division and the WMB took Fontanasecca.[69] Then from 22 November onwards Krauss and Scotti launched attacks all along the Grappa front, against Col della Berretta, Pertica, Col dell'Orso, Spinoncia and Tomba, and for the next four or five days some of the best troops in the Austrian and German armies attempted to advance up the steep slopes and high spurs to the summit ridge.

The fighting extended over the whole width of the massif. The summit of Pertica changed hands several times, but the Austrians were unable to hold their positions there because of Italian artillery fire from Monte Grappa.[70] Hence when the fighting ended on 25 November the summit was left unoccupied, with the Austrians and Italians lower down on either side of the hill.[71] Repeated Austrian attempts to take Col della Berretta all failed, notably on 26 November when units of the Edelweiss Division took possession of the summit only to be decisively thrown off by an Italian counter-attack.[72]

At the end of 26 November the XIVth Army had little to show for its latest effort. The Italians had maintained their positions on Col della Berretta, Pertica, Coll dell'Orso and Spinoncia. The only significant Austrian gain had been the capture of a length of the summit ridge of Monte Tomba, but the new positions and their supply line were subject to fire from heavy guns on Monte Pallon, and the Italians were still holding a line on the south slope somewhat below the ridge.

9.4   The Decision to Suspend the Offensive

Eugene's order of 4 November (Section 7.4) had set out new objectives for the XIVth Army and the adjacent Austrian armies on either side, namely to brush aside Italian attempts to stand on their new line and to advance at least to the line of the Brenta river. However, it became clear in the second half of November that the Italians were well established in their positions, and the Austrian and German armies were faced by an effective and determined resistance.

Throughout November several factors had weighed on the command of the XIVth Army. The Army's supply lines had been greatly extended and much effort was needed to maintain roads and bridges, and to avoid delay in bringing up supplies and ammunition.[73] The troops had been marching and fighting almost continuously since before 24 October and were becoming tired. The onset of winter would soon make conditions impossibly severe on the high ground at Asiago and on Grappa. In addition both von Below's diary and Krafft's account show a growing preoccupation with the presence of French and British troops in Italy. On 11 November von Below noted that the far bank of the Piave was now strongly defended and was supported by good French artillery.[74] On 15 November it was thought that the Allied presence would amount to three British and twelve or fifteen French divisions, constituted from some of the best assault troops in both armies. On 18 November artillery fire falling on a XIVth Army attack on Monte Tomba was apparently sufficiently troublesome that it was thought (incorrectly) to be either French or British.[75]

On 21 November von Below wrote in his diary that the XIVth Army offensive had come to a dead end, for any further advances would be slow with heavy losses. He complains that the Austrians had not known of the Italian defence preparations on Grappa, and fears that left to themselves the Austrians would 'melt as summer snow' before an Allied attack. Moreover, any 'opinion that another blow would lead to the collapse of Italy cannot be entertained, as the Allied forces can arrive here as they were not able to do in Serbia, Rumania and Russia'. However, it still remained necessary to stabilize the present positions by obtaining complete control of the Grappa massif.[76]

On 22 November the Austrian losses in the offensive at Asiago were so heavy that the Emperor Karl ordered a temporary suspension of the offensive to avoid further loss of life. On 23 November Karl visited General Krauss who appeared doubtful of obtaining any success on Grappa.[77] Karl then visited von Below on 24 November and sought to persuade him to end all the fighting immediately, including that on Grappa, but without success.[78] In fact, on 26 November von Below received a memorandum from the German High Command stressing the increasing risks arising from any further delays in the operations.[79]

Von Below himself was now increasingly concerned by the slow rate of progress being achieved by the XIVth Army, particularly by the failure of the Edelweiss Division to take Col della Berretta on 26

November, and also by the lack of action by Conrad's Group. His diary records his view that it was now necessary to finish with 'partial' offensives and replace them by a full-scale general action.[80] Hence on 26 November he sent Captain Fehr, a staff officer, to travel to Munich in order to talk with the Bavarian Minister of War.

Krafft and von Below were increasingly disenchanted with the performance of their Austrian allies, both in the Krauss Group and in the Austrian Armies on either side of the XIVth Army. On 27 November von Below's diary recorded his increasing concern over the slow build-up of ammunition supplies, due he suspected to their being diverted to Conrad's forces at Asiago.[81] The 195th German Division had been made available to Conrad at his request, but had then not been required, and on its way back to Germany had been blocked in a confusion of traffic in Val Brenta.[82] On 28 November von Below commented adversely on Krauss's control of his artillery, after it was reported that a group of seven Austrian howitzers was under the control of only one officer, and another group of five batteries under only a cadet officer. Nor was there any observation post on Fontanasecca, which offered excellent long-distance views.[83]

By 28 November Conrad's offensive in the Trentino appeared to have worn itself out, and von Below was informed by the German High Command that sixteen Franco-British divisions had arrived in Italy.[84] Hence he was now forced to conclude that the situation had changed to his disadvantage, and on 29 November suggested to the Archduke Eugene that the XIVth Army offensive be temporarily halted.[85]

Following Captain Fehr's visit to Munich, the German High Command sent a telegram on 29 November to the Austrian High Command, expressing views similar to von Below's. In their reply the next day the Austrians suggested that the XIVth Army front between the Piave and the Brenta be pushed forward to a line running from the Montello to Bassano. As this line lay totally in the plain at the foot of the Grappa massif, von Below 'declined with many thanks'.[86]

Finally, on the evening of 2 December von Below received orders from Eugene that the offensive be suspended.[87] However it was also ordered, at the insistence of the XIVth Army, that it remained necessary to improve their positions in the mountains, and to give the impression that the offensive was still continuing.[88] Hence the final run down of the offensive was accompanied by some considerable activity during the second half of December, both on the Asiago plateau and on Grappa, as described below.

Meanwhile the Germans prepared to leave. On 3 December orders were received that the 5th and 12th Divisions were to be withdrawn from Italy, and also the 26th Division after the completion of the operations on Grappa.[89] On 4 December von Below's diary records more complaints about the lack of Austrian traffic discipline 'not the result of ill will but of inability'.[90] Two days later the diary refers to 'a new spanner in the works' due to Conrad commandeering Krauss' food and ammunition supplies. This, notes von Below, was not an accident but a question of trust.[91] Finally on 14 December the German High Command decided that all their forces would be withdrawn from Italy.[92]

9.5 The Fighting in December

(a) Piave and Asiago

At the beginning of December, French and British forces were arriving in Italy in substantial numbers. By 4 December two French and two British divisions had relieved Italian divisions on the Piave between Pederobba and Nervesa, the French occupying positions from Monte Tomba to Pederobba and Crocetta (Map 12), and the British from Crocetta to the hill of the Montello and Nervesa. In addition, four more French and two British divisions were already in Italy, deployed on the plain as reserve forces behind the front line between Asiago and Nervesa, and were engaged in preparing a rear defence line in this region. A further British division was due to arrive on 17 December.[93] Hence, any attempt by the XIVth Army to cross the Piave would be immediately opposed by fresh and experienced troops, and in fact there was no further action on this part of the front apart from some patrol activity and artillery exchanges.

Below Nervesa the Austrian IInd and Ist Armies made several small-scale attempts to cross the river, but the general situation remained substantially unchanged. On 4 December the Italians opened an attack to displace the Austrians from the loop at Zenson by using artillery and floating mines to destroy their footbridge across the river. The Austrians delivered a counter-attack and maintained their position, but were eventually displaced on 1 January.[94] Other encounters occurred in the region of the delta. On 9 December the Austrians took the Italian bridgehead at Caposile, but it was retaken the next day by Italian arditi, commando-type units. Also on 9 December, the Austrians failed in an attempt to take the Italian bridgehead at Cortellazzo. On 18 and 19 December the Austrians made several attacks to cross the Italian line on the Sile but without much success.[95] Hence, on 1 January 1918, the Italians held the whole line of the Piave from Pederobba to the sea, except that they had been forced back from the Piave to the Piave Vecchia, where they held strong positions, even if uncomfortably near to Venice.

At Asiago, the Austrians launched heavy attacks against the line

Monte Sisemol – Monte Zomo – Monte Melette on 4, 5 and 6 December (Map 17). On 4 and 5 December the Italians were forced to withdraw from Zomo and Melette, and on 6 December from Sisemol but were able to establish new positions on the line Pennar – Monte Valbella – Col d'Ecchele – Val Frenzela. From 23 to 25 December the Austrians attacked and took Monte Valbella, Col di Rosso and Col d'Ecchele, but these three summits were retaken by the Italians between 27 and 31 January, and the line then remained unchanged for the rest of the winter.[96]

The losses of both sides at Asiago had been considerable. During November the Austrians suffered 23,000 casualties (dead, wounded, missing and ill).[97] During the attack on Melette on 4 and 5 December, the Italian 29th Division lost 539 officers and 14,263 men (including perhaps 11,000 taken prisoner).[98] The overall figures for the losses are less certain but were probably of the order of 30,000 on each side.

(b) Grappa

During November the resolute resistance of the Italian 4th Army on the Grappa massif had almost halted the XIVth Army. Von Below was particularly impressed by the failure of the Edelweiss Division to take Col della Berretta. He now decided that it was essential to improve and consolidate his positions by further operations, with greater coordination and more artillery support. After considerable reorganization, new attacks were launched on 11 December. The Austrian 4th Division was to capture Col della Berretta and Asolone (Map 13). The German 200th, Jäger and 5th Divisions were to cooperate in a combined operation against the stategic summits of Salarol and Col dell'Orso, attacking from three directions. The 200th Division would advance from the region of Fontanasecca, and the Jäger Division from Val Stizzon to the west, while the 5th Division would first take Spinoncia and then move up Val Calcino (Map 18).[99]

On 11 December the 4th Austrian Division captured the summit of Col della Berretta and established positions on one of the lower summits of Asolone.[100] The German divisions were less successful. The Grappa massif is not far from the sea and attracts mist and cloud even on a summer's day, and on 11 December the 200 Division found the mist so dense that they were unable to start. Without their support the Jäger Division failed to make any progress. The only German success during the day was the capture of Spinoncia by the 5th Division, made possible by supporting fire from guns brought up to positions on Fontanasecca. Krafft and von Below were unaccustomed to a day when the gains of one Austrian division exceeded the gains of three German divisions; Krafft's account of the day is very brief, and von

208

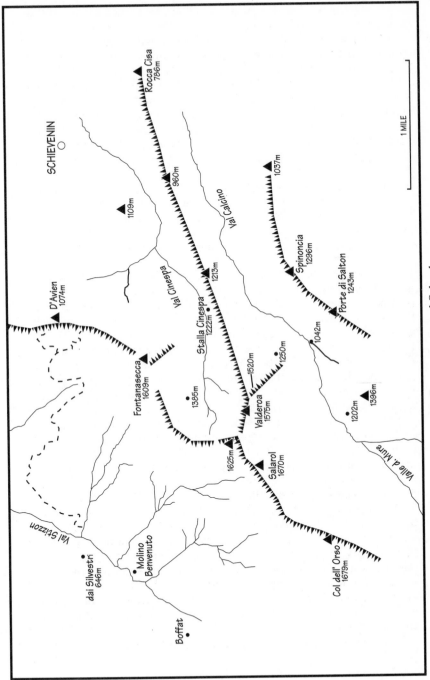

18. Fontanasecca and Salarol.

Below's diary records his displeasure at the failure of the 200th Division.[101]

After a day's pause the fighting for Salarol and its outlier Valdaroa resumed. On 13 December the Germans captured Italian defences below Valderoa at Height 1385, well below the summit,[102] but their drive towards Col dell'Orso continued to be held up at Valdaroa and Salarol. On 17 December the Germans took part of the north ridge of Salarol but the Italians continued to hold the summit, and block the way to Col dell'Orso.[103] On the west of the massif, the 4th Austrian Division finally captured the summit of Asolone on 18 December.[104]

The fighting had gained the XIVth Army some ground, but at the cost of heavy casualties, and without much improvement in its tactical position. It appeared to Krafft that any further gains that might be obtained were unlikely to justify the sacrifices that would be required. Already on 7 and 9 December von Below had commented in his diary that temperatures in the mountains had fallen to minus 20 and even minus 27 degrees, and on 17 December he ordered the cessation of all the offensive operations.

On 22 December von Below's diary recorded the fall of 60cm of fresh snow at Feltre and twice that in the mountains. The battle on Grappa was now almost over for the winter with the Italians still holding positions along or near the summit ridges. But one relatively large encounter was still to come. At the beginning of December the Italian line from Monte Tomba to Pederobba had been taken over by French mountain troops, the 47th Division Chasseurs Alpin, and on 30 December three battalions of these Chasseurs launched an attack to regain possession of the 2,500 yards or so of the ridge Tomba – Monfenera lost on 22 November.[105]

The French were holding inferior positions on the south-facing slope of Tomba somewhat below the summit ridge, while the Austrians were in good positions above. But this disadvantage was offset by careful planning and the support of some 450 guns of various calibres, including 68 French and 20 Italian of large calibre.[106] After five hours of artillery preparation the three battalions launched their assault at 14.05. According to the French Official History the 51st Battalion on the right reached its objectives in a few minutes; the 115th Battalion in the centre made equally good progress; the 70th Battalion obtained their objective despite having to traverse an artillery barrage. By 14.30 complete success had been obtained, for the Austrians made no attempt to retake the ground. Their losses had been severe: 500 dead in the abandoned positions, 1,546 prisoners, 8 guns, 6 mortars and 63 machine guns. The French losses were given as 54 dead, 205 wounded.[107]

The Austro-German forces on and adjacent to Tomba now had little choice but of retiring from the slopes of Tomba and Pallon towards the village of Alano. Finally on 15 January the Italian 66th Division attempted to retake Asolone but without success, partly because an order to delay the start time by an hour failed to reach all the units soon enough.[108]

By now winter had completely descended, and the fighting on Grappa had come to an end. The troops of the Italian 4th Army had maintained their line over the Grappa massif; the XIVth Army was being disbanded; and the German divisions were on their way to other fronts.

Rommel on Grappa

10.1　The Move to Grappa

The WMB spent 11 November in Longarone as a rest day and buried their dead. The Battalion had spent three weeks marching and fighting, and were to spend another six weeks in the Grappa massif before being withdrawn from Italy. During this time the Battalion was to be employed fairly continuously as a spearhead in attacks on the east flank of the Grappa massif.

The XIVth Army was now facing a much different situation from that on the Kolovrat and Matajur. The ground on Grappa was defended by troops of the 4th Army, well practised in mountain warfare, and not demoralized by the confusion of the breakthrough at Caporetto. Although their retirement had begun slowly, the 4th Army had arrived on Grappa in time to take up good positions protected by well-sited artillery. Moreover, the Italians were now fighting to halt the invasion of Italy. Fruili and part of Venezia had already been occupied, and on a clear day the sight of Venice and its lagoons was a reminder of former years under Austrian rule.

On 12 November the WMB marched down the Piave from Longarone, as part of Krauss's offensive to occupy the whole of the Grappa massif. The night was spent in Belluno, now largely deserted except for troops, and the following morning the Battalion moved to billets between Belluno and Feltre. That day, and the next two days, were spent mainly as rest days, because the speed of the advance was now determined by the slow progress of the 55(a) Division which was meeting determined Italian resistance in the narrow part of the Piave valley below Feltre (Section 9.3c). On 16 November the Battalion arrived at Feltre, and was assigned to the Jäger(g) Division. In the early hours of 17 November the 55 Division broke into the village of Quero (Maps 11 and 13) and the Jäger Division, which had been following on behind, took over as the lead division.

The advance so far had been confined by the narrow valley of the Piave, but beyond Quero the western side of the valley opens out, leading to three valleys running up between the ridges of Monte

Grappa. These valleys and their streams, the Cinespa, the Calcino and the Ornic, come together in the relatively flat ground east of Alano before entering the Piave. It was here, in the Alano Basin, that the Jäger Division arrived in the early hours of 17 November, and it soon became apparent that the whole basin was overlooked by a ring of high summits running from Tomba to Monte Pallon, Col dell'Orso, and Fontanasecca, where the Italians had deployed their main defence line complete with substantial artillery.

After Krauss issued his orders on 17 November for a comprehensive attack the next day (Section 9.3c), the WMB were ordered by the Jäger Division to advance 'over Spinoncia and then in the general direction of Col dell'Orso'.[1] Major Sproesser states that he was given a free choice as to how he would carry out these somewhat imprecise orders.[2] The Battalion orders issued at 13.00 followed the Divisional orders in that the WMB would go over Spinoncia, but added that it would break into the main Italian defence line on the summit ridge between Monte Grappa and Monte Pallon.[3] However, Sproesser subsequently changed his plan, so that only a detachment under Rommel consisting of the 2nd and 4th Rifle Companies, the 3rd Machine-Gun Company, part of the Signal Company, and two mountain batteries, would go by the route over Spinoncia. The greater part of the WMB (plus a Bosnian Company of 55 Division) would form another column and spend the night in the neighbourhood of Rocca Cisa (786m), on the ridge running up towards the summits on the north side of the Calcino stream (Map 18). Then the next day both groups would go forward to attack Monte Grappa.[4]

Having arrived just short of Quero during 17 November, the WMB waited until nightfall for the heavy Italian shelling to subside. The main group under Major Sproesser moved cautiously through Quero and reached the village of Schievenin about midnight. An advance guard consisting of the 6th Company and the Bosnian Company established positions on high ground near the summit of Rocca Cisa, and the rest of the group joined them during the night, the staff establishing themselves in dismal goat stalls and hay huts.[5]

Meanwhile the Rommel detachment had made its way through Quero and the Alano basin to the little village of Uson (Map 13) en route for Spinoncia. The conditions here were very different from those around Tolmin where the WMB had begun its march. At that time the Battalion and many other units of the XIVth Army had been concentrated near Tolmin for two nights within range of a great deal of Italian artillery, but the enemy guns had taken surprisingly little advantage of this opportunity. Now, however, powerful searchlights on the surrounding heights of Monte Tomba, Pallon and Spinoncia, swept and probed the Alano basin, and heavy artillery shells were falling on and around the deserted villages of Quero and Alano. (The Wurttembergers had dashed through Quero in small groups, seeing as they went craters from five to ten yards wide, and numbers of dead and wounded Jägers.)

After reaching Uson at the foot of Val Calcino without loss, Rommel sent out scouts to make contact with neighbouring units and assess the situation. Later he was to write that there could 'be no more talk of a brisk breakthrough over Monte Grappa to Bassano. The enemy front is strong and continuous, and we have arrived too late.' He also observed that 'six French and five English Divisions have been hurriedly inserted among the Italians to support them'.[6] With this inauspicious beginning the Rommel detachment set off from Uson in the early hours of 18 November towards Spinoncia, first for a mile or so up Val Calcino, and then on a track leading south to the east ridge of Spinoncia.

As dawn broke on 18 November, Sproesser at Rocca Cisa, and Rommel on the east ridge of Spinoncia, despatched squads to assess the terrain and the enemy positions. Sproesser sent 2nd Lieutenant Fuchtner with the 5th Rifle and 1st Machine-Gun Company to reconnoitre the route to the Valle delle Mure (Map 18).[7] Presumably Fuchtner followed the high-level track from Rocca Cisa high up on the south side of the ridge running towards Monte Valderoa. After about a mile and a half, this track crosses the ridge to drop down into Val Cinespa, where it follows the Cinespa stream uphill to some huts at Stalla Cinespa (1218m), and then leads into the Valle delle Mure.[8]

To appreciate the tactics of the situation we must note that in the region of Stalla Cinespa the ridge separating Val Cinespa from Val Calcino stands only about 50 metres above the stream in Val Cinespa. On arriving here Fuchtner would have seen that it was overlooked on one side by Fontanasecca and on the other by Spinoncia. Moreover, the Italians were already in good defensive positions around Stalla Cinespa supported by rifles and machine-gun squads on Fontanasecca. Fuchtner engaged the enemy and captured one post to the east of Stalla Cinespa, but could advance no further. In the late afternoon his detachment was reinforced by the arrival of the 1st Rifle Company and the Bosnian Company.

Meanwhile the forward units of the Rommel detachment had been reconnoitring the approach to Spinoncia along its east ridge. For the last half mile before the summit the ridge was narrow with precipitous slopes on either side, and was defended by troops and machine guns in good entrenched positions. There was no obvious way to circumvent these positions, and the whole area was subject to enemy artillery fire from Fontanasecca, Pallon and Tomba. As a first move Rommel sent the 4th Rifle and 3rd Machine-Gun Company to attempt to dislodge the Italians from some of their forward positions. But they failed to make any progress in the face of the superior enemy and machine-gun fire.[9] It then appeared to Rommel that 'Wir sind festgefahren!' (We have come to a dead end.)[10]

At about 04.00 the next morning (19 November) the Italians counter-attacked Fuchtner's Bosnian Company at Stalla Cinespa, and were forced to retire leaving numerous dead and wounded.[11] Then at 06.00 the Fuchtner detachment attacked the Italian positions below the summit of Fontanasecca and broke into the first Italian line, but was unable to proceed further because of very strong machine-gun fire from Spinoncia. During the afternoon and evening the Italians launched two further counter-attacks but failed to regain the lost positions, and it was learnt from captured prisoners that Fontanasecca was defended by at least four battalions. Meanwhile, Rommel on the east ridge of Spinoncia made further attempts to find a route to outflank the summit but without success.[12]

It was now clear that a major effort was required to gain control of Fontanasecca. During 20 November the WMB was joined by two battalions of the 1st Regiment Kaiserschützen (IIC Brigade, 22(a) Division) which had come down from the north, and preparations were made for a full-scale attack the next day. The Kaiserschützen would attack from the north-east, and the 5th and 6th Rifle Companies and the Bosnian Company from the south-east. Fire support would be given by two batteries at Rocca Cisa, and by the Rommel detachment with two mountain batteries on the ridge of Spinoncia.[13] The operation was to have been conducted by the senior officer, Lieutenant Colonel Florio commanding the 1st Regiment Kaiserschützen, but as he was ill the group came under the command of Major Sproesser, dependent on IIC Brigade 22 Division.[14] At the same time, XXV Brigade of the 94(a) Division in Val Stizzon on the west side of Fontanasecca was also preparing an attack for 21 November. Its first objective was to take Salarol from the north via Fontanasecca, after which the advance would continue to Col dell'Orso and beyond.[15]

Next day, 21 November, the attack by the Sproesser Group captured the summit of Fontanasecca. The Italian front line on the north-east slope of the mountain, initially about 300 yards below the summit, was forced back over the summit, and then another 300 yards down the ridge leading to Salarol.[16] However, neither the XXV Brigade in Val Stizzon nor the Rommel detachment on Spinoncia made any significant progress. Next day, the Commander of the IIC Brigade wished to continue, but the Kaiserschützen needed time to reorganize,[17] and Rommel failed in a further attempt to advance against Spinoncia.[18]

It was now clear that the WMB's projected drive across Grappa to Bassano was not making anything like the expected progress. The main body of the WMB had taken part in the capture of the summit of

Fontanasecca, but had not progressed much further. The Rommel detachment had spent five days, on precipitous ground dominated by the enemy artillery on Tomba, Pallon and Fontanasecca, attempting to take Spinoncia. Despite suffering casualties they had made no progress at all. Rommel records that on 21 November he was by the side of Sergeant Martin in a forward observation post when the latter was killed by a shell splinter.[19]

10.2   The Fiasco of 25 November

We now come to what was surely the least successful day experienced by Rommel, Sproesser and the WMB while in Italy. The Sproesser Group had taken the summit of Fontanasecca, but had still to obtain its first main objective, Monte Salarol. On 23 November Sproesser's group was reinforced by a battalion of the 2nd Regiment Kaiserschützen,[20] and two of its companies relieved the Rommel detachment on Spinoncia; the detachment returned to the main body of the WMB, and at the same time the Bosnian Company attached to the WMB returned to its own battalion. As Sproesser was now in command of three Kaiserschützen battalions as well as the WMB, Rommel was given command of the WMB.[21]

At 22.00 hours on 23 November Sproesser issued orders for a renewed attack on Salarol (Map 18).[22] These orders began by stating that the enemy was holding a line through Height 1385, the huts west of Stalla Cinespa, and Monte Spinoncia (Map 18). (Height 1385 is shown in Sproesser's sketch maps but is not readily identified with any points on the IGM maps, so its location on Map 18 is somewhat approximate.) The operation was to start in the early hours of 25 November, with attacks by the three Kaiserschützen battalions.

The instructions to the Kaiserschützen for the initial stage of the attack were quite brief. The two battalions of the 1st Regiment were to proceed against Height 1385, and the battalion of the 2nd Regiment against positions south of Stalla Cinespa; the main weight of the attack would be on the right. The order then continued that in the event of a 'successful assault' the forward advance would be vigorously and powerfully pursued. The WMB, hitherto in reserve, would advance along the line Monte Salarol – Col dell'Orso – Monte Grappa; the two battalions of the 1st Regiment Kaiserschützen would advance towards the main ridge of the massif between Pallon and Monte Grappa; and the battalion of the 2nd Regiment towards two positions described as Heights 1193 and 1509 (which we cannot identify on Sproesser's maps[23] or elsewhere).

Sproesser did not elaborate on the term a 'successful assault'. Did it mean the capture of the enemy positions around 1385 and Stalla

216

Cinespa, or did it include the capture of the defended positions on the summits of Salarol, three or four hundred metres higher. Nor was it clear when the WMB would come up from the reserve and pass through the Kaiserschützen. However, these obscurities were of no consequence, for in the event all the initial attacks were unsuccessful.

To follow the subsequent events of 25 November we must note that Monte Salarol lies on the long ridge which runs down from near the summit of Monte Grappa, via Col dell'Orso to Fontanasecca, Peurna and Tomatico (Map 13). The west side of Col dell'Orso, Salarol and Fontanasecca falls steeply for almost 1000 metres to Val Stizzon which hereabouts is a narrow V-shaped valley overlooked by impressive cliffs on the upper slopes of Fontanasecca (Plate 32).

We must also recall that the Krauss Corps was now organized in two groups (Section 9.3c). The first under General Wieden was aiming for the valley of the Brenta, the summits of Berretta and Asolone, and the long ridge leading from Roncone to Pertica. The other group under General Müller, including Sproesser's group, had been given the principal task of advancing over Monte Tomba to the plain, but was also to capture Spinoncia and the ridge between Fontanasecca and Salarol by moving up the valleys on its east side.[24] However, immediately to the west of the Salarol – Fontanasecca ridge the troops in Val Stizzon were part of the XXV Brigade of the 94(a) Division in General Wieden's group. Hence there was inevitably some possibility of poor communication and liaison between the two brigades on either side of the high ridge. In fact, although Major Sproesser's orders of 23 November had included instructions to ensure liaison between his four battalions during the attack on Salarol, no mention was made of any liaison with XXV Brigade. This was unfortunate, as XXV Brigade was also preparing to attack Salarol on 25 November.

The Sproesser Group launched its attack at 08.00 on 25 November. The Group Battle Report states, without much detail, that the Kaiserschützen made repeated attacks against the Italian positions for several hours, but no progress was made despite heavy Austrian casualties: 8 officers and 273 men in the 1st Regiment, and 8 officers and 140 men in the 2nd Regiment.[25] Meanwhile the WMB waited in reserve on the north-east slope of Fontanasecca, on a bitterly cold winter's day, and under some fire from enemy mountain batteries.[26]

About noon Rommel and Sproesser decided that it was time to bring the WMB into action. Accounts of subsequent events are given in the WMB Battle Report, in Rommel's book and in Sproesser's book, and are not entirely consistent with each other. Rommel's account states that at about noon he received a message from the Sproesser Group saying that the XXV Brigade had captured Salarol. What happened next is told in Rommel's own words.

217

I requested permission from the Sproesser Group to be allowed to move to the right of XXV Brigade towards Salarol, and then from there to strike in the direction of Grappa. Major Sproesser agreed, and soon the whole of the WMB was on its way. It was soon found that it was impossible to take the shortest route, that is to traverse the almost vertical wall of the west slope of Fontanasecca. So nothing remained to be done but to descend into Val Stizzon [Map 18]. We stepped out briskly, nevertheless it was dark by the time we reached Dai Silvestri.[27]

(Rommel gives the date of the attack as 24 November. This is clearly an error, as the 25th is confirmed by the Battalion Orders of 23 November, the Battalion Diary for 25 November and the Italian Official History.[28])

Although Rommel's account is very brief, the fact that his route was blocked by the cliffs of Fontanasecca, and that he intended to move to the *right* of XXV Brigade show unambiguously that his plan for the afternoon was for the whole WMB to advance towards Grappa by a traversing manoeuvre high up on the north side of Fontanasecca and Salarol, reminiscent of his successful traverse along the Kolovrat on 25 October. But Rommel also says that news had already been received that Salarol had been captured by XXV Brigade, and he appears quite unconcerned that this route would cross their lines of communication, for he makes no mention of any liaison with the Brigade. In fact the report of the capture of Salarol, mentioned by Rommel and only by Rommel, was incorrect. The fighting was still continuing, and any movement of the WMB across XXV Brigade's lines of communication would have been even more unwelcome.

After the WMB had arrived at Dai Silvestri, in the dark and 1000 metres below the summit of Salarol, Rommel decided that with an early start the next day, the Battalion could be on Salarol by daybreak to continue the battle.[29] While the exhausted battalion rested, he sent 2nd Lieutenant Ammann to find out the situation of 'our troops' on Salarol. Ammann's own account of his reconnaissance is quoted by Sproesser in his book (which like Rommel erroneously states the date as 24 and not 25 November). Ammann set out with a patrol up Val Stizzon for a short distance, and then followed a track leading up Salarol. He soon encountered a 2nd Lieutenant in a Jäger battalion of XXV Brigade who gave him a description of the present situation. The summit of Salarol was still held by the enemy; it was heavily defended; the Austrians had suffered heavy losses; they felt that they had no support.[30]

The Jäger officer, having heard that the WMB were also aiming for Salarol asked Ammann to accompany him to the Brigade Commander,

Colonel Wassenthal. The latter 'was very friendly to me and very enthusiastic about the reinforcements which would be provided by our Battalion. Using the map and the latest reports from the front, he discussed the situation with me thoroughly, and indeed the possible share of a combat sector'.[31]

When Ammann returned to report to Rommel, he was no doubt well pleased with the result of his reconnaissance. However, the WMB in crossing the ridge Fontanasecca – Salarol had arrived unannounced in the zone of another unit, not just the zone of another battalion, but of another division and of another group of divisions. Furthermore, the 94(a) Division had previously encountered the WMB at Longarone, when they had caught up with the Italian 1st Division and taken some of them prisoner, after Rommel had blocked the road out of Longarone. Without Rommel no one would have been captured at Longarone, but some members of the Austrian Division felt that their part in the operation had not been sufficiently recognized.[32] Be that as it may, the Commander of the 94 Division took great exception to the German intrusion into Val Stizzon.

Sproesser states in his book that

> Lieutenant Rommel was in the combat sector of the Austrian division and the fat was in the fire. One can understand the amusement of the High Command. It produced an amazing crisis, all the telephone lines in the area . . . . worked feverishly to defecate on this unheard of procedure of the WMB. The quarrel was so great that the Commander of the WMB had no option but to ask for its immediate detachment from its association with the 22 Schützen Division.[33]

Hence, by the time Lieutenant Ammann arrived to report to Rommel, the WMB had already received orders to descend Val Stizzon the next day and move to the region of Feltre.

The WMB Battle Report is a typescript document, the *Gefechts-Bericht*, covering the period 11 November to 9 December, which quotes relevant orders and summarizes events and actions. It states only that, after the heavy losses suffered by the Kaiserschützen, 'Lt Rommel received orders to descend with the entire WMB down mountain tracks towards Dai Silvestri [at the bottom of Val Stizzon], to capture Monte Salarol from the north breaking through the enemy defences, to liaise with the left flank of XXV Brigade and fill the gap between XXV Brigade and the 1st Regiment Kaiserschützen.'[34]

Thus the Battle Report, written after the event, acknowledges the existence of XXV Brigade, not mentioned in Sproesser's orders of

23 November which did not give any indication of how the WMB were to cooperate with the Brigade when both arrived on the summit of Salarol. However, this contingency did not arrive, as neither the WMB nor the XXV Brigade succeeded in reaching the summit. In fact, immediately after the above order to liaise with the XXV Brigade and the Kaiserschützen, the Battle Report concludes abruptly by saying that 'On its way there the Battalion received orders that it was removed from 22(a) Division and was to proceed through Arten and Feltre to join the German Jäger Division'![35]

Sproesser's account in his book includes details of a conversation with Rommel not recorded elsewhere. He states that in a verbal discussion, at a time not mentioned, he 'ordered the WMB to break through in the direction of Monte Grappa. . . . Major Sproesser had no doubt about it, the proved and brilliant Rommel would discover a way to break through, in a similar way as on the Kolovrat, on Kuk, on Craguenza, Matajur and on Forcella Clautana, at Cimolais and Longarone.' Hence, Sproesser ordered the WMB to take the ridge Monte Salarol – Col dell'Orso by an encircling movement on the west side of Fontanasecca, saying at the same time that the Battalion was to collaborate with the XXV Brigade in Val Stizzon.[36]

Immediately after the above, Sproesser's account continues by saying that 'Rommel was defeated in performing this order, so the WMB had to bivouac in a depression east of Fontanasecca, until Lt. Rommel had made his preparations for the breakthrough in the direction of Salarol.' This is immediately followed by Sproesser's next paragraph which begins 'Lt. Rommel immediately decided on the ascent of Salarol from above Molino Benvenuto [Map 18].'[37]

There are clear discrepancies in the accounts given by Sproesser and Rommel. Rommel says that he left the north-east slopes of Fontanasecca sometime after 12.00 with the intention of traversing towards Grappa, and because this proved too difficult he subsequently descended into Val Stizzon. On the other hand, Sproesser says that Rommel had previously failed to make this traverse, and that the WMB then bivouacked on the eastern side of Fontanasecca until Rommel gave the order to descend to Dai Silvestri.

Although some details of the failed operation remain obscure, it is clear that both Sproesser and Rommel, buoyed up by their previous successes, had become too optimistic, too regardless of the topography of the ground, and too regardless of the need to liaise with adjacent units. General von Below in his diary for 25 November commented that 'The 22 Division Schützen attacked heights 1385 and 1222 south of Fontanasecca but did not succeed to go further, because the Wurttemberg Mountain Battalion, charged to make an encircling movement, lost its way and ended in the depths of Val

Stizzon.'[38] These events were certainly the nadir of the WMB's campaign in Italy.

10.3 The Last Month

By the end of November it had become clear that all operations would have to be suspended during the winter, but before doing so Krafft and von Below aimed to achieve some tactical improvements in their positions. Perhaps also, after the failures of 25 November, they welcomed a further opportunity to demonstrate the effectiveness of the German forces. The scope and outcome of the consequent operations in December have already been outlined in Section 9.5b, and we now decribe the part played by Rommel and the WMB.

The slow progress of the XIVth Army during November, and particularly the failure to take Salarol, had brought home to Krafft and von Below the complexity of the ground, the strength of the Italian artillery, and the determination of the Italian infantry. Hence, there was now a pause while the XIVth Army made considerable preparations including the realignment of units, and the deployment of more and heavier artillery.

During the next few days all four divisions in the front line of the Krauss Corps were withdrawn, to give relief from both combat and the very severe winter weather. By 9 December the western sector of Monte Grappa was held by the 4(a) Division, the sector Pertica – Fontanasecca by the 200(g) Division, Fontanasecca by the 5(g) Division, and Monte Tomba by the Alpine Corps(g).[39]

Following these new arrangements, units of the 200(g)and 5(g) Divisions launched an attack on 11 December with the aim of taking Spinoncia, Salarol and Col dell'Orso. On the first day the Germans captured the summit of Spinoncia, and two days later gained the Italian positions at Height 1385 at the head of Val Cinespa, but the way beyond to Salarol and Col dell'Orso remained blocked by the Italian defences. (General von Below's diary for 13 December notes the capture of the subsidiary summit of Salarol at 1625m, known to the Germans as the Pyramidenkuppe, but this must be a confused reference to the capture of 1385, as four days later the diary notes that 'a new attempt by the 200 Division to take the summit of the Pyramide failed'.[40])

All this time the WMB were well behind the front line. After leaving Val Stizzon the Wurttembergers had spent a few days in different billets on the left bank of the Piave below Belluno, and then moved into the town of Belluno where they rested until 10 December. Then, marching in two stages, they spent the night of 11 December in a village outside Feltre. Here they received orders that the Battalion was

221

transferred from the Jäger to the 5(g) Division, and was to continue down the Piave the next day and take a track over Monte Cornella to reach Schievenin in the Alano basin (Map 13).

The route via Monte Cornella had been specified to avoid the road through Quero which was much exposed to enemy artillery fire. However, Sproesser judged that the mountain track would be under snow and ice and too difficult for both men and mules, so starting at 03.00 on 12 December the WMB passed safely along the road through Quero while it was still dark and reached Schievenin by 07.00. Here the Battalion was still some way from the combat zone, and during the next two or three days some squads helped to move stores up to the front.

The fighting at the head of Val Cinespa had now died away, and the Italians were reinforcing their positions on Valderoa and Hill 1625 (the Pyramidenkuppe), where the Germans were deployed on a line fifty to a hundred metres lower down, passing through the former Italian positions at 1385m. The XIVth Army was determined to make further progress, and another attack was planned for 17 December. This would be directed by the 200(g) Division, and would involve four and a half Jäger battalions, the WMB and II Battalion of the 52nd Infantry Regiment, both from 5(g) Division. Its aim would again be the capture of Salarol, starting from the higher positions won on 13 December.

Details of the plan of the attack were set out in the Divisional and Brigade Orders of 16 December, and in Major Sproesser's orders on the evening of the same day. The Divisional orders stated that the objective was Monte Salarol, and that an assault would be made by an attack group commanded by Major Sproesser, consisting of the XVII Reserve Battalion of the 5th Jäger Regiment, half the VI Reserve Battalion of the 4th Jäger Regiment, and the WMB. The group would 'Advance on both sides of Valderoa to Monte Salarol, storming the enemy positions. . . . Pyramidenkuppe will not be attacked, but will be held down during the attack by strong artillery fire.' At the same time the IInd Battalion of the 52 Regiment would attack enemy positions south-east of Valderoa, on the left flank of the Sproesser Group in 'immediate liaison with the Commanding Officer of the WMB'.[41]

Major Sproesser's orders laid down that the attack against Salarol would be led by the WMB and the XVII Jäger Battalion. The latter was to make for the summit of Valderoa from the north-east, spread out on either side of the rib between the north and east facing slopes of the mountain. Its left flank would be covered by a detachment of the WMB, the 1st and 5th Rifle Companies and the 2nd Machine-Gun Company under Lieutenant Fuchtner, which would work round on to the south slope of Valderoa. The rest of the WMB, four Rifle and two Machine-Gun Companies under Rommel, were to do no more than follow the attack 'in the 2nd line', and if necessary mop up the Pyramidenkuppe after the capture of Salarol by the Jäger Battalion.

In addition, Sproesser's orders began with two paragraphs which stated, inter alia, that 'The 200 Infantry Division captures on 17/12/17 Col dell'Orso and Salarol.', although neither the Division nor the Brigade orders had made any mention of Col dell'Orso. Hence it seems that, as on 25 November, Sproesser was planning that once Salarol had been captured, the WMB would swiftly move forward to Col dell'Orso and beyond.[42]

The Brigade orders had also introduced new arrangements not mentioned in the Divisional orders, nor in Sproesser's orders. In particular, another group of three battalions of the 3rd Jäger Regiment and one and a half battalions of the 4th Regiment, the 'Roll Group', was now to be involved. However, the orders defining the task of this large force said only that it would be 'responsible for the defence of Valderoa'. The Brigade orders also stipulated that 'the Groups Roll and Sproesser remain under the command of Colonel Thummel [3rd Jäger Regiment], the leader of the Infantry Attack Group'.[43]

Sproesser quotes all three sets of orders without comment and we are left wondering why the Brigade orders differ from the other two, and why the role of the Roll Group is set out so sketchily. It may be that the additional orders introduced by the Brigade can best be explained as an attempt by either Brigade or Division to keep a watching eye on Major Sproesser, who must by now have acquired a reputation for going off on his own. Hence the function of the Roll Group appears to have been primarily an excuse to insert Colonel Thummel above and in close contact with Sproesser!

For an account of the day's events we rely primarily on Sproesser's account[44] as Rommel's account is very brief. On 14 December Sproesser's attack group began to move up to an advance base near a blockhouse in the region of Stalla Cinespa (1222m) south of Fontanasecca. Frozen and slippery snow made the steeper parts of the track difficult and dangerous, particularly for the animals. The area around the blockhouse appears to have been shielded from enemy artillery shells, but the ground rose steeply on either side of the track,[45] so the troops had a hard time improvising what shelter they could from their groundsheets and sawn-up trees. The weather was now increasingly cold with rain and snow, and Sproesser mentions that the atmosphere was so damp that it was almost impossible to kindle a fire.

By the night of 16 December all the units of the Sproesser group were in position, with the XVII Jäger Battalion in the front line, having been substituted for the V Reserve Battalion earlier that evening.[46] Towards daybreak the Fuchtner detachment of the WMB, on the left of the Jäger Battalion, set off towards the south-east ridge of Valderoa and soon encountered hard frozen snow where the use of crampons was essential, and the Rommel detachment took up positions behind the Jäger Battalion.[47]

The German artillery preparation began at 07.30, and the Italians responded by reinforcing their front-line positions, including those around Height 1520 on the south-east ridge of Valderoa (sometimes referred to as the Nashorn). Then from 10.00 onwards their batteries on Grappa, Pallon and the south-west slopes of Spinoncia laid down a steadily increasing fire.

At 11.00, both the Fuchtner detachment and the XVII Jäger Battalion launched their attack. The Fuchtner detachment soon occupied enemy positions up to Height 1520, and the Italians began to withdraw their artillery on the south face. But then the Italians counter-attacked and the assault troops of the 5th Company WMB 'were thrown down the slope with a large number of casualties'.[48] The XVII Jägers fared no better, for their initial thrust was followed by a furious Italian counter-attack which drove them back to their start line. During the afternoon the Italians made repeated counter-attacks to drive the Germans still further back, but without success, despite heavy losses.

Meanwhile the Rommel detachment waited to go forward as soon as the Jägers had captured Valderoa, and as the Jägers were repulsed the detachment took no substantial part in the day's fighting. It was now becoming clear that the weather was too severe, and the opposing forces too evenly matched, for there to be much possibility of future progress, and the next day the Divisional orders stated that 'The attack, on account of the onset of winter will not be continued.' Sproesser quotes these orders and inserts a footnote after 'winter' saying: 'Read, on account of the French and British in Italy'.[49]

The WMB descended to Schievenin on the evening of 18 December and spent the next few days recovering from the effects of cold and frost-bite in cold and uncomfortable billets near Feltre. The XIVth Army units around the Alano basin were now to adopt a purely defensive strategy on the line of their forward advance. But the Italians still held the line of the summits, Salarol – Pallon – Tomba – Monfenera, except for 2500 yards near the summit of Tomba where they had been forced back some way down the south-facing slope (Section 9.3c). Thus, the Austro-German positions were now generally sited uncomfortably below the Italians on the summits encircling the Alano basin, and were dominated by an arc of Italian guns.

Towards the end of December the WMB were sent to relieve units of the Jäger Division on the right of the Austrian 50 Division on Tomba. On 25 December half the Battalion, under Rommel, moved into positions immediately to the right of the Austrian positions, and were followed on 29 December by the rest of the Battalion under

Lieutenant Fuchtner which occupied the line further to the right. When the Rommel detachment first arrived the front was fairly quiet, which was just as well, as the rifle and machine-gun nests forming the basis of their defences were no more than 'small hollows on the bare precipitous slopes'.[50] The ground was covered by snow, and tracks had to be avoided or brushed away; no one was allowed to show themselves by day; lighting fires was forbidden.

The apparent calm was not to last. Since the end of November the Italians had been much concerned at the enemy occupation of part of Monte Tomba, for they feared that a renewed attack at this point might break through their poor positions below the ridge, capture the whole of Tomba and Monfenera, and so turn the defences of the Piave. Therefore they were determined to regain the lost length of ridge, and the task was entrusted to the French 47th Division of specialist mountain troops, the Chasseurs Alpins, who had taken over these Italian positions on 5 December.

As described above, the Chasseurs Alpins regained the ridge in a short but decisive action on 30 December, inflicting very heavy casualties on three Austrian battalions. In fact, the French had now completed their programme, but the Austro-German Command was much concerned that they might push through the gap torn in the Austrian line, and threaten the XIVth Army guns near Alano and Quero. Austrian reserves were sent up the next day to close the gap but found themselves in an impossible position on a bare mountain slope, under fire from the French immediately above and from the Italian artillery on Pallon. Hence, by the evening all the XIVth Army troops had been ordered to draw back to a line from Spinoncia to Faveri, about a thousand yards south of Quero. The winter campaign on Grappa was over, and soon Rommel and Sproesser were en route back to home leave in Germany.

Epilogue

Caporetto had been a brilliant Austro-German success. Krafft had seen, appreciated, and seized a great opportunity which led to one of the outstanding military successes of the war. As an immediate consequence Austria remained in the war at the side of Germany, and more than 200,000 French and British troops were directed away from the Western Front. Yet the outcome was not entirely what Hindenberg and Ludendorff would have wished, for it led directly to other less desired consequences.

One of the most immediate results was that Cadorna, Porro, Capello, Cavacciocchi and Bongiovani were all removed from their commands. Cadorna was appointed as the Italian representative on the new Joint Allied War Council at Versaille; Capello after discharge from hospital was given the command of the Reserve 5th Army engaged in rebuilding the pieces of the 2nd Army; Porro, Cavacciocchi and Bongiovani retired to relative obscurity. Cadorna was replaced as Chief of Staff by Diaz, and Porro by two Deputy Chiefs, Badoglio and Giardini, and as already mentioned Gatti has recorded the improvements at the Comando Supremo (Section 9.2).

Perhaps the greatest effect of the Austro-German success was to provide Italy with a new and more evocative war aim. The enemy was now in control of all Fruili-Venezia Giulia and part of the Veneto and very close to Venice, facts more evocative and compelling than the prospect of continuing a war to gain the Trentino and Trieste which for two and a half years had made virtually no progress. There was certainly a reduction in defeatism and political agitation against the war, and this together with the improved conditions of service in the army ensured that there was no military collapse such as had occurred in France and Russia in 1917.

For Austria the eventual outcome of Caporetto was disastrous. The Germans left Italy but insisted that Austria either continue the war against Italy or send troops to the Western Front. Hence in June 1918 Austria launched the largest of all its offensives in Italy, at the Tonale Pass in the mountains of the Trentino, at Asiago, on Grappa and across the Piave, and everywhere was totally rebuffed. This conspicuous failure was no doubt a further indication to the various subject peoples of the Austro-Hungarian Empire that the time had come to go their own ways.

The WMB returned to the Vosges, and from February to May took part in the fighting at Hartmannswillerkopf. Then in May during the Michael Offensive they were involved in the fighting on the Chemin des Dames and suffered their heaviest casualties in the war (203 dead, 798 wounded). After the war the Battalion, now a Regiment, was disbanded. Major Sproesser was badly wounded in the hand in France, but remained in the German Army and was eventually promoted Major General. He continued to take a deep interest in his old battalion, editing and writing its history and organizing an association of old members. When he died in 1933 his funeral was attended by 800 old members of the Battalion.[1]

Rommel had won a great reputation. After his leave in January 1918 he was posted away from the WMB to a new position as a member of a large staff on the Western Front. No doubt the appointment was made to ensure that he survived the war, and to give him experience of the wider aspects of military command, but he writes in his book of his sorrow at leaving the WMB.[2]

For Rommel the most important outcome of Caporetto was the book he published twenty years later. This masterly book went through at least twelve editions in seven years; is said to have been read by General Patton until he knew it by heart;[3] and it is still in use today. More importantly for Rommel it was read by Hitler, and Rommel was in command of Hitler's personal guard during the invasion of Poland. Subsequently he asked Hitler for an active command, and on being offered an infantry division, asked for a Panzer division even though all his experience was with the infantry. Such a highly unusual appointment was not approved by the Army Appointments Office and was only made on Hitler's personal authority.[4] Rommel took up his appointment on 7 February 1940, and in three months this remarkable man took over his division, learnt the mechanics of commanding tanks and mobile columns, and trained the division to work with infiltration tactics not greatly different from those he had employed as an infantry officer twenty years previously.

Finally it would seem that the Germans did not draw quite the right conclusions from their victory. They were clearly soldiers of the very first order, but they tended to ignore at least three points which were a warning that similar victories might not come as easily in the future. There would seldom be a tactical situation so readily leading to a breakthough as at Caporetto. It would always be difficult to avoid cooperation with less able allies. Nor at any time in Italy were they in

227

combat with troops with experience of German methods on the Western Front.

Von Below and Krafft were quite aware that this was the case, but Krafft ends his book with his belief that Germany would do better next time. 'In all the German races the memory of that time of victory can strengthen the support for unification, with the awareness that the genuine Germans of the future will be invincible.'[5]

Rommel probably felt rather the same way, but not exactly so. He ends his book by reference to those German soldiers who died for their country. 'In the West, East and South lie the German Schützen [soldiers], who faithfully went on performing their duty for Fatherland and Home until the bitter end. They always remind us, the survivors, and future generations that we must not be untrue to them when it is a question of making a sacrifice for Germany.'[6] However, on the same page, writing of his mountain troops who were the victors of Cosna, Kolovrat, Matajur, Cimolais and Longarone, Rommel makes the comment that only a small part were able to return to their native land. 'Nur ein kleiner Teil von ihnen darf die Heimat wiedersehen.'

109 Ibid, 100
110 Ibid, 101
111 IOH (IV, 3), 129; IOH (IV, 3, Doc), 106
112 IOH (IV, 3 Doc), 108
113 Ibid, 137; IOH (IV, 3), 112
114 IOH (IV, 3), 152
115 IOH (IV, 3, Doc), 111
116 IOH (IV, 3), 130
117 Caviglia (1933), 81
118 IOH (IV, 3, Doc), 147
119 IOH (IV, 3), 117
120 Ibid, 147
121 Capello (1920), 364
122 Faldella, Vol. 2, 53; CI Vol II, 131
123 IOH (IV, 3) Schizzo 6
124 IOH (IV, 3, Doc), 116
125 IOH (IV, 3), 296
126 Ibid, 156

Chapter 3 (pp. 47–65)
1   Krafft (1981), 397
2   Ibid, 99
3   Ibid, 109
4   Ibid, 113
5   Ibid, 88ff
6   Caviglia (1933), 144ff
7   IOH (IV, 3), 301
8   Ibid, 250
9   Faldella, Vol. 2, 140
10   IOH (IV, 3), 301, 333
11   Krafft (1981), 84ff
12   Young, 322
13   Caviglia (1933), 271
14   IOH (IV, 3), 288
15   Ibid, 305
16   Ibid, 280
17   Ibid, 282
18   Ibid, 321
19   Ibid, 322
20   Ibid, 321, 323
21   Caviglia (1933), 269
22   IOH (IV, 3), 322

23 Ibid, 240
24 Ibid, 286
25 Ibid, 306
26 Ibid, 307
27 IOH (IV, 3), Carta 3
28 IOH (IV, 3), 326, 324
29 Ibid, 326
30 Ibid, 324
31 Ibid, 331
32 Ibid, 327
33 Ibid, 330
34 Ibid, 328
35 Ibid, 330
36 Krafft (1981), 93, 128
37 Ibid, 130
38 Ibid, 131
39 IOH (IV, 3), 285
40 IOH (IV, 3, Doc), 283
41 IOH (IV, 3), 286
42 Ibid, 357
43 Ibid, 404
44 Ibid, 357 358
45 Ibid, 333
46 Ibid, 204, 162
47 Ibid, 336, 337
48 Ibid, 339, 340
49 Ibid, 340
50 Ibid, 338
51 Ibid, 340
52 Ibid, 336
53 Ibid, 341
54 Ibid, 335
55 Ibid, 336
56 Krafft (1981), 135
57 IOH (IV, 3), 341
58 Krafft (1981), 144
59 IOH (IV, 3), 361
60 Ibid, 362
61 Ibid, 411
62 Ibid, 360
63 Ibid, 365
64 IOH (IV, 3), 363; Faldella, Vol. 2, 230

65 IOH (IV, 3 Doc), 289
66 Krafft (1981), 142
67 Ibid, 142
68 Ibid, 144
69 Faldella, Vol. 2, 237
70 IOH (IV, 3), 459; IOH (IV, 3, Doc), 290
71 IOH (IV, 3, Doc), 291
72 Ibid, 293
73 IOH (IV, 3), 405ff
74 Ibid, 377
75 Ibid, 382
76 Krafft (1981), 383
77 IOH (IV, 3, Doc), 294–8
78 Faldella, Vol. 2, 240–1

Chapter 4 (pp. 66–90)
1 IOH (IV, 3), 668
2 Krafft (1981), 74–5
3 Ibid, 83–6
4 IOH (IV, 3, Doc), 101
5 Krafft (1981), 121
6 Rommel (1979), 227
7 Falls, 38
8 Edmonds, 28
9 Trevelyan, 176
10 IOH (IV, 3), 156
11 Melograni, 335ff
12 IOH (IV, 3), 156
13 Gatti, 146–8
14 Wilks & Wilks, 38
15 IOH (IV, 3), 46, 72
16 IOH (IV, 3), 102; (IV, 3, Doc), 65
17 Melograni, 395
18 IOH (IV, 3), 106
19 Villari, 150
20 CI Vol II, 279
21 CI Vol II, 279; Mangone, 109
22 CI Vol II, 282
23 Martini, 1036
24 Gatti, 12–13
25 Faldella, Vol. 2, 88
26 Ibid, 35

27 IOH (IV, 3), 236
28 Capello (1967), 233
29 IOH (IV, 3), 119
30 Ibid, 361
31 Ibid, 325
32 CI Vol II, 294
33 Baedeker (1913), 298
34 CI Vol II, 294
35 Malagodi, 191
36 Viazzi (1981), 57
37 Pieropan (1988a), 211
38 Gatti, 110
39 IOH (IV, 3, Doc), 54
40 Gatti, 424
41 IOH (IV, 3, Doc), 92
42 Ibid, 99
43 Silvestri (1965), 345; Faldella, Vol. 2, 103
44 IOH (IV, 3), 116
45 Ibid, 117, 133–4
46 IOH (IV, 3, Doc), 82
47 Ibid, 116
48 IOH (IV, 3), 119
49 Ibid, 120
50 Ibid, 302
51 Ibid, 299
52 Ibid, 299
53 Ibid, 238
54 Ibid, 238, 299
55 Ibid, 295
56 Ibid, 297–9
57 Ibid, 300
58 Ibid, 288
59 Ibid, 301
60 Bencivenga (1997), 82
61 Pieri & Rochat, 61
62 IOH (IV, 3), 301
63 Faldella, Vol. 2, 141
64 Krafft (1981), 118
65 CI Vol II, 110
66 Pieri & Rochat, 189
67 Ibid, 189
68 Ibid, 191

69 IOH (IV, 3, Doc), 67
70 IOH (IV, 3), 176
71 Ibid, 304
72 Ibid, 230
73 Ibid, 305
74 Ibid, 305
75 Ibid, 306
76 Ibid, 306, 267f
77 Ibid, 306
78 Ibid, 307
79 IOH (IV, 3, Doc), 276
80 IOH (IV, 3), 307
81 Ibid, 308
82 Ibid, 308
83 IOH (IV, 3, Doc), 101–2
84 IOH (IV, 3), 228, 263
85 Travers, 70–84, 178
86 Melograni, 421
87 IOH (IV, 3), 144; (IV, 3, Doc), 126
88 IOH (IV, 3), 112
89 Ibid, 151
90 Ibid, 153
91 IOH (IV, 3, Doc), 138
92 Ibid, 139
93 IOH (IV, 3), 156
94 Mack Smith (1989), 217ff
95 Caviglia (1952), 111
96 IOH (IV, 3), 310
97 IOH (IV, 3, Doc), 114
98 IOH (IV, 3), 311
99 Ibid, 313
100 Ibid, 314
101 Ibid, 314
102 Ibid, 231
103 Capello (1967), 292
104 IOH (IV, 3), 236
105 Ibid, 120
106 Ibid, 239
107 Ibid, 106
108 IOH (IV, 3, Doc), 72
109 Faldella, Vol. 2, 60ff
110 Caviglia (1933), 298

111 IOH (IV, 3), 227
112 Pieri and Rochat, 319ff
113 IOH (IV, 3), 233, 201
114 Ibid, 228
115 Krafft (1981), 90
116 Ibid, 97
117 Faldella, Vol. 2, 292
118 IOH (IV, 3), 305
119 Capello (1967), 292
120 Faldella, Vol. 2, 221
121 IOH (IV, 3), 231
122 Fadini, 255
123 Ibid, 293–4
124 IOH (IV, 3), 670
125 Gatti, 268
126 Ibid, 446
127 Ibid, 447
128 Page, 303; Rodd, 344; Trevelyan, 167
129 Caviglia (1933), 278
130 IOH (IV, 3), 237; Melograni, 406
131 Edmonds and Davies, 65

Chapter 5 (pp. 91–116)
1   Rommel (1942), 260
2   Krafft (1926), Map 3
3   Krafft (1981), 81
4   Rommel (1942), 257
5   IOH (IV, 3), 224
6   Rommel (1979), 217
7   Krafft (1926), Map 3
8   Krafft (1981), 99
9   Sproesser (1933), 276
10   Rommel (1942), 281
11   Ibid, 286
12   Rommel (1979), 230; IOH (IV, 3), 311
13   Rommel (1942), 289
14   Ibid, 289
15   Ibid, 298
16   Rommel (1979), 245
17   Rommel (1942), 313
18   Ibid, 326
19   Ibid, 322

20 Ibid, 323
21 Ibid, 324
22 Ibid, 323
23 IOH (IV, 3), 342
24 Ibid, 440
25 Ibid, 440
26 Rommel (1942), 330
27 Ibid, 330
28 Ibid, 331
29 Rommel (1979), 269
30 Ibid, 269
31 Rommel (1942), 333
32 Ibid, 335
33 Ibid, 336–7
34 Rommel (1979), 274
35 IOH (IV, 3), 345
36 Schittenhelm, 75
37 Krafft (1981), 124
38 Pieropan (1988a), 438
39 Fadini, 251
40 Krafft (1981) 148
41 Fadini, 252

Chapter 6 (pp. 117–44)
1   Epstein, 19ff
2   Edmonds and Davies, 63
3   IOH (IV, 3), 411
4   Ibid, 411
5   Ibid, 411
6   Krafft (1981), 179
7   Ibid, 181
8   Ibid, 163
9   Ibid, 164
10 Ibid, 186ff
11 Ibid, 189
12 Ibid, 193
13 Ibid, 191
14 Fadini, 257
15 Krafft (1981), 196
16 Ibid, 184
17 Krafft (1981), 185; Rommel (1979), 278
18 Krafft (1981), 182

19 Ibid, 183
20 Uboldi, 121ff
21 Trevelyan, 179ff
22 Krafft (1981), 205
23 Ibid, 205, 206
24 Ibid, 208
25 Ibid, 212
26 Ibid, 212
27 Ibid, 210
28 Ibid, 212
29 Ibid, 213
30 IOH (IV, 3, Doc), 324
31 IOH (IV, 3), 404
32 Caviglia (1933), 191ff
33 Ibid, 204
34 Ibid, 225
35 Trevelyan, 169
36 Caviglia (1933), 203
37 Krafft (1981), 201
38 Ibid, 202
39 Ibid, 203
40 Ibid, 199
41 Ibid, 200
42 Ibid, 206
43 Ibid, 225
44 Ibid, 209
45 Ibid, 213
46 Ibid, 216
47 Krafft (1981), 220; Fadini, 259
48 IOH (IV, 3), 429
49 Krafft (1981), 223
50 IOH (IV, 3), 429; Bencivenga (1997), 109; Edmonds, 69
51 Fadini, 260
52 IOH (IV, 3), 427; IOH (IV, 3, Carta), 21
53 Caviglia (1933), 223
54 Ibid, 209
55 Krafft (1981), 207; Rommel (1979), 279
56 Krafft (1981), 241
57 IOH (IV, 3), 449
58 Ibid, 445
59 Krafft (1981), 252; Fadini, 262; Pieropan (1988a), 493
60 Silvestri (1984), 212ff

61   IOH (IV, 3), 159
62   Ibid, 358, 368
63   Ibid, 393
64   IOH (IV, 3), 359, Schizzo 11, Carta 20
65   IOH (IV, 3, Doc), 346
66   Ibid, 440
67   Krafft (1981), 119
68   Ibid, 119
69   IOH (IV, 3), 319
70   Krafft (1981), 138
71   Ibid, 159
72   Ibid, 160
73   Ibid, 177
74   Ibid, 178
75   Ibid, 181
76   Ibid, 198
77   Ibid, 216
78   Ibid, 224
79   Ibid, 228
80   Ibid, 233
81   IOH (IV, 3), 394
82   Krafft (1981), 160
83   Ibid, 200
84   Ibid, 183
85   Ibid, 238
86   Ibid, 239
87   Ibid, 256
88   Ibid, 262
89   Ibid, 296
90   IOH (IV, 3), 440; IOH(IV, 3, Doc), 199ff
91   IOH (IV, 3, Carta), 25
92   LFDE, 134
93   IOH (IV, 3), 440
94   Ibid, 415
95   Trevelyan, 185
96   Reynolds, 87ff
97   IOH (IV, 3, Doc), 289
98   Ibid, 317
99   Forcella & Monticone, 305
100 IOH (IV, 3) 647
101 Mack Smith (1981), 35
102 Uboldi, 129

103 Melograni, 442ff
104 De Simone, 270
105 Ibid, 271
106 *The Times*, 6 Nov 1917, 7f
107 Ibid, 7 Nov 1917, 7f

Chapter 7 (pp. 145–63)
1   Krafft (1981), 66
2   Ibid, 231
3   Ibid, 267, 286
4   Ibid, 268
5   Ibid, 268; IOH (IV, 3), 432
6   Krafft (1981), 258
7   Ibid, 260
8   IOH (IV, 3), 457
9   IOH (IV, 3, Doc), 336; IOH (IV, 3), 447
10   Krafft (1981), 286
11   IOH (IV, 3, Doc), 342
12   Ibid, 401
13   IOH (IV, 3), 488, 500
14   IOH (IV, 3, Doc), 336
15   Fadini, 265
16   IOH (IV, 3), 485, 511
17   IOH (IV, 3, Doc), 346
18   IOH (IV, 3), 477
19   IOH (IV, 3, Doc), 349
20   IOH (IV, 3), 455
21   Ibid, 455–6
22   Krafft (1981), 290
23   Ibid, 290
24   Ibid, 290
25   IOH (IV, 3), 477; IOH (IV, 3, Doc), 346
26   Krafft (1981), 291
27   Fadini, 268
28   IOH (IV, 3), 467
29   Krafft (1981), 294
30   IOH (IV, 3), 471
31   CI Vol II, 170
32   LFDE, 134
33   IOH (IV, 3), 521
34   Ibid, 440
35   Ibid, 459

36　Villari, 48
37　IOH (IV, 3), 458
38　IOH (IV, 3, Doc), 359
39　Ibid, 290
40　Ibid, 297
41　Andreoletti & Viazzi, 264
42　IOH (IV, 3), 458
43　IOH (IV, 3, Doc), 350
44　Ibid, 353
45　IOH (IV, 3), 460
46　Caviglia (1933), 243
47　IOH (IV, 3, Doc), 335
48　IOH (IV, 3), 461
49　Ibid, 462
50　Ibid, 462
51　Ibid, 463
52　Ibid, 463
53　Viazzi (1974), 275; Andreoletti & Viazzi, 271
54　Krafft (1981), 287; Fadini, 264
55　Krafft (1981), 265
56　Ibid, 284
57　Ibid, 284, 265
58　Ibid, 288
59　Fadini, 266
60　Krafft (1981), 291
61　Ibid, 294
62　Ibid, 287
63　Ibid, 294
64　Ibid, 307
65　Ibid, 302
66　Wilks & Wilks, 25
67　Ibid, 176
68　Krafft (1981), 293
69　Ibid, 303
70　Wilks & Wilks, 187
71　Krafft (1981), 303, 306
72　IOH (IV, 3, Carta), 25
73　IOH (IV, 3), 676
74　IOH (IV, 3, Doc), 297
75　IOH (IV, 3)), 468
76　Ibid, 559–60; IOH (IV, 3, Carta), 25
77　IOH (IV, 3), 464

78   Ibid, 473
79   Marchetti, 274

Chapter 8 (pp. 164–88)
1   Krafft (1981), 264
2   Sproesser (1933), 293
3   Ibid, 294
4   Fadini, 266
5   Krafft (1981), 288
6   Sproesser (1933), 295; Rommel (1979), 280
7   Krafft (1981), 291
8   Rech (1998), 105
9   IOH (IV, 3, Carta), 32
10   Sproesser (1933), 298
11   Ibid, 298
12   Ibid, 299; Map 44
13   Rommel (1979), 280
14   Sproesser (1933), 299
15   Rommel (1942), 347
16   IOH (IV, 3), 472
17   Sproesser (1933), 299
18   Ibid, 299
19   Ibid, 300
20   Ibid, 300
21   Rommel (1979), 286
22   Sproesser (1933), 300
23   Rommel (1942), 354
24   Sproesser (1933), Map 45
25   HStASt. M1/11 Bü 773
26   Rech (1998), 75
27   Rommel (1979), 292
28   Merlin, 147ff
29   Rommel (1942), 363
30   Ibid, 365
31   Ibid, 366
32   Sproesser (1933), 303
33   G-B (Sproesser), (A), p.17; Rech (1998), 121ff
34   Sproesser (1933), 303ff; Rommel (1979), 297ff;
35   Rommel (1979), 299; Schittenhelm, 120; Rech (1999), 5
36   Rommel (1979), 300
37   Sproesser (1933), 305
38   Ibid, 304

39 Sproesser (1933), 305; Rommel (1979), 304
40 Rommel (1979), 305
41 Ibid, 305
42 Ibid, 305
43 Rommel (1942), 376
44 Ibid, 378
45 Rommel (1979), 308
46 Ibid, 308
47 Sproesser (1933), 306
48 Rommel (1979), 314
49 Rommel (1942), 381
50 Ibid, 384
51 Sproesser (1933), 306
52 Ibid, 307
53 Ibid, 306
54 Ibid, 308
55 Ibid, 308
56 Rommel (1979), 317
57 Schittenhelm, 33, 137
58 CI Vol I, 370
59 CI Vol II, 177ff
60 CI Vol I, 370
61 Riassunta, 418
62 Sproesser (1933), 300; Rommel (1979), 301
63 Sproesser (1933), 300
64 Ibid, 300
65 Ibid, 302
66 Ibid, 306
67 Ibid, 307
68 Ibid, 311–4
69 Ibid, 330
70 Ibid, 303
71 Rommel (1979), 115
72 Sproesser (1926)

Chapter 9 (pp. 189–211)
1   IOH (IV, 3), 521
2   IOH (IV, 3, Carta), 25
3   Wilks & Wilks, 28
4   Edmonds, 90
5   Hardie & Allen, 14
6   Barnett, 5

7   Edmonds, 100
8   Melograni, 478
9   IOH (IV, 3), 575, 594; IOH (V, 1, Carta), 1
10 *The Times*, 5 Nov. 1917, 7f
11 Ibid, 9 Nov. 1917, 8c
12 PRO FO 371, 2948, p.216
13 Rodd, 350
14 *The Times*, 8 Nov. 1917, 9f
15 CI Vol I, 374
16 Uboldi, 129
17 Hardie & Allen, 14
18 Melograni, 479 ff
19 Wilks & Wilks, 31
20 Mack Smith (1989), 230
21 Gatti, 317
22 Ibid, 110
23 Caviglia (1933), 254
24 Villari, 170
25 IOH (IV, 3), 544
26 Gatti, 148
27 Caviglia (1934), 49
28 Wilks & Wilks, 29
29 Gatti, 403
30 Ibid, 146–8
31 CI Vol II, 326
32 Baldini, 51
33 CI Vol II, 326
34 Pieropan (1988a), 175
35 Melograni, 501; *The Times*, 20 December 1917, 6c Baldini, 53;
36 Baldini, 38–9
37 Ibid, 55ff
38 Krafft (1981), 305
39 Ibid, 308
40 Ibid, 320
41 IOH (IV, 3), 577; Pieropan (1988a), 534
42 IOH (IV, 3), 578
43 Ibid, 578
44 Ibid, 577
45 IOH (IV, 3, Carta), 25
46 IOH (IV, 3), 577
47 IOH (IV, 3, Carta), 24
48 IOH (IV, 3), 546

49   Ibid, 547
50   Caviglia (1934), 27
51   Krafft (1981), 313
52   Ibid, 313
53   Ibid, 314
54   Ibid, 315
55   Ibid, 318
56   Ibid, 314
57   Ibid, 317–8
58   Ibid, 317
59   Ibid, 320
60   Ibid, 321
61   Ibid, 321
62   Ibid, 325
63   Ibid, 323
64   Ibid, 326
65   Fadini, 271
66   Krafft (1981), 330
67   Pieropan (1988a), 542
68   Krafft (1981), 322, 321
69   Ibid, 332; IOH (IV, 3), 556; Sproesser (1933), 324
70   Krafft (1981), 332
71   Pieropan (1988b), 32
72   Fadini, 276
73   Krafft (1981), 336
74   Fadini, 269
75   Krafft (1981), 309, 329
76   Fadini, 273
77   Krafft (1981), 339
78   Fadini, 275
79   Krafft (1981), 340
80   Fadini, 276
81   Ibid, 276
82   Ibid, 276, 279
83   Ibid, 277
84   Krafft (1981), 340
85   Ibid, 342
86   Fadini, 278
87   Ibid, 278
88   Krafft (1981), 342
89   Fadini, 278
90   Ibid, 279

91   Ibid, 280
92   Krafft (1981), 344
93   Wilks & Wilks, 50
94   IOH (IV, 3), 604
95   Ibid, 603
96   IOH (V, 1), 239
97   Riassunta, 429
98   IOH (IV, 3), 593; Schierini, 82
99   Krafft (1981), 343; Fadini, 282
100 Fadini, 282
101 Krafft (1981), 343; Fadini, 282
102 Fadini, 283
103 Ibid, 284
104 Krafft (1981), 344
105 FOH Tome VI, Vol 1, 118
106 Pieropan (1988a), 565
107 FOH Tome VI, Vol 1, 118
108 Pieropan (1988a), 604

Chapter 10 (pp. 212–25)
1   G-B (Sproesser), (B), p. 2
2   Sproesser (1933), 321
3   G-B (Sproesser), (B), p.3
4   Sproesser (1933), 321
5   Ibid, 322
6   Rommel (1942), 394
7   Rech (1998), 158; Sproesser (1933), 322
8   Sproesser (1933), Map 48
9   G-B (Sproesser), (B), p.6
10   Rommel (1942), 395
11   G-B (Sproesser), (B), p.6
12   Ibid, p.7
13   Ibid, p.9
14   Ibid, p.8
15   Rech (1998), 162
16   Sproesser (1933), Maps 49, 50
17   G-B (Sproesser), (B), p.11
18   Rommel (1979), 321
19   Ibid, 321
20   G-B (Sproesser), (B), p.12
21   Rommel (1979), 322
22   G-B (Sproesser), (B), p.12

23 Sproesser (1933), Maps 48–51
24 Krafft (1981), 331
25 G-B (Sproesser), (B), p.14
26 Rommel (1979), 322
27 Rommel (1942), 396
28 G-B (Sproesser), (B), pp.12, 14; IOH (IV, 3), 575
29 Rommel (1942), 396
30 Sproesser (1933), 326
31 Ibid, 326
32 Rech (1998), 131ff
33 Sproesser (1933), 326
34 G-B (Sproesser), (B), p.14
35 Ibid, p.14
36 Sproesser (1933), 325
37 Ibid, 325
38 Fadini, 275
39 Krafft (1981), 343
40 Fadini, 283–4
41 Sproesser (1933), 332
42 Ibid, 333, Map 51
43 Ibid, 332
44 Ibid, 333
45 Verein Württemberg Gebirgsschützen, p.168, (photograph)
46 Rech (1998), 192
47 Sproesser (1933), Map 51
48 Ibid, 334
49 Sproesser (1933), 338
50 Rommel (1942), 397

Epilogue (pp. 226–8)
1 Rech (1998), 19
2 Rommel (1942), 324
3 Rommel (1979), v
4 Irvine, 36; Fraser, 151
5 Krafft (1981), 360
6 Rommel (1942), 399

Bibliography

Official Histories

IOH The Official Italian History: *L'Esercito Italiano nella Grande Guerra*,
Stato Maggiore dell'Esercito, Ufficio Storico, Rome
Vol. IV Tome 3 *Gli avvenimenti dall Ottobre a Decembre (1917)*, 1967
Vol. V Tomo 1 *Gli avvenimenti dal Gennaio al Guiguno (1918)*, 1980

A particular tome of the narration is indicated by its volume and tome
number, e.g. IOH (IV, 3). The accompanying document and map
(carta) sections are denoted by IOH (IV, 3, Doc) and IOH (IV, 3,
Carta).

Krafft (1926) *Der Durchbruch am Isonzo*, Krafft von Dellmensingen, K.,
Berlin (1926), being volumes 12a and 12b of the German Official
History *Schlachten des Weltkrieges* issued by the Reichsarchiv.
Krafft (1981) *1917 Lo Sfondamento dell'Isonzo*, an Italian translation of
the above by G. Pieropan, Milan, 1981

Riassunto *Riassunto della Relazione Ufficiale sulla Guerra 1914–1918*. A
600-page résumé of the official Austrian history, edited by
A. Bolloti, Stato Maggiore dell'Esercito, Ufficio Storico, Rome, 1946

FOH The Official French Account: *Les Armées Françaises dans la Grande
Guerre*, Ministre de la défense, Paris Tome VI: Vol. 1 (1931), Vol. 2
(1935). Each volume is accompanied by one or more volumes of
Annexes

Abbreviations
CI   *Relazione della Commissione d'Inchiesta, Dall'Isonzo al
                Piave*, Rome, 1919
G-B (Rommel)   *Gefechts-Bericht* (Battle Report of the Rommel
                Detachment, 6–10 November), HStASt., M660,
                Nachlass Rommel

G-B (Sproesser) *Gefechts Bericht* (Battle Report of the Württemberg
Mountain Battalion), HStASt., M130, Bü5, Gefechts-
Bericht. (A): 1–10 November, 1917; (B): 11 November
– 9 December, 1917

HStASt   Hauptstaatsarchiv Stuttgart
LFDE   La Forza dell'Esercito (Italian Military Statistics) Min.
della Guerra, Rome, 1927.
PRO   Public Record Office
SMEBE   Statistics of the Military Effort of the British Effort of the
British Empire during the Great War; Part XXIII,
Discipline, London, 1922

Battalion History and Photographs

Sproesser, T., *Die Geschichte der Württembergischen Gebirgsschützen*,
Stuttgart, 1933
Verein Württemberg Gebirgsschützen, *Bilder zur Geschichte der
Württembergischen Gebirgsschützen*, Stuttgart, 1928.

List of other Books

Albrecht-Carrié, R., *Italy at the Peace Conference*, New York, 1938
Andreoletti, A., & Viazzi, L., *Con glio alpini sulla Marmolada*, Milan, 1977
Babington, A.P., *For the Sake of Example*, London, 1983
Baedeker, *Northern Italy*, Leipzig, 1913
Baldini, A., *Diaz* (translated W.J. Manson), London, 1935
Barnett, G.H., *With the 48th Division in Italy*, Edinburgh and London, 1923
Bean, C.E.W., *The Official History of Australia in the War 1914–1918*,
Sydney, 1923
Bencivenga, R., *Saggio critico sulla nostra guerra; Appendice: La Sorpresa
Strategica di Caporetto*, Rome, 1932
—— *La Sorpresa Strategica di Caporetto*, edited by G. Rochat, Udine,
1997
Berti, A., *1915–1917 Guerra in Comelico*, Milan, 1985
Britannica, *Encyclopaedia Britannica*, Chicago, 1947
Buchan, J. (ed.), *Italy*, New York, 1923
C.A.I. Sezione di Bassano del Grappa., *Il Grappa un Patrimonio ambien-
tale*, Bassano del Grappa, 1985
Cadorna, L., *La Guerra alla Fronte Italiana*, Milan, 1923 (2 Vols)
—— *Altre pagine sulla grande guerra*, Milan, 1925
Capello, L., *Note di Guerra*, Milan, 1920a
—— *Per la Verita*, Milan, 1920b
—— *Caporetto, Perche*, Turin, 1967

Caviglia, E., *La Dodicesima Battaglia (Caporetto)*, Verona, 1933
—— *Le tre battaglie del Piave*, Milan, 1934
—— *Diario 1925–1945*, Rome, 1952
Cechin, G., *Caporetto e la Ritirata*, Bassano del Grappa, 1996
Cervone, P.P., *Enrico Caviglia, l'anti Badoglio*, Milan, 1992
Cruttwell, C.R.M.F., *A History of the Great War*, 2nd Ed., 1936
Dalton, E.H.J.H., *With British Guns in Italy*, London, 1919
De Simone, C., *L'Isonzo Mormorava*, Milan, 1995
Douhet, G., *Diario Critico di Guerra*, Turin, 1922
Edmonds, J.E. and Davies, H.R., *Military Operations Italy 1915–1919*, London, 1949
Ellis, J., *The Sharp End of War*, Newton Abbot, 1980
Epstein, R., *Prince Eugene at War*, Arlington TX, 1984
Fadini, F., *Caporetto dalla parte del Vincitore*, Milan, 1992
Faldella, E., *La Grande Guerra*, 2 volumes, Milan, 1965
Falls, C., *Caporetto*, London, 1966
Ferris, J., *The British Army and Signals Intelligence during the First World War*, Army Records Society, Stroud, 1992
Fiala, P., *Il Feldmaresciallo Franz Conrad von Hötzendorf*, Vicenza 1990, translated from the German by G. Pieropan
Forcella, E., & Monticone, A., *Plotone di Esecuzione*, Bari, 1998
Fraser, D., *Knights Cross: A Life of Field Marshal Erwin Rommel*, London, 1993
Gatti, A., *Caporetto, Diario di Guerra*, Bologna, 1964
Giardino, G., *Rievocazioni e Riflessioni di Guerra*, 3 volumes, Milan, 1929–1935
Goldsmid, C.J.H., *Diary of a Liaison Officer in Italy*, 1920
Gudmundsson, B.I., *On Artillery*, London, 1993
Hammerton, J.A., *A Popular History of the Great War*, Vol III, London
Hardie, M. and Allen, W., *Our Italian Front*, London, 1920
Hemingway, E., *A Farewell to Arms*, London, 1929
Irvine, D., *The Trail of the Fox: The Life of Field Marshal Erwin Rommel*, London, 1977
Jones, H.A., *War in the Air, Vol 6, Italy*, London, 1937
Krauss, A., *Das Wunder von Karfreit*, Munich, 1926
Lichem, H., Massignani, A., Maltauro, M., Acerbi, E., *L'Invasione del Grappa*, Valdagno, 1993
Liddell Hart, B.H. (ed.), *The Rommel Papers*, London, 1953
Ludendorff. E., *My War Memories*, London, 1919
Mack Smith, D., *Mussolini*, London, 1981
—— *Italy and its Monarchy*, London, 1989
Malagodi, O., *Conversazioni della Guerra 1914–18*, Milan-Naples, 1960
Mangone, A., *Luigi Capello*, Milan, 1994
Marchetti, T., *Ventotti anni nel Servizio Informazioni Militari*, Trento, 1960

Martini, F., *Diario (1914–1918)*, Milan, 1966

Melograni, P., *Storia Politica della Grande Guerra*, Bari, 1972

Merlin, T., *Sulla Pelle Viva*, Verona, 1997

Musizza, W. & De Dona, G., *Dalle Dolomiti al Grappa*, Seren del Grappa, 1999

Page, T.N. *Italy in the World War*, London, 1921

Papafava, N., *Badoglio a Caporetto*, Turin, 1923

Pieri, P., *L'Italia nella Prima Guerra Mondiale (1915–1918)*, Turin, 1965

—— and Rochat, G., *Pietro Badoglio*, Turin, 1974

Pieropan, G., *1914–1918 Storia della Grande Guerra*, Milan, 1988a

—— *Monte Grappa guida breve a un Campo di Battaglie*, Valdagno, 1988b

Rech, M., *Da Caporetto al Grappa*, Vicenza, 1998

—— *Da Forcella Clautana al Piave*, Seren del Grappa, 1999

—— *La Battaglia di Longarone*, 9–10 Novembre 1917, Seren del Grappa, 1999

Reynolds, M., *Hemingway's First War*, Princeton, 1976

Rocca, G., *Cadorna*, Milan, 1985

Rochat, G., *L'Italia nella Prima Guerra Mondiale*, Milan, 1976

—— *Gli Arditi della Grande Guerra*, Milan, 1981

Rodd, J.R., *Social and Diplomatic Memories*, Vol. 3, London, 1925

Rommel, E., (1937), *Infanterie greift an*, Potsdam, 1937

—— (1944) *Infantry Attacks*, an English translation by the American Army, in the *Infantry Journal*, Washington, 1944

—— (1979), *Attacks*, an English translation by J.R. Driscoll, Vienna (Virginia, USA), 1979

—— (1990) *Infantry Attacks*, a reprint of the 1944 translation, Toronto, 1990

Schaumann, W., *Grappa quel Monte Invalicabile*, Bassano del Grappa, 1989

Schiarini, P., *La Battaglia d'Arresto sul Altopiano d'Asiago*, Stato Maggiore dell'Esercito, Ufficio Storico, Rome, 1934

Schittenhelm, H., *Rommel sul Fronte italiano nel 1917*, edited by M. Rech., Udine, 2000 (translated by M.G. Jussig from *Wir Zogen nach Friaul*, 1929)

Seth, R., *Caporetto*, London, 1965

Silvestri, M., *Isonzo*, Turin, 1965

—— *Caporetto*, Milan, 1984

Spriano, P., *Torino operaia nella Grande guerra*, 1960

Sproesser, T., *Die 12te Isonzo-Schlacht 24–27.10.17*, Selbstverlag, Stuttgart-Cannstatt, 1926

Stark, Freya, *Travellers Prelude*, London, 1950

Stone, N., *The Eastern Front*, London, 1975

Tomaselli, C., *Gli 'ultimi' di Caporetto*, Udine, 1997

Travers, T., *How the War was Won*, London, 1992

Trevelyan, G.M., *Scenes from Italy's War*, London, 1919

Uboldi, R., *Pertini Soldato*, Milan, 1984

Ungari, A., *Caporetto: uno scandalo italiano*, Nuova Storia Contemporanea III, 2, (March–April), Rome, 1999

Viazzi, L., *Le Aquile delle Tofane*, Milan, 1974

—— *I Diavoli dell'Adamello*, Milan, 1981

—— & Caravati, P. (eds), *Muli e Alpini*, Chiari, 1999

Villari, L., *The War on the Italian Front*, London, 1932

Wilks, J. & Wilks, E.M., *The British Army in Italy 1917–1918*, Barnsley, 1998

Young, G.W., *The Grace of Forgetting*, London, 1953

Zabecki, D.T., *Steel Wind*, Westport, Conn. 1994

Zandonella, I., *Alta Via Degli Eroi*, Bologna, 1975

Zivojinovic, D.R., *The United States and the Vatican Policies 1914–1918*, Boulder, Colorado, 1978

Index of Names

Wedel, Gen. von, 125, 126, 138
Weygand, Gen., 68
Wieden, Gen. E. von Alpenbach,
    120, 128, 139, 140, 201–4,
    217

William, Kaiser of Germany, 187
William, King of Wurttemberg,
    21, 187
Willisen, Major L.W. von, 165,
    169, 186

Index of Units